THE
ESSENCE

A GUIDED JOURNEY
OF DISCOVERY THROUGH THE BIBLE

JOHN PASQUET

innovo
PUBLISHING

Published by Innovo Publishing, LLC
www.innovopublishing.com
1-888-546-2111

Providing Full-Service Publishing Services for Christian Authors, Artists & Ministries:
Hardbacks, Paperbacks, eBooks, Audiobooks, Music, Screenplays & Curricula

THE ESSENCE
A Guided Journey of Discovery through the Bible

Library of Congress Control Number: 2021931403
ISBN: 978-1-61314-608-8

Cover Design & Interior Layout: Innovo Publishing, LLC

Printed in the United States of America
U.S. Printing History
First Edition: 2021

To Adam, Seth, Clark, Sam, Aaron, Bo, Wesley, Mike, Carrie, Papri, and everyone else in my life with whom I have ever read the Bible or talked about Jesus, . . . and to you, the reader.

CONTENTS

PART III: THE PROMISE OF PARADISE RESTORED: POETS AND PROPHETS

PART IV: PARADISE RESTORED: THE BEGINNING

PART V: PARADISE RESTORED: THE CULMINATION

ACKNOWLEDGMENTS

T his book is really the culmination of a lifetime of learning, and I have been truly blessed in the places I have had to learn.

My parents have long been faithful Christians. My dad has been a student of the Word since college, so I grew up learning about God and His Word from infancy. My mom has spent a lifetime praying for me, so much so that I actually might hold the record for most prayers offered for one person all-time. For this I am eternally grateful.

My brother Hank has also been a faithful friend and companion to me for my entire life.

In college, the influences of Larry Glabe and Mike Jordahl were immeasurable. That is where my faith became my own, and I truly learned to study the Scriptures for myself.

I also found a wonderful church during my college years where I could really learn the Scriptures. My pastor, Michael Burt, became a lifelong mentor and friend. I cannot measure how much I have learned from him.

For the past decade or more, I have also had the immense privilege of reading the Bible with people from around the world as part of a ministry led by Craig and Shirley Colbert. I can't thank them enough for letting me come alongside them.

As a computer science major in college, I had never written much of anything aside from a high school term paper in Mr. Francis's English class. As such, writing a book seemed to be an insurmountable task that I put off for many years.

I am very grateful for those who critiqued the earlier versions and gave input and encouragement. These people include Mom, Dad, Hank, Mathew Vroman, Ann Russell, Garlett Avery, Pam Martin, Jason Gentry, Mike Whitely, Dr. Terri Woods, and Robert and Linda Murdock.

I am also truly grateful to Bart Dahmer, Rachael Carrington, Yvonne Parks, and Innovo Publishing for partnering with me in this project.

Most of all, I am eternally grateful to Jesus Christ for His salvation.

PREFACE

Why am I here?
You have asked that question before, haven't you? So have I. It is one of the most important questions we can ever ask. Indeed, it is so universal that we might wonder if it is written somewhere deep inside the heart of every one of us. Perhaps we should wonder who it was who wrote it there.

The very question itself reveals something quite significant about *us*—we *expect* there to be an answer. Our hearts instinctively reject the notion that there is *no answer* because that would mean there is no purpose to our existence. Meaninglessness is wholly detestable to the human heart. Our minds may be capable of entertaining such a notion and be somehow comfortable with it, but not our hearts. Our hearts passionately long for deep meaning and purpose, and they will be satisfied with nothing less.

So we do not ask *if* there is a reason why we are here. We already believe that there is. Our question is only concerned with *what* that reason might be.

DOES GOD EXIST?

Yet, why exactly do we expect there to be a reason for our existence? Why do we assume that meaning and purpose exist?

This leads us to another question: *Does God exist?* This is really the heart of the issue. If there is no God, then we must be merely the product of random, mindless processes. If this is true, then there would be no reason for why we are here. Chance cannot produce design or intent. It only produces accidents. There can be no ultimate meaning or purpose for accidents.

To be sure, we can certainly try to create our own meaning and purpose—and many people do. But why would we even want to do this? What does it matter? To do so would be completely inconsistent with a purely accidental existence and a blatant denial of our true origins. Meaning and purpose can only arise from design and intent. Yet it is not what is *designed* that decides what those are. Only the *designer* can do that.

If a group of small rocks were to wash up onto a sidewalk, there would be no meaning in their placement. It would be merely accidental. However, if someone came along and arranged those rocks to form the word *hello*, then there would be meaning. Yet that meaning would not have arisen from the rocks but from the one who arranged the rocks—the designer.

Thus, if our lives do have real meaning and purpose, that does not and cannot come from ourselves. It can only come from the designer and creator—from God.

If there is no God, then there is no creator.
If there is no creator, then there is no designer.
If there is no designer, then there is no design.
If there is no design, then there is no purpose.
If there is no purpose, then there is no meaning.[1]

Thus we are left with two options. Either the question of why we are here does have an answer, or it does not. If there is no answer, then life ultimately has no real meaning or purpose. Yet if there *is* an answer—if there *is* true meaning and purpose in life—then there must be a God.

Now, I am not suggesting that our desire for meaning and purpose is the only reason to believe that God exists or is even sufficient evidence for that—far from it. There are many other compelling reasons to draw this conclusion. I am suggesting, though, that our inherent belief in meaning and purpose is certainly one of the reasons that supports this conclusion.

So if there is a God, then there is ultimate meaning and purpose. This is good news, indeed! However, merely being assured that such things exist is insufficient. We must know *what* they actually are.

WHERE ARE THE ANSWERS?

If God is the Designer, then He is the one who has the answers to our questions about meaning and purpose. He is the one who defined them at the very beginning.

We must not, then, seek these answers from any other source. To do so would be to risk getting answers that are incorrect. Wrong answers could be much worse than no answers at all. Thus we must look to God and to God alone. This is the only way we may be sure the answers we receive are the correct ones.

Now, the questions regarding meaning and purpose are extremely important, but they aren't our only questions, are they? They certainly aren't mine.

---

1. From a presentation by Pastor Ronnie Collier Stevens in January 2002, in Budapest, Hungary.

Where do I come from? Where am I going? Who am I? Why is there so much pain and suffering in the world? Why is there so much hate and so little love? Why is there so much violence and so little peace? Why is there so much hurt and so little joy? Why do the innocent suffer? Why do the guilty prosper? Why does everyone I love have to die? What happens after death?

I could go on and on, and so could you. Because God does exist, there *are* answers to all these questions, and we find them in the same place—in God alone.

Admittedly, I am not going to try to answer all of these questions in this book, as that is not my purpose here. I do believe, though, that what we will cover together will provide a solid foundation from which these questions may be answered.

WHO IS GOD?

So we understand that we have to look to God Himself to find the answers to our questions and to make sense out of life. But who is God anyway? It does a weary traveler little good to know that a well does exist somewhere. He has to know where it is.

There are many different religions in the world with very different ideas about who God is and what He is like. So, how can we possibly know which one is true?

There are many reasons why I myself am convinced that the God of the Bible is the one true God, but a presentation of the evidence for that is not the purpose of this book either. However, what we will cover in this book will certainly support that conclusion, as it will show just how remarkable the Bible is. No other sacred text even comes close to it.

I am convinced that the one who honestly studies Christianity and compares it to any other religion will find the evidence for it to be quite overwhelming. If you are interested in this particular topic, please see the appendix for some helpful resources.

Even if you do not share my opinion about the God of the Bible at this point, it should still be acknowledged that Christianity is certainly *one* of the most prominent religions in the world today, if not the *most* prominent. So, at the very least, we should consider the God of the Bible as a good candidate for being the one true God. We should also consider the Bible as a good candidate for revealing the truth about God. That will be our focus in this book.

THE BIBLE

The Bible is most definitely the one and only authoritative text for Christianity. It presents itself as not merely the words of men but the revelation of God Himself. Again, there is ample reason to accept this claim as true, but I am not going to deal with that topic here either. The appendix will list some great resources on this topic.

I will say this, however. If there really is a God who is so powerful that He could create the universe and everything in it, then He certainly would also have the power to communicate His message to mankind and prevent that message from being distorted or corrupted over time.

For the purposes of our discussion here, I will be treating the Bible as the divine revelation of God and the source for all spiritual truth. Again, you do not need to agree with me at this time, but I want to be clear about the perspective from which I am coming.

If you have ever tried to read the Bible for yourself, you have probably noticed that it is quite a lengthy book, and I would certainly agree with you. Even if you sat down and read it through from cover to cover, you might still find it quite difficult to truly understand, especially if it were your first time. Reading through the Bible in one year is something that a good number of Christians attempt to do from time to time. However, many of these attempts fail when the reader comes to certain parts of the Bible known as Numbers, Leviticus, or Chronicles. Oftentimes, the big picture is lost and the relevance of the stories is obscured. This can lead to confusion and a loss of interest.

Perhaps it is a little bit like going to a city you have never been to before. There are monuments, statues, and buildings in various places. You know there must be great significance to each of them, but as a visitor you have no idea what that might be. So you pass on by and miss out on a deeper understanding that could have been yours.

However, it could all make a lot more sense if you had a really good tour guide. A good tour guide knows well the history, language, and culture of the city and has probably lived there for many years. As such, he or she is uniquely qualified to pass that on to the newcomer and unveil the deeper meaning behind the many landmarks there.

In the following pages, I hope to serve as your tour guide through the Bible. We won't look at everything, and we won't even go into great depth on some of the things we do cover. I hope and expect, though, that, by the end of our journey together, you will understand and appreciate the Bible and God's message to you on a much deeper level.

The Bible is, indeed, a book of matchless wonder and beauty, and my desire is to help you catch a glimpse of that.

INTRODUCTION

I have already mentioned that the purpose of this book is not to give a presentation of the evidence for Christianity or for the Bible as the revelation of God. So you might be asking, *What exactly is its purpose?* Well, that's a fair question, and it is certainly time I gave you an answer.

The purpose of this book is to help you understand from the Bible the very *essence* of God's message to you and me. That message is God's revelation of His ultimate purpose and plan of restoration for mankind. Essentially, it is His guide for us to come back into relationship with Him.

There is certainly a lot more in the Bible than just this. It reveals who we are, who God is, why the world is like it is today, the origin of death, what happens after we die, and a host of other thing as well. It holds the answers to all of life's deepest questions. Still, the overall message is the restoration of our relationship with God.

If you are new to the Bible, you will be interested to know that it has quite a unique format. It is actually a collection of sixty-six different books with a total of 1,189 chapters. These chapters are further divided up into verses. A verse is oftentimes one sentence or a part of a sentence. There are just over thirty-one thousand verses in the Bible containing more than eight hundred thousand words. By comparison, one of the longest books with which you may be familiar is the novel *Les Misérables*, by Victor Hugo, which is just over six hundred fifty thousand words. So the Bible is a little less than twenty-five percent longer than that.

To read through the entire Bible from start to finish would take approximately seventy hours. If you read for ten hours a day, then you could read it through in one week. Still, that's a lot of time, so we're not going to do that here. Instead, I have chosen a little over fifty passages for us to read together (a little less than thirteen hundred verses total). This amounts to just over four percent of the entire Bible.

Before each passage, I will give a brief introduction and sometimes point out certain things to look for in the text. Then, we will read through the passage from the Bible itself. After that, we will discuss what we have read, and I'll try to unveil some of the deeper meaning.

Now, I am not suggesting that the other chapters in the Bible are not as important or as essential as these. However, I do believe that, in these particular passages, we can gain a really good understanding of the Bible in its entirety. It certainly was no easy task to decide which chapters to include and which chapters to leave out. I wanted to provide as complete a picture as necessary in as few passages as possible.

As we begin, you may sense that we are going pretty slowly, and you will be right. The reason for this is that the first few passages are foundational for everything else. Without a solid understanding of these events, it is very difficult to understand the significance of the Bible as a whole.

This is true of any story. If we were to begin watching a movie three-fourths of the way through, it would be difficult to understand what is really going on. There might be a lot of interesting and exciting things happening, but we really wouldn't understand how it all fits together and what's really going on.

With that being said, I hope you read this book through to the end. I hope you come to a good understanding of what God's message is for both you and me, and I hope you can see what a truly wonderful book the Bible is.

PART I

PARADISE LOST

THE BEGINNING
GENESIS 1:1

O n December 24, 1968, the crew of Apollo 8 became the first people in history to leave the earth's gravity and then orbit the moon. On one of their orbits, they saw what no one had ever seen before—the *earthrise*. Later, they would also be the first to see the *lunar sunrise*. As they gazed out at the awesome beauty of creation, the crew read the first ten verses from the book of Genesis. We will read all of those verses very soon, but we begin now with the very first verse that was read on that day—the first verse of the Bible.

> "In the beginning God created the heavens and the earth." (Genesis 1:1 NIV)

TIME, SPACE, AND MATTER

This verse and the book of Genesis were probably written about thirty-five hundred years ago by a Jewish man named Moses, who is one of the most prominent figures in the Bible. We will read much more about him later.

You might wonder how anything written so long ago can have any relevance for you and me today. After all, aren't we living today in the age of information, science, technology, and reason? Aren't we far more advanced now than ever before?

Well, you actually might be surprised at how much ancient man knew. After all, they built the Pyramids of Egypt and Stonehenge, so they had to be quite intelligent and creative. Remember also that the Bible presents itself not as the words of men but as the words of God. If this is true, then the message of the Bible would be timeless and just as meaningful today as it was the day it was revealed.

In this modern world of ours, we understand that the physical universe in which we live consists of time, space, and matter. Each particle of matter occupies a particular point in space at a particular time in history. With that in mind, let us take a closer look at that very first statement in the Bible.

> "In the beginning God created the heavens and the earth." (Genesis 1:1 NIV)

The "beginning" is a reference to time. The "heavens" is a reference to space. The "earth" is a reference to matter. Thus, here in the very first sentence of the Bible, we are introduced to the nature of the physical universe—a universe that consists of time, space, and matter. This perfectly corresponds to our modern scientific understanding today. The Bible has contained this truth for thirty-five hundred years!

May I suggest then, that the Bible may not be merely the primitive ramblings of ancient people? In fact, it may have a great deal of relevance for you and me today. It may even be the very words of God.

Its relevance goes far deeper than this. The Bible does not merely address physical realities but spiritual realities as well. This includes the deepest longings of our hearts and the answers to the most essential questions of our souls.

THE BEGINNING

So we live in a physical universe of time, space, and matter, but what is the origin of the universe? To this question, there are only two possible answers. Either the physical universe had a beginning, or it did not.

While some still dispute this, there is more than ample reason to conclude that the universe did have a definite beginning in the finite past. One reason has to do with the second law of thermodynamics, or the Law of Entropy. This states that the amount of disorder in the universe is always increasing. It follows that the amount of usable energy is decreasing.

If there were an infinite past, then all the usable energy would have been used up long ago. Well, my laptop is still on right now, and there is soft music playing in the background. So there certainly seems to be usable energy available today. Thus the universe must have had a definite beginning in the finite past.

A second interesting piece of evidence has to do with the fact that we cannot traverse infinity. We can never start from now and arrive at the infinite future. We can get far into the future, but we can never arrive at the *infinite* future. In the same way, we could never get from an infinite past to today. The distance would essentially be the same.

So, based on this and a lot of other evidence, it is reasonable and rational to conclude that the physical universe did have a beginning.

Ok, so what difference does that make? Well, a universe with a definite beginning and not an infinite past raises the question of what exactly caused it to come into existence in the first place. It hasn't always existed, so why does it exist now?

Some might suggest that there was no cause—that it just came into existence out of nothing because of nothing. Yet the notion that something can come from nothing is certainly not scientific by any stretch of the imagination. The scientific method requires a test that can be replicated, and no experiment can replicate *nothing* creating *something*. Everything that begins to exist has a cause. The universe began to exist, so the universe must have a cause.

But what would the nature of such a cause have to be—a cause great enough that the universe is its effect? First of all, it would have to be something that is not itself a part of the physical universe. If it were, then we would have something creating itself. This is a logical absurdity. So it must, of necessity, have been something that is outside the physical universe—outside of time, outside of space, and outside of matter.

We also note that every cause is greater than its effect. An effect cannot be greater than its cause. When we examine the effect itself—the physical universe—and we look at mankind specifically as part of that universe, we observe that we ourselves are personal, moral, and relational beings, among other things.

Thus the cause behind the creation of mankind as part of the physical universe must not only be outside of time, space, and matter, but also personal, moral, and relational. A being that is less than that would not have been great enough to have created the universe.

Some may attempt to ascribe some other word to such a cause as this, but the word *God* certainly fits quite well. This is particularly true when we look at the God who reveals Himself in the Bible.

Once again, the very first statement in the Bible affirms that it was, in fact, God who created the heavens and the earth in the beginning. God presents Himself in the Bible as being outside of time, outside of space, and outside of matter. He is also presented as being personal, moral, and relational.

God created the heavens and the earth in the beginning.

THE MAP

ACTS 17:22B-31

N ot far from where I live, there is a corn maze—a field of corn with a maze cut into it. The corn stalks grow to perhaps eight or nine feet tall, and there are various places inside the maze that the visitor is somehow supposed to find.

I remember well the very first time I went through it. I had been given a map of the maze with my ticket, but I paid absolutely no attention to it at all. I just boldly marched in, turned left, then right, then left again, and then I don't really remember which direction after that. It wasn't long before I realized my folly. I had no idea where I was, where I had been, or where I was going. I was completely lost!

It was at that moment when I began to notice the map that I was still holding in my hand. I realized that there may have been a very good reason why they had given it to me. I began studying it very intently. After a few minutes, I was able to locate where I was. Then, after a bit of trial and error, I began to be able to navigate the maze quite well. I knew where I was, where I had been, and where I was going. The map was essential, though. Without it, I was lost.

I have returned many times to the maze since then and have enjoyed taking others through it for their first time. Though the maze is different every year, I can pretty easily navigate to wherever I want to go with great ease. I can also help others learn to do the same—as long as we have the map.

The same principle applies to navigating our way through the Bible. We desperately need some kind of map to guide us through all the different places and events. Without one, it is easy to get completely lost and feel quite helpless.

We find such a map in the 17th chapter in a book of the Bible called Acts. It is the account of a man named Paul who is visiting the city of Athens in ancient Greece some two thousand years ago. Paul is a believer in the God of the Bible, but the people of Athens are not. They have never even heard of Him. Instead, they worship just about every god imaginable except the God of the Bible, and their city is full of idols to these false gods.

Paul is grieved to see so many people who do not know the one true God, so he decides to introduce them to Him for the very first time.

This is what he says to them.

22 "...People of Athens! I see that in every way you are very religious. 23 For as I walked around and looked carefully at your objects of worship, I even found an altar with this inscription: to an unknown god. So you are ignorant of the very thing you worship—and this is what I am going to proclaim to you.

19

[24] *"The God who made the world and everything in it is the Lord of heaven
and earth and does not live in temples built by human hands. [25] And
he is not served by human hands, as if he needed anything. Rather, he
himself gives everyone life and breath and everything else. [26] From one
man he made all the nations, that they should inhabit the whole earth;
and he marked out their appointed times in history and the boundaries
of their lands. [27] God did this so that they would seek him and perhaps
reach out for him and find him, though he is not far from any one of
us. [28] 'For in him we live and move and have our being.' As some of
your own poets have said, 'We are his offspring.'*

*[29] "Therefore since we are God's offspring, we should not think that the
divine being is like gold or silver or stone—an image made by human
design and skill. [30] In the past God overlooked such ignorance, but
now he commands all people everywhere to repent. [31] For he has set
a day when he will judge the world with justice by the man he has
appointed. He has given proof of this to everyone by raising him from
the dead." (Acts 17:22b-31 NIV)*

THE UNKNOWN GOD REVEALED

Paul begins his address to the people of Athens by commending
them for being very religious. They already believed in the divine. This
was a good thing, even though what they believed was not true. They
had even set up an altar to a god that they didn't know, seemingly in
acknowledgement that they might be missing something. It is this
unknown God who is the only true God, whom Paul reveals to them.

He explains that the one true God is much different than any of
the other gods they knew. Each of their idols needed its own temple for
shelter and people to take care of it, but the one true God had no such
needs. He didn't need anyone to give Him anything at all. In fact, He is
the one who gives life and breath to everything else. We are dependent
on Him. He is not dependent on us. It is He who determines the times
and places in which we all live, and He had a specific purpose for this
that is of immense importance. That purpose is that we would seek Him,
that we would reach out for Him, and that we would ultimately find Him
(Acts 17:27). It isn't enough that we merely seek Him. It isn't enough
that we reach out for Him. The final step is essential. He wants us to
find Him.

So why are we here? The answer to that question, at least in part,
is that you and I are on a journey that is intended to culminate in finding

God. The fact that God intends for us to find Him does not only reveal something about us. It also reveals something about God. God wants to be found. He wants to be known. And He specifically wants to be found and known by you and me!

God's desire to be known reveals His personhood. Personhood refers to a being who has a mind, a will, and emotions. This describes us as humans, but it also describes God. He is not merely an impersonal force but a personal Creator who has feelings, thoughts, and volition.

This is what makes it possible for you and me to know Him, and this is what Paul is saying here. Indeed, knowing God is at the very heart of our purpose and meaning in life. But how exactly can we know Him?

Paul goes on to explain more about the differences between the one true God and the ideas that they held. God is nothing like the idols of gold or silver or stone, who had mouths but could not speak, eyes but could not see, and ears but could not hear (Psalm 115:5-6). By contrast, God is the Lord of heaven and earth, who can see and hear and speak. If He sees, then He can see you and me as we walk through all the sorrows and joys of this life. If He hears, then He can hear us, and we can express ourselves to Him. If He speaks, then we can know Him by listening to (or reading) what He says.

In the past, God had overlooked mankind's ignorance about God, but Paul explains that He does so no longer. God now requires that all people repent—change their way of thinking—from believing what is false about God to embracing what is true.

This is critical, Paul explains, because a day of judgment is coming. On that day, all people will be held accountable to God for their beliefs and their actions. The only questions that will matter on that day are these: *Did you and I seek God? Did we reach out for Him? Did we find Him?*

THE EVIDENCE OF THE RESURRECTION

So why should we believe that the God of the Bible is real and everything else is false? What evidence does Paul give to prove what he is asserting? Surely we should not believe something this momentous without sufficient evidence.

Paul answers this question in his final statement. He declares that God Himself gave proof that this was true, and that proof was extraordinary. In fact, it was such that only God could have provided it.

What was this proof? The proof was that God raised a particular Man from the dead. Though Paul does not mention His name here, he later identifies Him as Jesus.

Is this evidence sufficient? People certainly don't naturally come back from the dead. Of course, some have had their hearts stop beating for a few minutes at a time and have then been revived, but Paul is talking about something different here. Jesus was dead and buried for three days before He came back to life. That is humanly impossible. Only God could perform such a miracle. Indeed, only the one true God, who gives all men life and breath, could restore life and breath again to one who had been dead for so long.

All of Christianity rests upon the historical fact that Jesus was resurrected from the dead. If the resurrection is true, Christianity is true. If the resurrection is false, Christianity is false.

The Bible teaches that it is through Jesus and His death and resurrection that mankind has the ability to know the one true God. Furthermore, Jesus is the key that unlocks the mysteries of the Bible. He is the central figure from beginning to end. Without Him, it's just a collection of random and often peculiar accounts of obscure people throughout history with strange customs.

But with Jesus as the key, all the stories come together as a beautiful masterpiece, painted by none other than God Himself. This is what I hope to help you see as we continue.

So that's the map. The Bible is God's revelation to mankind, and the key to understanding it all is Jesus, through whom you and I can know God.

Let's continue!

THE CREATION
GENESIS 1:1-2:3

So far, aside from the map in the book of Acts, we have only covered the very first sentence in the Bible. We will now look at the first chapter of the Bible in its entirety (and a few verses from the second).

The first sentence, as we have already noted, describes the creation of the physical universe of time, space, and matter. The very next sentence describes the state of creation at that point. It describes it as being "formless and empty." To say it another way, the earth was unformed and unfilled. It was as yet incomplete. The remainder of the chapter describes its completion.

You will see that the account describes a very orderly creation, identifying six distinct days in which creation takes place. These six days split well into two groups. The first three days are dedicated to forming what was yet unformed. The second three days describe the filling of what was then formed, but as yet unfilled.

The order of the three days of forming and the three days of filling match up to each other. What is formed on the first day is filled on the fourth day. What is formed on the second day corresponds to what is filled on the fifth day, and what is formed on the third day will be filled on the sixth day.

The seventh day marks the completion of God's creative work. It is not considered a part of the six days of Creation because nothing was created on that day. Still, it holds a significance all its own, as we will see.

Now, you may be wondering, *We have time, space, and matter, but what about energy?* We certainly can't have a universe without energy, and God certainly didn't forget about that. You will see that God creates that on the very first day when He says, "Let there be light" (Genesis 1:3 NIV).

There are a few other important things to note as well. In the course of Creation, God (1) names, (2) separates, and (3) calls His creation good. He also gives certain commands and blessings that are very important, so pay attention to those as well.

The sixth day is of immense importance, as that is the day on which God creates us. Take special note of exactly how we are created, as that begins to answer one of the questions you and I both have—the question of, *Who am I?*

Forming: Day 1

¹In the beginning God created the heavens and the earth. ²Now the earth was formless and empty, darkness was over the surface of the deep, and the Spirit of God was hovering over the waters.

³And God said, "Let there be light," and there was light. ⁴God saw that the light was good, and he separated the light from the darkness. ⁵God called the light "day," and the darkness he called "night." And there was evening, and there was morning—the first day.

Forming: Day 2

⁶And God said, "Let there be a vault between the waters to separate water from water." ⁷So God made the vault and separated the water under the vault from the water above it. And it was so. ⁸God called the vault "sky." And there was evening, and there was morning—the second day.

Forming: Day 3

⁹ And God said, "Let the water under the sky be gathered to one place, and let dry ground appear." And it was so. ¹⁰ God called the dry ground "land," and the gathered waters he called "seas." And God saw that it was good.

¹¹ Then God said, "Let the land produce vegetation: seed-bearing plants and trees on the land that bear fruit with seed in it, according to their various kinds." And it was so. ¹² The land produced vegetation: plants bearing seed according to their kinds and trees bearing fruit with seed in it according to their kinds. And God saw that it was good. ¹³ And there was evening, and there was morning—the third day.

Filling: Day 4

¹⁴ And God said, "Let there be lights in the vault of the sky to separate the day from the night, and let them serve as signs to mark sacred times, and days and years, ¹⁵ and let them be lights in the vault of the sky to give light on the earth." And it was so. ¹⁶ God made two great lights—the greater light to govern the day and the lesser light to govern the night. He also made the stars. ¹⁷ God set them in the vault of the sky to give light on the earth, ¹⁸ to govern the day and the night, and to separate light from darkness. And God saw that it was good. ¹⁹ And there was evening, and there was morning—the fourth day.

Filling: Day 5

²⁰ And God said, "Let the water teem with living creatures, and let birds fly above the earth across the vault of the sky." ²¹ So God created the great creatures of the sea and every living thing with which the water teems and that moves about in it, according to their kinds, and every winged bird according to its kind. And God saw that it was good. ²² God blessed them and said, "Be fruitful and increase in number and fill the water in the seas, and let the birds increase on the earth." ²³ And there was evening, and there was morning—the fifth day.

Filling: Day 6

²⁴ And God said, "Let the land produce living creatures according to their kinds: the livestock, the creatures that move along the ground, and the wild animals, each according to its kind." And it was so. [25] *God made the wild animals according to their kinds, the livestock according to their kinds, and all the creatures that move along the ground according to their kinds. And God saw that it was good.*

[26] *Then God said, "Let us make mankind in our image, in our likeness, so that they may rule over the fish in the sea and the birds in the sky, over the livestock and all the wild animals, and over all the creatures that move along the ground."*

[27] *So God created mankind in his own image,*
in the image of God he created them;
male and female he created them.

[28] *God blessed them and said to them, "Be fruitful and increase in number; fill the earth and subdue it. Rule over the fish in the sea and the birds in the sky and over every living creature that moves on the ground."*

[29] *Then God said, "I give you every seed-bearing plant on the face of the whole earth and every tree that has fruit with seed in it. They will be yours for food.* [30] *And to all the beasts of the earth and all the birds in the sky and all the creatures that move along the ground—everything that has the breath of life in it—I give every green plant for food." And it was so.*

[31] *God saw all that he had made, and it was very good. And there was evening, and there was morning—the sixth day.*

Resting: Day 7

[2:1] *Thus the heavens and the earth were completed in all their vast array.*

[2] *By the seventh day God had finished the work he had been doing; so on the seventh day he rested from all his work.* [3] *Then God blessed the seventh day and made it holy, because on it he rested from all the work of creating that he had done. (Genesis 1:1-2:3 NIV)*

THE TRINITY

You may have noticed a peculiar use of pronouns used by God in this passage. He says, "Let *us* make mankind in *our* image, in *our* likeness"

(Genesis 1:26 NIV, emphasis added). He uses the plural pronoun three times in that one statement. So to whom is He referring? Is there more than one divine being? Is the Bible teaching polytheism—that there are many gods?

If we stopped reading here, we certainly could draw that conclusion. However, the Bible as a whole is emphatically monotheistic, teaching that there is one and only one God. So how do we make sense of the plural pronouns here?

In the Scriptures, there are many different words for God, but to add to the confusion, the word being used here—*Elohim*—is actually in the plural form in the original language. Furthermore, at the beginning of the passage we are introduced to the Spirit of God as well. Who or what is that?

To makes sense of all this, it is helpful to look at Creation itself. We have already identified that the physical universe consists of (1) time, (2) space, and (3) matter. This is a trinity of sorts—three distinct realities that are an intricate part of one reality. They are each components of the physical universe, and without each of them, the physical universe could not exist.

Time is also a trinity of sorts. It consists of (1) past, (2) present, and (3) future. The past is time. The present is time. The future is time. However, each one is distinct from the other.

Space also has three dimensions: (1) length, (2) width, and (3) height. Matter also exists most commonly in three states: (1) solid, (2) liquid, and (3) gas. (Some of you might be wondering about plasma, and yes, that is a fourth state that is fairly rare. There is also a fifth state of matter. Still, in our world, matter most commonly exists in just three states.)

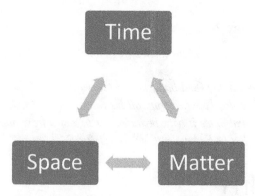

Figure 1: The Trinity of the Physical Universe

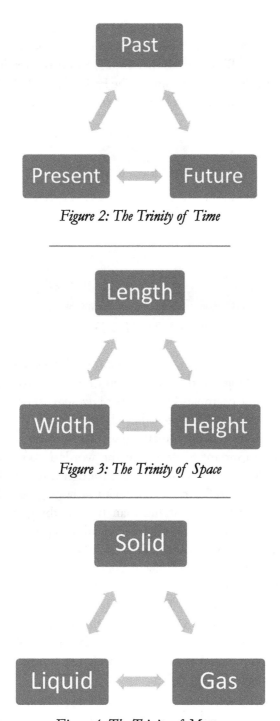

Figure 2: The Trinity of Time

Figure 3: The Trinity of Space

Figure 4: The Trinity of Matter

None of this is new, of course. We are all taught this from childhood. However, this can perhaps help us make some sense of the nature of God. The Bible reveals that God Himself is a Trinity consisting of the Father, the Son, and the Spirit. The Father is God, the Son is God, and the Spirit is God, but each is distinct from the other.

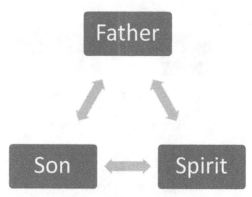

Figure 5: The Holy Trinity

Now, in no way am I suggesting that the relationship of the Father to the Son is anything like the relationship of the past to the present or like any other of the examples I gave. What I *am* suggesting is that the idea of one reality consisting of three other distinct realities is not something bizarre or absurd. It's actually something we see all around us every day.

It is also important to note that the words *Father* and *Son* imply procreation within the physical universe, though this is not always the case. Someone might refer to an older man as having been like a father to him. He doesn't mean that the man had anything to do with his conception, but that there was a certain relationship that he fulfilled in his life which corresponds to the role of a father.

In the movie *Braveheart*, William Wallace addresses the soldiers as, "Sons of Scotland." He certainly doesn't mean that the land or nation itself gave birth to those men. He is merely using the word *sons* to imply a relationship to the culture and history of the Scottish people.

We must remember, too, that biology is a physical reality. It was God who created that reality, but He Himself exists outside of it. There is no biology in the spiritual realm.

We refer to the Father, Son, and Spirit as distinct Persons of the Trinity, each possessing all of the attributes of God. The Father is God. The Son is God. The Spirit is God. Yet the Father is not the Son, and the

Son is not the Father. The Father is not the Spirit, and the Spirit is not the Father. The Son is not the Spirit, and the Spirit is not the Son.

The Trinity is sometimes referred to as "God in Three Persons." *God* refers to *what* He is, while the *Father, Son,* and *Spirit* refer to *who* He is. Later in the Bible, in what is known as the *Shema*, we find the affirmation of God's Oneness. It reads, "Hear, O Israel: The LORD our God, the LORD is *one*" (Deuteronomy 6:4 NIV, emphasis added). It is again possible to read this verse in English and conclude that God must not, after all, be a Trinity. However, to do so would be a mistake.

Two different words in the original language of that passage may be translated into English as "one." The word that is used here also appears in the very next chapter of the Bible. In that place it is speaking of marriage when it says a man and woman "become one" (Genesis 2:24 NIV). This, of course, doesn't mean that on their wedding day a man and a woman cease to be individuals and are fused into one being. What it does mean is that two distinct individuals become united in marriage as one couple and should never be separated.

So, too, the Trinity is united as One and is inseparable. Thus, when God says, "Let *us* make man in *our* image," it implies that the Father, Son, and Spirit were all involved in Creation from the beginning.

So why does this matter? Well, the nature of God as a Trinity indicates that He is community in Himself. He is relational. He is love. Even before anything else existed, this was His unchanging nature. He didn't become these things once something else existed. Creation didn't give Him the opportunity to commune, relate, or love. He already possessed those abilities within Himself. Creation merely gave Him more opportunities to express them.

Perhaps the most beautiful thing about this is that love is not something that God merely does. It's much more than that. Love is something that God is! "God *is* love." (1 John 4:16 CSB, emphasis added). Thus He loves us, not because of who *we* are—but because of who *He* is!

THE IMAGE OF GOD

The creation of mankind in this passage is of immense importance to us. Here we see that God created us very differently from everything else. We are truly special—the crowning achievement of God's creation—for it is mankind alone who bears the very image of God.

But what exactly does this mean—that we are created in His image? It probably includes several things. Mankind stands alone in this world as being extremely creative, and this certainly reflects the creativity of God as the ultimate Creator. We are also moral beings, and this reflects the moral nature of God.

There is something at the very core of our nature, though, that is perhaps even more reflective of the image of God. The Bible speaks about three different aspects of the nature of mankind: the *body*, the *soul*, and the *spirit* (1 Thessalonians 5:23). We ourselves, then, are a kind of trinity, and in this we reflect the image of God.

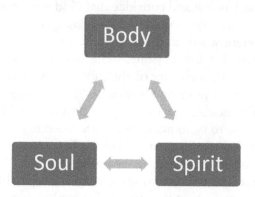

Figure 6: The Trinity of Mankind

Many times when I have mentioned the nature of mankind to someone, the first question I get is, *What's the difference between the soul and the spirit?* The confusion likely comes from the fact that these are both non-physical realities. Thus it is a little more difficult to distinguish between the two.

This is the way I myself have thought about the distinction. There are three main types of living things: plants, animals, and mankind. A plant has only a body but not a soul or a spirit. An animal is certainly more than a plant, but not quite a human. They exhibit distinct personalities, even though they are certainly not persons. This may be ascribed to the presence of a soul.

However, it is only mankind that has a spirit. This is where we get our sense of morality and virtue and also where worship takes place.

	Plants	Animals	Mankind
Body	✓	✓	✓
Soul		✓	✓
Spirit			✓

Table 1: The Body, Soul, and Spirit in Relation to Created Life

As we have discussed before, God exists completely outside of the physical reality. He exists in what we refer to as the spiritual realm. Yet we, too, have a spirit. It seems, then, that God created mankind, in particular, as not only physical beings but as spiritual beings as well.

At the very core of who we are is the desire for relationship. Though we can care for plants, we can't have relationships with them. Animals are different. We *can* have a relationship with our pets, but those can still only go so deep. We can never relate to them on the spiritual level because they do not have spirits. It is only with other spiritual beings that we can relate at this deepest of levels.

We find this most often in our relationships with other people. However, as spiritual beings, we were not made merely for relationships with each other. Ultimately, we were made for a relationship with God Himself. Remember, too, that God desires to be known by us. Nothing short of knowing God will ever satisfy our deepest longings. If we fail to experience that relationship, our lives will ultimately be lacking and unfulfilled.

THE BLESSING OF MAN

We also see in this passage that God gives a blessing to mankind immediately after He creates us. Intriguingly enough, this blessing comes in the form of a command. We are commanded to be fruitful, increase in number, fill the earth, subdue it, and rule over it.

The filling of the earth is notable, and this will be repeated throughout the Bible. God's heart is to see the world filled with people, yet He is not merely concerned with numbers. God desires a certain kind of people to fill the earth. He is looking for people who reflect the image of God and are living in relationship with Him. That is who He created us to be.

We also note that God gives mankind authority over the earth. Indeed, it seems that God created this amazingly beautiful world full of wonder and then just gave it to us to enjoy. Mankind was not created for the sake of the earth—the earth was created for the sake of mankind.

That certainly doesn't mean we should abuse the earth in any way. On the contrary, we should both enjoy and preserve this precious gift God has given us. After all, the best way to honor the Giver is to honor the gift.

JUST SIX DAYS?

So, did God really create everything in just six days? What about the hundreds of millions and even billions of years we've been told about?

Well, first, it should be understood that the God of the Bible is so powerful that He certainly didn't even need six days. While some may ask how God could have possibly made everything in such a short amount of time, those who understand the awesome power of God might wonder why He took so long.

A discussion of the age of the earth and evolution is beyond the scope of this book, but it is important to note that this passage does describe exactly what we observe today. Plants and animals reproduce after their own kinds, generation after generation. We do not observe them reproducing after other kinds. In the appendix, I have included some resources that cover this topic in much greater detail.

TIMES AND SEASONS

On the fourth day, God created "lights in the vault of the sky." The purpose of these, among other things, was to mark "sacred times, days and years." That is also exactly what we find today. The solstices and equinoxes mark the changing of the four seasons. The time it takes for the earth to make one orbit around the sun marks one year. The time it takes the moon to orbit around the earth marks, roughly, one month. Many cultures still use the lunar calendar to this day. The time it takes for the earth to revolve around its axis marks one day. So we have astronomical realities that mark days, months, and years, just as the Bible says.

But what about the week? Where does that come from? What in astronomy gives us an explanation for that? In reality, there isn't anything that corresponds to it. It seems, then, that the seven-day cycle that exists all over the world today is likely rooted in the Creation account revealed to us by God in this passage.

THE CREATION OF MAN
GENESIS 2:4-25

While the first chapter of the Bible records the creation of everything in the universe, the second chapter focuses on the creation of mankind. The two accounts are complementary—what the former describes in general about the creation of mankind, the latter describes in detail. The first chapter is a view from far away, while the second chapter is a close-up.

As you read this second account, take note of how attentive God is to the needs of mankind. After the man is created, he needs a place to live, food to eat, something to do, and someone to share it with, among other things. God specifically provides for each of those needs. God is seen here as the Great Giver of all good things.

You will also encounter various names of places and things. These can prove quite difficult to pronounce, but don't let that be a distraction. Just do the best you can and don't worry about it. The places and names are important, though, as this amount of detail shows that these are not just made-up stories. Rather, they describe actual events that occurred in real places at specific times in history.

Finally, pay close attention to the two named trees and the command that pertains to one of them. These will prove to be of great significance.

God Gives the Gift of Life

[4] This is the account of the heavens and the earth when they were created, when the LORD God made the earth and the heavens.

[5] Now no shrub had yet appeared on the earth and no plant had yet sprung up, for the LORD God had not sent rain on the earth and there was no one to work the ground, [6] but streams came up from the earth and watered the whole surface of the ground. [7] Then the LORD God formed a man from the dust of the ground and breathed into his nostrils the breath of life, and the man became a living being.

God Gives a Home and Food

[8] Now the LORD God had planted a garden in the east, in Eden; and there he put the man he had formed. [9] The LORD God made all kinds of trees grow out of the ground—trees that were pleasing to the eye and good for food. In the middle of the garden were the tree of life and the tree of the knowledge of good and evil.

[10] A river watering the garden flowed from Eden; from there it was separated into four headwaters. [11] The name of the first is the Pishon; it winds through the entire land of Havilah, where there is gold. [12] (The gold of that land is good; aromatic resin and onyx are also there.) [13] The name of the second river is the Gihon; it winds through the entire land of Cush. [14] The name of the third river is the Tigris; it runs along the east side of Ashur. And the fourth river is the Euphrates.

God Gives Work

¹⁵ The LORD God took the man and put him in the Garden of Eden to work it and take care of it.

God Gives a Command and a Warning

¹⁶ And the LORD God commanded the man, "You are free to eat from any tree in the garden; ¹⁷ but you must not eat from the tree of the knowledge of good and evil, for when you eat from it you will certainly die."

God Gives a Task

¹⁸ The LORD God said, "It is not good for the man to be alone. I will make a helper suitable for him."

¹⁹ Now the LORD God had formed out of the ground all the wild animals and all the birds in the sky. He brought them to the man to see what he would name them; and whatever the man called each living creature, that was its name. ²⁰ So the man gave names to all the livestock, the birds in the sky and all the wild animals.

God Gives a Wife

But for Adam no suitable helper was found. ²¹ So the LORD God caused the man to fall into a deep sleep; and while he was sleeping, he took one of the man's ribs and then closed up the place with flesh. ²² Then the LORD God made a woman from the rib he had taken out of the man, and he brought her to the man.

²³ The man said,
  "This is now bone of my bones
    and flesh of my flesh;
she shall be called 'woman,'
  for she was taken out of man."

²⁴ That is why a man leaves his father and mother and is united to his wife, and they become one flesh.

²⁵ Adam and his wife were both naked, and they felt no shame. (Genesis 2:4-25 NIV)

THE INSTITUTION OF MARRIAGE

The first of all human relationships God created was the marriage relationship. We saw in the previous chapter that God had repeatedly said that His creation was *good*. However, here God says that something is *not good*, at least not initially.

This is not to suggest that God created something deficient or bad or evil. That would be unthinkable. What God is saying is that man alone is incomplete. He was made for relationship with God but also with other human beings. He was made for community and a relationship of love. The most important of these human relationships is the one he has with his wife.

God created the man first and then specifically made a woman to be the perfect complement to him. You will recall that God's blessing of mankind in the previous chapter instructed them to have children. This could only occur with the union of a man and a woman. Yet the compatibility surely goes much further than biology, perhaps encompassing the entirety of our beings—body, soul, and spirit.

So the man and the woman were made to be different, complementary, and equal. We saw in the previous chapter that both the man and the woman bear the image of God, and not one more than the other. Yet how can things that are different be equal?

Being equal and being the same are two different things. Today, a farmer could purchase a new combine for harvesting wheat, while someone else, with the same amount of money, could purchase a house. Both are, at least initially, of equal value, but they are in no way the same. So it is with men and women. They are obviously different, yet each is of equal value and worth in the eyes of God.

There is an old poem that puts it quite well:

The woman came from a man's rib,
Not from his feet to be walked upon,
Not from his head to be superior,
But from his side to be equal,
Under his arm to be protected,
And next to his heart to be loved.
—Unknown

THE DUST OF THE EARTH

In this passage we see that the man whom God created has now been referred to by a specific name—Adam. This is translated as both "Adam" and "man" in different places. It's the same word, so context is the only distinction. Its root is apparently tied to the color red, which could be a reference to the color of the dust of the earth from which he was made. Thus his name identifies both who he is and what he is.

A COMMAND TO OBEY

Many have wondered why God would even make a tree from which mankind was forbidden to eat. After all, wouldn't it have been better if there had never been the opportunity for man to disobey God at all? Actually, no. It wouldn't have been better.

In God's command, the first three words are of supreme importance: "You are *free*" (Genesis 2:16 NIV, emphasis added). God created mankind as free beings with their own individual wills—not as slaves or robots with no will of their own. Having free will is a very good thing, as it enables us to truly experience love—being able to both offer and receive it. Love can only be love when it is by choice. It cannot be bought, and it cannot be taken. It can only be given and received. God created us for relationship, both with each other and with Himself, and He intended for those to be relationships of love. Thus we needed to be able to freely choose—to have *free will*.

This is the reason behind the forbidden fruit. For God to create us with the ability to love, He had to also endow us with the freedom to choose. Of course, the freedom to choose allows us to choose evil and not just good. Mankind has certainly made that dreadful choice time and time again. Thankfully, that is not the end of the story. There is nothing too broken that God cannot restore. But I'm getting ahead of myself. We will discuss much more about this later.

ADAM'S TASK

After God declares that it is not good for man to be alone and before He forms the woman, He gives Adam the task of naming the animals. Previously, it was God who had named the day, the night, the sky, the land, and the seas. Yet when He created the animals, He left them unnamed. He did this so that later He could assign this high honor to mankind. This affirms that He was giving mankind dominion over them.

We carry on that great honor today, naming children, cities, roads, mountains, and even stars. That all started here in the Garden.

ADAM AS A PICTURE OF CHRIST

As we discussed previously, the Bible is all about Jesus from beginning to end. As we continue on our journey, we will see specific prophecies of His coming. We will also see what is referred to as "pictures of Christ" or "foreshadowing." What is meant by this is that a specific person actually lived and experienced certain things at various times. Those events and experiences, however, are also a picture or foreshadowing of what would one day take place in the life of Jesus.

Jesus is the central figure of the Bible. Everything else is merely a shadow. The prophecies foretell events that will occur hundreds and even thousands of years in the future. These are quite impressive and are profound evidence to the authenticity of the Bible as the Word of God.

Still, the foreshadowing of Christ in the actual historical events is just as compelling. I say this because the authors who recorded what they saw and experienced probably had no idea that they were foreshadowing the coming of Jesus. Indeed, it is only as we look back in time that we can marvel at how everything fits together so beautifully in the masterpiece of God's story, which we refer to as *history*. History is, indeed, *His story.*

So how does Adam fit into this? How does he foreshadow the coming of Jesus? We note that in this account, Adam falls into a deep sleep. A rib is then removed from his side. Finally, from that rib, a bride is created for him.

The Bible later refers to believers in Jesus as His "bride" (Revelation 19:7 CSB). Jesus was crucified and died before He was raised to life again. Death is sometimes referred to euphemistically as "falling asleep." After that, His side is pierced, just as Adam's side was presumably pierced to remove his rib. Because of that piercing of Jesus and the "falling asleep" that accompanied it, believers can be brought back into relationship with God. Jesus receives His own bride!

If that seems a bit obscure, I believe it will become much clearer as we see the story of Jesus continue to unfold.

NAKED AND UNASHAMED

The last sentence in this chapter states that Adam and his wife were both naked and yet unashamed. This time in human history is commonly referred to as the *Age of Innocence.* There was no sin in the world then.

Sin refers to anything contrary to what is holy and right. This does not merely refer to what we do but also includes what we think and even feel. Put another way, there are sins of the heart, the mind, and the will. However, mankind was originally created in innocence. Even though they were given the freedom to choose, their original state was one free from any immoral choice or inclination.

Death would begin only as the consequence of disobedience to God's command. Thus it seems that if there had never been any disobedience, death would have never entered into creation. Of course, in His infinite knowledge, God knew full well that mankind would sin. As such, this was never a real possibility.

So why were they naked? That seems a bit odd, doesn't it? We should note, though, that this was the reality for every living thing and not something unique to mankind. In fact, nothing else in all creation wears clothing to this day. The key point here, though, is not that they were just naked, but that they were naked *and unashamed*. Shame was not a part of God's original creation. They were innocent and free from shame. The exposure of their bodies was not a reason for embarrassment. Everything was pure and holy.

Several years ago, some friends of mine had a small child that was around a year old. To his parents' great embarrassment, he seemed to despise being clothed and was constantly removing every piece of clothing they tried to put on him. The reality was that this child, like most children his age, felt absolutely no shame. He wasn't embarrassed by his body in the least, nor did his exposure of himself come from any impure or immoral thoughts. Perhaps this is a remnant of the Age of Innocence and a little glimpse of what it might have been like for Adam and his wife.

THE PURPOSE OF MANKIND

At this point, we can begin to answer the question regarding our purpose in life: *Why are we here?*

We observe that Adam's life was incomplete without companionship, so that seems to establish the reality that we already know in our hearts—that we were made for relationship. As I have mentioned before, this involves relationships with each other but also a relationship with God. Apart from a relationship with God, our lives will ultimately be lacking, no matter how much we fill them with other things, and even other *good* things.

Another way to put this is that we were made for love. We all know by experience that the greatest joy this life has to offer is the joy of loving and being loved. This is also intended to be experienced in the relationship that each of us has with God. We can receive love from other people, but the greatest love we can ever experience comes from God alone. His love is far greater than ours.

We also observe that we were created for tasks or work—to be industrious, creative, productive, and responsible. A life lived without these things will also be lacking and ultimately unfulfilling.

So if you seek to live a life of deep meaning and purpose, seek for God until you find Him, grow in a love relationship with Him, live a life of love toward others, be industrious, creative, productive, and responsible. That kind of life is truly a life worth living. It is a life that is not in vain.

THE FALL OF MANKIND
GENESIS 3:1-13

T he world at this point in history could well be described as paradise. There was no shame, no death, no pain, and no sickness—nothing bad of any kind. It was full of life and beauty and joy and peace. God Himself had proclaimed that it was very good, even by His standards. The relationship that Adam had with his wife at that time was also perfect, devoid of any hindrance, jealousy, or insecurity.

In this chapter, however, all of that changes when Adam and his wife choose to reject God. The consequences of this could not have been more severe.

The passage begins by introducing us to a being who is referred to as the serpent. In the context of the entirety of the Bible, we understand that this was not just a reptile. To fully understand who this is, though, we need to understand something about angels.

Now, the Bible doesn't tell us a great deal about angels, but it does give us some information. Angels are spiritual beings that may or may not have been a separate creation from our physical universe. They may have even been witnesses to Creation (Job 38:4, 7). It seems that they are quite numerous, but it seems that they do not reproduce (Matthew 22:30). When they were created, they were innocent like us. They also saw God face to face in all His glory.

At some point after their creation, one of the most beautiful and powerful angels rejected God and sought to be worshiped as God himself. This angel is known as Satan, Lucifer, or the devil. The Bible seems to be quoting his statement of rebellion in this passage:

13 "...I will ascend to the heavens; I will raise my throne above the stars of God; I will sit enthroned on the mount of assembly, on the utmost

heights of Mount Zaphon. ¹⁴ I will ascend above the tops of the clouds;
I will make myself like the Most High." (Isaiah 14:13b-14 NIV)

Note that there are five "I will" statements, culminating in his aspiration to be *like God*. That will come up again in this passage.

For any created being to be like God in all His glory is, of course, impossible. We are called to imitate His character but not His attributes. God is infinite, self-existent, self-sufficient, all-knowing, all-powerful, and eternal. No created being could ever become any of those things.

At the time of Satan's rebellion, it also appears that one-third of the angels joined him in opposing God. All of them were cast out of heaven as a result (Revelation 12:4). We now refer to these "fallen angels" as *demons* or *devils* to distinguish them from the angels who did not rebel, whom we still refer to as angels.

It is Satan who appears in this chapter and is referred to as "the serpent." As one who led the first rebellion against God, he now seeks to attack something God loves—mankind.

The Deception of Evil

¹ Now the serpent was more crafty than any of the wild animals the LORD God had made. He said to the woman, "Did God really say, 'You must not eat from any tree in the garden'?"

² The woman said to the serpent, "We may eat fruit from the trees in the garden, ³ but God did say, 'You must not eat fruit from the tree that is in the middle of the garden, and you must not touch it, or you will die.'"

⁴ "You will not certainly die," the serpent said to the woman. ⁵ "For God knows that when you eat from it your eyes will be opened, and you will be like God, knowing good and evil."

The Fall of Mankind

⁶ When the woman saw that the fruit of the tree was good for food and pleasing to the eye, and also desirable for gaining wisdom, she took some and ate it. She also gave some to her husband, who was with her, and he ate it.

The Consequences of Sin

⁷ Then the eyes of both of them were opened, and they realized they were naked; so they sewed fig leaves together and made coverings for themselves.
⁸ Then the man and his wife heard the sound of the LORD God as he was walking in the garden in the cool of the day, and they hid from the LORD God among the trees of the garden.

God's Pursuit of Mankind

*⁹ But the L*ORD *God called to the man, "Where are you?"*

¹⁰ He answered, "I heard you in the garden, and I was afraid because I was naked; so I hid."

The Blame Game

¹¹ And he said, "Who told you that you were naked? Have you eaten from the tree that I commanded you not to eat from?"

¹² The man said, "The woman you put here with me—she gave me some fruit from the tree, and I ate it."

*¹³ Then the L*ORD *God said to the woman, "What is this you have done?"*

The woman said, "The serpent deceived me, and I ate." (Genesis 3:1-13 NIV)

THE TEMPTATION OF MANKIND

The tactics Satan uses in his temptation of mankind are quite interesting, and these are the same ones he still uses today. He begins by questioning the very words of God, and he intentionally misquotes His command. Next, he completely contradicts God regarding the consequences of sin. He even suggests that it would be beneficial for mankind to disobey God. Finally, he directly attacks the character and goodness of God. He suggests that God is withholding good from them and depriving them of true fulfillment, happiness, and joy.

Again, these are the same tactics Satan uses today with you and me. Satan and God promise us the very same things—fulfillment, love, joy, peace, happiness, meaning, and fulfillment. However, Satan possesses none of these, and he can't give what he does not have. His promises are just lies. God alone is the source of all that is good, so He alone is the One from whom we can receive such things.

Nonetheless, Satan's lies were persuasive then just as they so often are today. Adam and his wife chose to eat the fruit. In doing so, they rejected God Himself.

Admittedly, it seems like a small thing. All they did was eat fruit from the wrong tree. How bad could that be? We say that today, though, in the context of a world full of evil. Theirs was a world of absolute purity without even the slightest hint of anything unholy.

All sin is a rejection of God and His authority and plan. In eating the fruit, Adam and his wife were attacking the character of God, believing

Satan's allegation that God was not good—that He was not to be trusted as the source of fulfillment. Indeed, the notion that the One who is completely holy and righteous and pure and loving and gracious and benevolent is, in fact, evil, is the gravest of sins. It would not go unpunished.

God is so holy and righteous and pure that even the smallest sin will most assuredly be judged, yet God is also so loving and merciful and gracious that even the greatest sin can most assuredly be forgiven.

THE DECEPTION OF SIN

In the fall of mankind, the woman saw that the fruit of the tree was (1) good for food, (2) pleasing to the eye, and (3) desirable for gaining wisdom. Yet God had already made all kinds of trees grow out of the ground that were "pleasing to the eye and good for food" (Genesis 2:9 NIV). So we have to wonder in what possible way she was lacking. Indeed, she was only offered what she already possessed. The reality was that she didn't lack anything at all. She was only deceived into believing that she was lacking.

As far as "gaining wisdom," Satan's promise was that they would become like God, knowing both good and evil. You will recall that this was exactly what Satan himself sought after when he had rebelled against God. It did not end well for him. Still, Adam and his wife had already been made in the image of God—something that Satan certainly had never possessed.

Regarding the knowledge of both good and evil, it seems that until this point, they had only known good. The knowing here suggests the experience of something and not merely intellectual knowledge. The only thing they were gaining was the knowledge or experience of evil. This was certainly not to their gain. It was only to their loss, regardless of how good it may have sounded.

Temptation is never successful by telling the truth, but by obscuring it, twisting it, or hiding it altogether. Thus it wasn't until after they had eaten the fruit that they realized it had all been a lie. Unfortunately, by then it was too late. They had already made their choice, and they would surely face the consequences.

THE TALE OF TWO TREES

Ultimately, it came down to a choice between two trees. Eating from the tree of the knowledge of good and evil would bring death. As such, it is appropriate to refer to it as just that—*the tree of death.*

So there was the tree of life and the tree of death. Adam and his wife had the freedom to choose either one of them. They were under no obligation. They could either believe God and put their trust in Him and in His character, or they could believe Satan and put their trust in him and his character.

They chose the tree of death.

Four thousand years later, on a hill outside the city of Jerusalem, there would be another tree. This tree would be both a tree of death and a tree of life. It was the tree of death for the One who would be nailed to it, but the tree of life to all those who would put their faith in the One who died upon it.

But I'm getting ahead of myself again. We will look at this more closely when the time comes.

MAN'S ATTEMPT TO HIDE HIS SIN

The first consequence of sin was that their "eyes were opened." Had they been closed? No, of course not, but this is perhaps not speaking of physical sight. After they sinned, they began to perceive the world very differently than they ever had before, and different was not a good thing. What was different was not something physical but something spiritual. The colors and shapes of things hadn't changed. *They* had changed.

They now felt shame for the very first time. Oh, what a dreadful feeling this is! You and I can both remember horrific moments in our lives when we have experienced shame in significant ways. Those memories still haunt us, don't they? We go to great lengths to avoid having to experience such shame ever again.

Adam and his wife were no different. Their response was much the same as ours is today. They first attempted to hide from each other, making clothes to cover the shame of their bodies. Yet their physical nakedness was a mere symptom of the problem. The real issue was far deeper than that.

BUT THE LORD GOD CALLED TO THE MAN

Then they "heard the sound of the LORD God as he was walking in the garden" (Genesis 3:8 NIV). When God had visited them previously, it had likely been an occasion for great delight as they could walk in the wonderful presence of their Creator. They could know Him and be known by Him.

But there was no delight on that day. Their self-made clothing that had seemed sufficient in each other's presence was worthless in the presence of a holy God.

How would God respond to this treason? Would He abandon His creation and leave them to die in their sin? Would He destroy them in His righteous anger? Would He terrify them with His wrath? Would He cast them away from His presence as He had done before with the angels who had rebelled against Him?

No, He wouldn't.

*"But the L*ORD *God called to the man..." (Genesis 3:9a NIV)*

This is one of my favorite verses in all of Scripture! It reveals that it is God who takes the first step in restoring our broken relationship with Him—not us. He does not wait for man to come to Him, nor does He leave him to wallow in his shame. Instead, He reaches out to sinful man in the depths of his sin and shame and calls him back to Himself. This is who God is, and this is great news for you and me—for I, too, am a sinful man!

WHERE ARE YOU?

It is so beautiful that God calls out to Adam, and it is quite fascinating to see what God actually says in His call. He simply asks the question, "Where are you?"

We should understand that whenever the all-knowing God asks a question, it is not for the purpose of gaining information. That would be impossible. The reason for the question, then, is not for God's benefit but Adam's. Indeed, it was the question itself that revealed the grave reality.

Where was Adam? He was now separated from God. He had never experienced that before.

ADAM'S RESPONSE

Adam's response to God's question is also quite profound. He says, "I heard you in the garden, and I was afraid, because I was naked, so I hid" (Genesis 3:10 NIV).

"I heard You in the garden." The presence of his wife had not had the same effect on him as the presence of God. After all, she was just as sinful as he was. Yet in the presence of the One who alone is holy, Adam realized that something was very wrong—and that something was himself.

"I was afraid." Fear was a new emotion for Adam. Before their sin, there had been nothing to fear. The presence of God had never evoked any fear because mankind had been created in innocence. Now that innocence was gone, and fear became a grave reality.

"I was naked." We must note that neither Adam nor his wife were truly naked physically. They had already clothed themselves with fig leaves. Yet it seems unlikely that Adam is attempting to tell a lie here, as the truth would be blatantly obvious. It seems that he is merely expressing his true feelings. He *felt* naked. His nakedness, however, was not merely physical in nature. His nakedness was his shame, and this is a spiritual reality—not a physical one.

"So, I hid." Having failed to cover over the shame of his own sin before God with the fig leaves, Adam had resorted to fleeing from His presence altogether. Yet how can anyone hide from the One who fills heaven and earth (Jeremiah 23:24)? It is a foolish endeavor, to be sure—destined to fail at the outset.

So why did he do that? And why do you and I still do that today? Adam's response is really the statement of all mankind from that moment on. When we as sinful beings encounter the presence of a holy God, we cannot help but feel shame and guilt. This leads to fear—fear of being found out and fear of being punished. Our response is to flee in desperation and hide from God however we can. Some hide in the philosophy of atheism, denying that there is any God whose presence we must encounter. After all, if there were no God, then there would be no judgment either.

Others hide by denying that God is both loving and just at the same time. They prefer to imagine that He is only loving and nothing else or that His love drowns out everything else about Him. This would mean He would never bring judgment upon anyone, so this again would mean there is nothing to fear.

Still others deny that they are truly sinful, or at least not as sinful as others. It seems that they imagine there is some large scale and that they are probably in the top twenty-five percent of the good people. Their reasoning is, somehow, that this top quartile of "least offensive sinners before God" will somehow be left unpunished.

This notion is quite absurd, though. We certainly do not experience that in our own justice systems. A judge does not compare a defendant's life on a scale of everyone in society and give him a pass if he places above a certain percentile. He is judged by a scale that is absolute—not one that is relative.

It is the same with our sins against God. As previously mentioned, God is so holy that even the smallest sin will surely be punished, but He is so loving that even the greatest sin can be forgiven.

Thus man's response to sin should not be to hide from God but rather to seek the forgiveness that He offers. We should not run *from* Him but *to* Him.

THE BLAME GAME

God continues the conversation by asking how Adam came to realize that he was naked. He specifically asks if Adam had eaten from the forbidden tree. Adam's response is to shirk responsibility for his own actions.

"The woman you put here with me…." (Genesis 3:12a NIV)

Adam actually tries to put the blame on his wife and make her suffer the consequences. He even goes so far as to suggest that *God Himself* is partially to blame since it was He who gave her to him.

When God turns his questioning to the woman, she follows the example of her husband and tries to blame Satan. However, despite the attempts to shift the blame, both Adam and his wife acknowledge that they have, indeed, eaten the forbidden fruit. Having confessed, they now await the judgment of God, which we will read about in the next passage.

THE DEVASTATION OF SIN
GENESIS 3:14-24

You will recall that when God came into the Garden after Adam and his wife had sinned, He directed His questioning first to Adam, then the woman, who blamed Satan. God's judgment proceeds in the opposite direction, beginning with Satan, then the woman, and finally Adam. The specific judgments given to each of them are of tremendous importance, and we will discuss these in detail afterward.

The Judgment of the Serpent

[14] *So the LORD God said to the serpent, "Because you have done this,*

"Cursed are you above all livestock
and all wild animals!
You will crawl on your belly
and you will eat dust
all the days of your life.
[15] *And I will put enmity*
between you and the woman,

and between your offspring and hers;
he will crush your head,
  and you will strike his heel.' "

The Judgment of the Woman

16 *To the woman he said,*
"I will make your pains in childbearing very severe;
with painful labor you will give birth to children.
Your desire will be for your husband,
and he will rule over you. "

The Judgment of Adam

17 *To Adam he said, "Because you listened to your wife and ate fruit*
from the tree about which I commanded you, 'You must not eat from it,'

"Cursed is the ground because of you;
through painful toil you will eat food from it
all the days of your life.
18 *It will produce thorns and thistles for you,*
and you will eat the plants of the field.
19 *By the sweat of your brow*
you will eat your food
until you return to the ground,
since from it you were taken;
for dust you are
and to dust you will return. "

A Name for Adam's Wife and the Clothing of God

20 *Adam named his wife Eve, because she would become the mother of*
all the living.

21 *The* LORD *God made garments of skin for Adam and his wife and*
clothed them.

Separation from God

22 *And the* LORD *God said, "The man has now become like one of*
us, knowing good and evil. He must not be allowed to reach out his hand
and take also from the tree of life and eat, and live forever." *23* *So the* LORD
God banished him from the Garden of Eden to work the ground from
which he had been taken. *24* *After he drove the man out, he placed on the*
east side of the Garden of Eden cherubim and a flaming sword flashing
back and forth to guard the way to the tree of life. (Genesis 3:14-24 NIV)

THE FIRST GOSPEL

The significance of the judgment of Satan cannot be overstated. While in the first part of the judgment, the curse is actually for the serpent, the second part is directed at Satan. The meaning of this is not obvious at first, but it should become clearer as we walk through it together.

God said to Satan, "And I will put *enmity* [make enemies] between you and the woman, and between your offspring and hers; he will crush your head, and you will strike his heel" (Genesis 3:15 NIV, emphasis added).

So what does this mean? God establishes that Satan and the woman, in particular, would now be enemies. Satan is certainly the enemy of both men and women, as he seeks to destroy all mankind and rob us of our relationship with God. Yet the woman is specifically mentioned here.

God then states that this enmity will extend to the offspring of both Satan and the woman. It is peculiar, here, that the offspring of the woman is not the offspring of both a man and a woman. We also observe that the offspring of the woman is identified in the next phrase with the masculine pronoun *he*, so this will be a man who is uniquely born of a woman. Satan and this man will make war against each other. In that battle, Satan will inflict a wound on the man by striking his heel. However, the man will crush the head of Satan.

The difference of the wounds is important. A strike to the heel is an injury, but it is not fatal. A strike to the head, however, is a death blow that gains the victory. Thus this man—this offspring of a woman—will one day defeat Satan. He will be wounded in that battle, but not mortally.

Through his deception, Satan had brought death to all mankind. However, there would be a day when a man would bring death to Satan.

At this time, Adam and his wife could not have grasped what this all meant. Today, however, we know that the man who conquers Satan is Jesus. We will see later that He was born of a virgin. Thus He alone in all of human history is uniquely the offspring of a woman and not the offspring of both a man and a woman.

The Bible teaches that Jesus conquered Satan through His own death and resurrection. His death was by crucifixion. Intriguingly enough, three nails were used in crucifixion—two pierced each of the person's hands, and one pierced both feet. At the crucifixion of Jesus, Satan did strike the heel of Jesus, the Offspring of the woman. That wound did not achieve the victory, though, as Jesus rose from the dead, triumphing over Satan and over death itself. This prophecy in the judgment of Satan is commonly known as *the First Gospel*.

The word *gospel* is a word that means "good news." During the Roman Empire, whenever a new emperor (Caesar) took power, an edict was sent out to proclaim the gospel (good news) that he was now lord (ruler), savior, and a son of the gods. Yet he would one day die, and his rule would come to an end.

When Jesus rose from the dead after paying the penalty for the sins of the whole world, He established that He Himself was the true Lord of all, the Savior of all mankind, and the one true Son of God. He will never die again and will rule forever.

THE JUDGMENT OF MANKIND

While God specifically cursed Satan, He did not curse either Adam or his wife. They were judged but not cursed, and the distinction is important.

The judgments are both similar and different at the same time. Both would experience pain as a result of their sin, yet the pain would come in different forms. For the woman, it would taint the wondrous miracle of childbirth as well as her relationship with her husband. What had originally been a perfect and pure relationship would now be corrupted with insecurity, jealousy, distrust, and various forms of brokenness.

For the man, the work that had originally been a blessing would now become a burden. Much effort would be exerted to merely maintain what had previously been built. Everything would now see decay. The ground would now begin to produce thorns and thistles instead of only things that brought nourishment. Man would have to continually fight this battle with the ground. His toil would eventually end in death, when he would return to the ground from which he had been taken. There would be a sense of vanity in all the work of his hand.

We must also note the significance of thorns in this passage. We observe that they were a direct consequence of sin and are thus symbolic of sin itself. Many years later, when Jesus, the Offspring of the woman, hung on a cross, a crown of thorns would be placed upon His head. This symbolized the reality that our sin was truly placed upon Jesus, just as the crown of thorns—a direct result of sin—was placed on His head.

THE MOTHER OF ALL THE LIVING

Up to this point, Adam's wife had not been named. Adam had only referred to her as "a woman" because she had been "taken out of the man" (Genesis 2:23 NIV). Yet that was not her name. Now, as he gives her a name, Adam does not look to her past or to her origin, but to her future.

Their sin had brought death to all mankind, yet the name he chose for her is not one of despair but one of hope. She would be called Eve, which means to give life, because she would be the mother of all the living. She would also be the mother of all the *dying*. However, God had promised a Savior who would one day overcome sin and death. Thus the name of Adam's wife embodied the hope of that promise.

THE SECOND GOSPEL

The Scriptures record that God made garments of skin for Adam and Eve. They had previously made garments of fig leaves for themselves, so they were not unclothed.

What, then, was the purpose of this new clothing? We remember that the clothing they had made for themselves was wholly insufficient for covering up their shame, and this is a universal principle. It is impossible for mankind to cover over his sin and shame by his own efforts. God's provision of clothing for Adam and his wife was of a different kind than what they had made for themselves. He made garments of skin.

So where did He get the skins? Obviously, He would have had to get them from some type of animal, so at least one animal had to have died that day. The Bible does not detail exactly how this happened, but it seems that it must have been God who also performed the act of killing.

Now imagine, for a moment, that you are in the place of Adam and Eve. It was you who had rejected God, you who had charged Him with evil, you who had sinned against Him, and you who had sought to be equal with God. You are now standing in the presence of God, ashamed and frightened, awaiting the full force of His vengeance.

But then, something very strange and unexpected happens. God turns away from you and seizes an animal instead. To your horror, He then proceeds to kill that animal. It was the first death in all creation.

Your heart cries out in agony, "What are you doing? What did that animal do? We are the guilty ones. That animal did nothing wrong." And you would be right. Yet in this peculiar act, God introduces the radical and glorious concept of a *substitute*. One that was innocent would die in the place of the one who was guilty. It was Adam and Eve who deserved to die, yet a substitute was offered that day. The sacrifice of the innocent animal covered the shame of their sin.

As we have noted previously, shame was not the real issue but merely a symptom of it. The real issue was the sin itself. While the death of an animal could cover their shame, it could never account for the sin that caused the shame. That would require something far greater—not merely the death of one that was innocent, but the death of One who was righteous.

Only God Himself is truly righteous. Thus God would one day become a man—the Offspring of the woman. He would die as a substitute for our sins. We are the ones who sinned, but He would be the one who would die in our place to pay our penalty.

So the garments of skin are really the "Second Gospel"—the second indication that Someone would one day come to pay the penalty for sin and redeem mankind.

SEPARATION FROM GOD

Later in the Bible, the Jewish nation would observe many different animal sacrifices as part of their worship. The idea was always the same—the innocent died in place of the guilty. Yet again, the sacrifice of animals was never sufficient to cover over sin, and the evidence of that is seen in the last paragraph of this chapter.

God had sacrificed an animal to make the garments of skin. If that sacrifice had been sufficient, we would expect Adam and Eve to have remained in the Garden and in the presence of God. That did not happen.

Instead, God banished them from His presence and from the home He had made for them. He even placed an angel at the gate to keep them away. The presence of God was lost, but not forever. There was still the promise and the hope that it would one day be restored.

The creation of mankind ended with Adam and Eve being unclothed, yet unashamed. The fall of mankind ends with them being clothed, yet ashamed. Adam and Eve could never have imagined the depths of evil and depravity to which mankind would fall as a result of sin. Nonetheless, they would soon experience it for themselves firsthand.

FIRST MERCY

It is intriguing to note that this is the first time in all of history when mercy was shown. When the angels had rejected God, each of them received the punishment they deserved. There had been no mercy—only justice. In fact, they may not have even known what mercy was.

When Adam and Eve rebelled against God, the angels may have expected to see God's justice again. After all, that's the only response they had ever seen to sin and rebellion. Imagine their wonder, then, when God withheld the punishment that Adam and Eve deserved. How could this be? What was happening? How could judgment be left undone?

Again, it is the beauty of the substitute. The punishment would surely come—it just wouldn't come on them.

They would receive mercy. Jesus would receive justice in their place.

WHY DIDN'T THEY DIE?

Now, you may be wondering why it was that Adam and Eve did not die on the day they ate from the forbidden tree. After all, hadn't God specifically warned them that they would? Was Satan telling the truth after all? Had God told a lie?

Of course not! Mankind is not merely physical in nature. We are not just a body, but a body, a soul, and a spirit. Furthermore, it is our spirits that are the truest parts of who we are—not our bodies. So just because Adam and Eve did not die physically on the very day that they ate the fruit does not mean that they didn't die in any other way—or even in the most significant way. Indeed, had the consequences of their sin been merely physical, that would have been a pretty light judgment. In fact, the death they experienced that day was spiritual. They were separated from the presence of God.

When we attend a funeral, we typically don't refer to the body of the deceased by that person's name. We merely refer to it as his body. The truest part of who he was is no longer there. Physical death, then, is separation—separation of the body from the soul and spirit.

Spiritual death is also separation, but of a different kind. It is the separation of the whole person from God. This was the death Adam and Eve experienced on the day they ate from the tree. From that very moment on, sin impacted their souls and bodies as well. They did become mortal, and their souls were also tainted with sin. Still, these were secondary to the spiritual death they suffered.

PARADISE LOST

As we look at the world around us today, a lot of difficult questions arise, as we discussed before. Why is there so much suffering? Why is there so much evil and so little good?

The world today is a world full of pain, heartache, brokenness, hatred, violence, abuse, addictions, disease, disasters, and ultimately death. This is certainly not how God had described the Garden of Eden at Creation. It had been a place that could well be described as *paradise*. God Himself proclaimed it to be good—even very good. It was a place full of life and joy and peace and beauty and love and harmony—devoid of hate and corruption and strife and despair and death.

The world today seems to be almost the exact opposite of that. It could well be described as *paradise lost*, and that is exactly what it is.

So why is the world so messed up today? Because mankind is sinful and in desperate need of a Savior. Many people attempt to deny this reality. They suggest that if we just had a better environment to grow up in, then it wouldn't be this way. Perhaps if we just controlled things better or passed the right laws, then we could have a world with only good and no evil. Yet mankind has been trying to create a world like this for thousands of years and has failed miserably. I would suggest to you that all the evidence of the world around us points to the truth found in the Bible. Mankind is, indeed, sinful.

I am painfully aware that I myself am sinful. No matter how much I desire to be someone who lives a holy and righteous life, I still struggle with envy, selfishness, impatience, pride, and many other sins. I am entirely unable to make myself become who I truly desire to be. The only answer to this seems to be that I need Someone else to save me from my sin, and that is precisely the promise we have from God.

THE ULTIMATE STORY

We have seen that the story of the Bible, and the story of us, began in unimaginable beauty. God created a world that was very good, full of life and joy and peace and beauty and harmony. However, an enemy invaded that paradise and threatened all that was good in it. Relationship was broken, and Adam and Eve fell under the curse of sin and death.

Then, Jesus came forward as the Hero, valiant and strong. Risking everything, He rescued us from the hand of the enemy. Relationship was restored, and with it, all the love and joy and beauty that we first had.

The Bible reveals that after our lives are over, we who have put our faith in Jesus will spend eternity in His presence. We refer to this as heaven. It is a place of ultimate love and joy and beauty and peace and everything good.

In this life, however, the reality is that we are no longer in Eden, but not yet in heaven. The world is still broken. There is still evil and suffering that God allows on a temporary basis. But why does He do this? Why doesn't He make all the suffering just go away? Isn't He powerful enough to do that?

Indeed, He is. However, the world we live in with all its horrors serves to show us the reality of our separation from God and our desperate need for Him as our Savior. If God were to take away all the suffering now, we likely would not recognize our need for Him and would fail to come to Him for His salvation. After all, this is not our permanent dwelling place, so we shouldn't get too comfortable here anyway.

The same is true about physical pain itself. In reality, pain is a great blessing. It lets us know that something is wrong. If we didn't experience pain, we would do far more damage to our bodies without ever knowing it. In the same way, the spiritual and emotional pain in this world helps us to see that something is very wrong, and it prompts us to look for One who can heal us.

Thus God does allow suffering to exist temporarily. Rest assured, though, He will one day put an end to all sin and pain and suffering and death.

THE STORY RETOLD

It is quite fascinating to see how the ultimate story of our relationship with God is so frequently retold in our world—not only today but throughout history. The pattern of the story is essentially this:

- Beauty Established
- Beauty Threatened
- Beauty Restored (by a great Hero)

Quite a few years ago now, a blockbuster movie called *The Matrix* was released. Intriguingly enough, it follows this pattern quite remarkably. It begins with a world of people who are enslaved to machines, but this hadn't always been the case. They had once been gloriously free. A great battle had been fought against the machines, and mankind had lost. The harsh reality was that they were now slaves. Finally, a hero arises to defeat the forces of evil and make everything right again, ultimately setting the world free. In his quest to accomplish this, he even dies and then comes back to life.

Part of me wants to smile and, with a twinkle in my eye, say, "That would never happen!" But I would be joking because that is exactly what happens in the Bible. *The Matrix* follows the storyline precisely!

Another well-known blockbuster movie is *Titanic*. Jack and Rose have fallen in love during their journey. This is the original beauty. However, the boat hits an iceberg and begins to sink. The beauty is threatened. Jack and Rose, along with over fifteen hundred other people, have missed the lifeboats and are freezing to death in the frigid waters of the Atlantic. They find some debris that allows them to get partially out of the water, but they soon realize it is not enough to support them both. Jack slips back into the water so that Rose can lift herself onto the debris. In doing so, Jack gives up his own life to save the one he loves.

In the last scene of the movie, Rose is now an old woman lying in her bed, and then she passes away. The cameras plunge to the bottom of the ocean, and you see the ruined remains of Titanic. The mood is one of sadness and despair. The viewer mourns that the beauty of the love between Jack and Rose was not merely threatened but lost forever. We wish the story didn't have to end that way.

At this point, you might be objecting to this example. After all, how does this mirror the pattern of original beauty, beauty lost, and beauty restored? There was no beauty restored, and we don't really like that. As an American, I expect there to be a happy ending, and I'm pretty upset if there isn't one.

Yet the movie does not end with death. As the cameras continue to move along the ruins of Titanic, something truly wonderful begins to happen. The water drains away from the hallway. Light begins coming through the windows again. Color returns. Then the incredible majesty of the ship is restored. You soon realize that you are seeing everything from Rose's perspective as she walks through what is being made new once again. She is young again—and beautiful. The doors are opened for her. She approaches the main staircase in all its grandeur. All the people from the ship are gathered together welcoming her, smiling and full of joy. She is smiling too.

Then, there he is—her beloved Jack—waiting for her halfway up the stairs. He turns around and smiles. They are separated no more. He takes her hand, and then they kiss. She is wearing white, and it's almost as if they are now finally married. Everything is good. Everything is right. Everything is joy. Everything is love. Everything is beauty. It's a glimpse of heaven.

We didn't want the story to end with a love that was lost and a joy that was shattered. We wanted to see a love that would last forever and a joy and beauty that would be restored. We wanted the *ultimate story*, and that's what they gave us. And I am glad they did. The ultimate story is not merely reflected in these few examples either. It is everywhere—not always complete, but present nonetheless.

In *The Gladiator,* Maximus is reunited in death with his loving wife and beloved son. Simba regains the throne as *The Lion King* and restores peace to the land. In *Braveheart,* William Wallace, as he is about to die, sees his murdered wife again from beyond the grave, walking in the crowd, smiling, and waiting for him to join her. Aslan, in *The Chronicles of Narnia,* rises from the dead, conquers the evil witch, and brings peace to Narnia again. In *Pride and Prejudice,* Mr. Darcy returns to ask for Elizabeth's hand in marriage.

Beauty restored is, indeed, the greatest story ever told. It's what our hearts long for most passionately. It's what our souls crave most deeply. It's what our spirits so desperately need. It is the ultimate story. It's God's story. It's our story.

THE BIBLE

In the third chapter of the Bible, everything has changed. Paradise is lost. Mankind has sinned against God and is now separated from Him and subject to physical death as well. Still, God has already begun to speak of a Savior—the Offspring of the woman—who will defeat the power of Satan and rescue mankind from sin. This gives us sufficient background to begin to understand the message of the Bible as a whole.

55

If you have never picked up a Bible before, it will be helpful to know some basic information. If you are familiar with the Bible, then this chapter may not offer anything new.

There are two main divisions to the Bible—the Old Testament and the New Testament. The word *testament* refers to a covenant or promise that God has made with mankind. Sometimes these are like a contract where God promises to do something and mankind is obligated to do something as well. Other times, they are just promises that God makes, and there is nothing mankind has to do.

To be a bit more precise, we might refer to the first of the two divisions as the Old Testaments (plural), as it contains several major promises God makes to mankind.

There are a total of seven main covenants mentioned in the Old Testament, and we have already seen two of them. The first was God's covenant with Adam in the Garden of Eden, which is commonly referred to as the Edenic Covenant. In this covenant, God gives Adam all the trees of the Garden for food except one. Adam's responsibility is to obey, and the consequence of his disobedience would be death.

The second covenant came in God's cursing of the serpent after Adam and Eve sinned. This is a covenant where God promises to send a savior—the Offspring of the woman. This covenant makes no demands on mankind at all. God makes this covenant based not on an expectation of mankind's future obedience but in response to mankind's previous disobedience. This is commonly referred to as the Adamic Covenant.

In the remainder of the Old Testament, God makes covenants with Noah, Abraham, Moses, and the entire nation of Israel. Each of these covenants begins in the Old Testament.

However, one final covenant is only mentioned in the Old Testament, but its beginning is never recorded. It is referred to simply as the *new covenant*. This new covenant is to be a better covenant than any of the previous ones. The New Testament is the revelation of this new covenant.

WHO WROTE THE BIBLE?

You might be wondering at this point who exactly wrote the Bible? Admittedly, God Himself did not pick up a pen and paper and write the Bible from cover to cover. However, even though it was written by men, the Bible is absolutely unlike any other book regarding its authorship.

It was written by about forty different authors—not just one—so that is pretty unique. These authors lived at different times in history as well, spanning around sixteen hundred years (from about 1500 B.C. to

100 A.D.). It was also written on three different continents and in three different languages. So it is very unlike any other book, indeed!

Nonetheless, the Bible asserts that it is not merely the speculations of men but is rather the revelation of God through men. It specifically asserts that men "spoke from God as they were carried along by the Holy Spirit" (2 Peter 1:21 NIV). Thus God is the author, and men are merely His secretaries.

THE LANGUAGES OF THE BIBLE

The Old Testament was written almost entirely in the Hebrew language, which is and was the language of the Israelites (the Jewish people). It is intriguing that the Hebrew language was a dead language for 1,800+ years but was resurrected in 1914. Of course, Jesus Himself also died and was resurrected.

A small portion of the Old Testament from the book of Daniel was written in Aramaic.

When the New Testament was being written, the nation of Israel was under the control of the Roman Empire. The language of trade at that time was Greek—a carryover from the Greek Empire that had preceded the Romans. To make its message accessible to the entire world of their day, the New Testament authors wrote in Greek.

BOOKS, CHAPTERS, AND VERSES

Some of the authors wrote a lot, and some wrote very little. The Bible is actually a collection of sixty-six individual works, which we call books of the Bible. There are thirty-nine Old Testament books and twenty-seven New Testament books. Each book is typically named either for its content, its author, or its recipients.

So far we have read primarily from the first book of the Bible, which is entitled Genesis. This name refers to its content, as it is the book of beginnings. We have also read from the book of Acts, which again is named for its content. It is sometimes referred to as the Acts of the Apostles because it describes primarily what two of Jesus' apostles did. (The word *apostle* refers to a follower of Jesus who has specifically been sent out on a mission.)

We will see that most of the prophetic books as well as the biographies of Jesus are named for their authors. Finally, there are many books that appear later in the New Testament that are named for their recipients.

Originally, there were no chapter or verse divisions in the Bible. Over time, these were added to make it easier to identify a specific statement or passage. Today, you will commonly see a reference from the Bible look something like this: Genesis 1:26-27.

Genesis refers to a particular book of the Bible. The first number refers to the chapter in that book, and the number or numbers after the colon refer to the particular verses being referenced. If there is no colon and no other numbers, then the entire chapter is being referenced. Sometimes a reference will be made to just a portion of a verse. In this case, the letter "a" or "b" will follow the verse number, indicating either the first or last part of the verse.

BIBLE OVERVIEW

Now we know enough to provide a simple overview of the entire Bible that will hopefully be helpful to you.

1. God created.

2. Man destroyed.

3. God restores.

Yes, it really is that simple!

We have actually already covered the first two parts of this. Creation is recorded in the first two chapters of Genesis. The fall of man is recorded in the first few verses of chapter 3. Then, the full account of God's restoration is recorded, starting in the middle of chapter 3 and continuing for the next 1,186 chapters.

We could also label these to reflect the ultimate story that we discussed previously: (1) God created beauty, (2) man destroyed beauty, and (3) God restores beauty. Here it is in a little more detail:

- *God created beauty* (Genesis 1–2): God created the universe, made mankind in His own image, and made a covenant with him that included a command to obey. Everything was right and pure and good. Everything was beautiful.

- *Man destroyed beauty* (Genesis 3:1-8): Mankind disobeyed God's command and incurred His judgment. This included physical death and separation from God. Beauty was destroyed.

- *God restores beauty* (Genesis 3:9 to the end): God promised that He would restore mankind's relationship with Himself through the Offspring of the woman. For thousands of years after this, God continued to speak of the coming of this Savior. Then, Jesus was born, died in our place to pay the penalty for our sins, rose from the dead, and ascended into heaven. After this, the message of God's restoration began to be proclaimed to the whole world. Finally, God spoke of

His completed restoration, which will occur sometime in the future. Beauty will be fully restored one day.

The Bible is ultimately the story of God's restoration of mankind from sin—beauty restored. This restoration unfolds in three different phases.

1. God comes to be *near* us.
2. God comes to be *with* us.
3. God comes to be *within* us.

Each of these steps involves primarily a different Person of the Trinity. Throughout the remainder of the Old Testament, we observe the glory of God the Father who comes to be near us. In the first part of the New Testament, it is God the Son who comes to be with us. This occurred when Jesus, the Son of God, entered into the world. After the resurrection and ascension of Jesus, it is the Holy Spirit who comes to be within us.

In the future, there remains what may be considered a fourth phase where we will go to be with God in heaven. Heaven is where those who have put their faith in Jesus, the Son of God, will live after they pass through physical death. Death is not the end.

The Old Testament, after the first three chapters, covers just the first of these three steps, namely God the Father coming to be near us. This happened progressively, as God appeared to certain people at various times and places but eventually made His presence dwell in the temple in Jerusalem.

The books in the Old Testament fall into three main categories: history, poetry, and prophecy. We will spend the majority of our time in the historical books. The poetic and prophetic books all fit into different places within the historical books.

The final steps of God drawing near to us will occur in the New Testament.

THE DESCENT OF MAN

GENESIS 4

We now return to the unfolding story of God's restoration following the sin of Adam and Eve in the Garden.

The idea of knowing both good and evil had sounded so appealing to them. They were deceived into thinking they could actually be like

God Himself. Yet, as we saw, that was a complete lie. As we already mentioned, *knowing* typically refers to an experiential knowing and not merely intellectual comprehension. Growing in knowledge is certainly a good thing, but experiencing evil is not.

Adam and Eve would now see firsthand just how devastating the experience of evil could be as it invades the lives of their own children.

Cain and Abel

¹ The man was intimate with his wife Eve, and she conceived and gave birth to Cain. She said, "I have had a male child with the LORD's help." ² She also gave birth to his brother Abel. Now Abel became a shepherd of flocks, but Cain worked the ground. ³ In the course of time Cain presented some of the land's produce as an offering to the LORD. ⁴ And Abel also presented an offering—some of the firstborn of his flock and their fat portions. The LORD had regard for Abel and his offering, ⁵ but he did not have regard for Cain and his offering. Cain was furious, and he looked despondent.

⁶ Then the LORD said to Cain, "Why are you furious? And why do you look despondent? ⁷ If you do what is right, won't you be accepted? But if you do not do what is right, sin is crouching at the door. Its desire is for you, but you must rule over it."

⁸ Cain said to his brother Abel, "Let's go out to the field." And while they were in the field, Cain attacked his brother Abel and killed him.

⁹ Then the LORD said to Cain, "Where is your brother Abel?"

"I don't know," he replied. "Am I my brother's guardian?"

¹⁰ Then he said, "What have you done? Your brother's blood cries out to me from the ground! ¹¹ So now you are cursed, alienated from the ground that opened its mouth to receive your brother's blood you have shed. ¹² If you work the ground, it will never again give you its yield. You will be a restless wanderer on the earth."

¹³ But Cain answered the LORD, "My punishment is too great to bear! ¹⁴ Since you are banishing me today from the face of the earth, and I must hide from your presence and become a restless wanderer on the earth, whoever finds me will kill me."

[15] Then the LORD replied to him, "In that case, whoever kills Cain will suffer vengeance seven times over." And he placed a mark on Cain so that whoever found him would not kill him. [16] Then Cain went out from the LORD's presence and lived in the land of Nod, east of Eden.

Lamech

[17] Cain was intimate with his wife, and she conceived and gave birth to Enoch. Then Cain became the builder of a city, and he named the city Enoch after his son. [18] Irad was born to Enoch, Irad fathered Mehujael, Mehujael fathered Methushael, and Methushael fathered Lamech. [19] Lamech took two wives for himself, one named Adah and the other named Zillah. [20] Adah bore Jabal; he was the first of the nomadic herdsmen. [21] His brother was named Jubal; he was the first of all who play the lyre and the flute. [22] Zillah bore Tubal-cain, who made all kinds of bronze and iron tools. Tubal-cain's sister was Naamah.

[23] Lamech said to his wives:
Adah and Zillah, hear my voice;
wives of Lamech, pay attention to my words.
For I killed a man for wounding me,
a young man for striking me.
[24] If Cain is to be avenged seven times over,
then for Lamech it will be seventy-seven times!

Seth

[25] Adam was intimate with his wife again, and she gave birth to a son and named him Seth, for she said, "God has given me another offspring in place of Abel, since Cain killed him." [26] A son was born to Seth also, and he named him Enosh. At that time people began to call on the name of the LORD. (Genesis 4 CSB)

TWO OFFERINGS

The first question that arises from this passage is why God accepted the offering of Abel but rejected the offering of Cain. At first glance, it certainly seems that both of them were doing something good—bringing to God an offering from the fruit of their chosen professions. It's important to remember, though, that there were two types of garments in the Garden that were used to cover the shame of Adam and Eve's sin. One of them was sufficient, and one was not. The garment that was acceptable came from the sacrifice of an animal.

Something had to die. This symbolized what was to come. Sin could never be covered over by good works. The penalty for sin is death, and only through the death of a substitute could sin be forgiven. We must come to God on *His* terms—not ours.

Abel's offering recognized this in that it included the death of an innocent. Cain's offering did not. This lack of recognition of the seriousness of sin and of its penalty seems to have been what made Cain's offering unacceptable to God.

Cain responded in anger at his rebuke and refused the correction given by God Himself. His reaction was not to change his own behavior but to attack and murder the one whose behavior was righteous. Thus Adam and Eve saw for the first time the reality of death that their own sin had brought into the world.

However, even after this horrific sin, God showed great mercy to Cain. He pronounced judgment but spared his life. This provided him with at least the opportunity to repent of his sin and honor God with the rest of his life, even though that does not appear to have happened.

LAMECH AND POLYGAMY

It only got worse from there. Lamech, the great-great-great grandson of Cain, also committed murder. He not only showed no remorse for his sin, but he was even defiant in his own self-righteousness.

We also see the first mention of polygamy as Lamech took two wives. It is important to understand that the Bible records the fact that polygamy occurred. However, this was certainly not God's design from the beginning. When God saw Adam's need in the Garden, He only created one woman to meet that need—not two or three or more. If God had intended for polygamy to be practiced, He would surely have also provided for that in the ratio of births between males and females. As it is, the number of boys born every year is virtually the same as the number of girls.

We also note here that polygamy is first attributed to an unrighteous man—not to a man who walked with God and was pleasing to Him. Most of the key figures in the Bible either practiced monogamy or did not marry. In the few cases where polygamy did occur, it always gave rise to major problems.

WHERE DID CAIN GET HIS WIFE?

A common objection to the truth of the Bible is the question of, *Where did Cain get his wife?* The Bible clearly states that all people came from Adam and Eve, so who could he have married?

The answer is quite simple. He married one of his sisters. As we will see in the next chapter, mankind appears to have been quite fruitful at this time. The world was apparently quite healthy, even as it suffered under the curse of sin. People also lived very long lives. We know that mutations accumulate in each successive generation, but in the very first few generations, there would have been a very small number. For this reason, marrying a close relative would not have caused the genetic problems that we would experience today.

In fact, it wasn't until the time of Moses more than two thousand years later that God gave the command to the Israelites that prohibited marriage between close relatives (Deuteronomy 27:22).

NOAH, A RIGHTEOUS MAN
GENESIS 5

The next chapter in our journey details the family line of Adam down to a man named Noah, spanning nine generations and about sixteen hundred years.

You will no doubt notice that the ages given here are enormously large, and you may wonder how that could even be possible. Yet the numbers are anything but random, and the author records them merely as a matter of fact. He seems to feel no burden to offer an explanation or excuse but just assumes that his audience will accept them as they are presented without question.

Six chapters after this, though, the line of Noah is picked up again through his son Shem and carried out for another ten generations down to a man named Abram. In that account, we observe the recorded ages decreasing quite rapidly. The book of Genesis ends with the death of Abram's great-grandson Joseph, who dies at the age of 110. This is still quite old by today's standards, but certainly not impossible. It is only rare. From the time of Joseph on, the ages recorded are completely consistent with what we see today. Thus it seems that something significant may have happened between the time of Noah and the time of Abram that would account for this drastic decline in life expectancy.

We find just such an event in the next three chapters which give the account of God's judgment of the world's sin through a catastrophic global flood. Such an event would certainly have had a devastating impact on the earth, and that is exactly what we find.

As you read through the line of Adam, be sure to take note of the man named Enoch. Something extraordinary in his life distinguishes him from all the others, and God makes special mention of that.

¹ This is the document containing the family records of Adam. On the day that God created man, he made him in the likeness of God; ² he created them male and female. When they were created, he blessed them and called them mankind.

³ Adam was 130 years old when he fathered a son in his likeness, according to his image, and named him Seth. ⁴ Adam lived 800 years after he fathered Seth, and he fathered other sons and daughters. ⁵ So Adam's life lasted 930 years; then he died.

⁶ Seth was 105 years old when he fathered Enosh. ⁷ Seth lived 807 years after he fathered Enosh, and he fathered other sons and daughters. ⁸ So Seth's life lasted 912 years; then he died.

⁹ Enosh was 90 years old when he fathered Kenan. ¹⁰ Enosh lived 815 years after he fathered Kenan, and he fathered other sons and daughters. ¹¹ So Enosh's life lasted 905 years; then he died.

¹² Kenan was 70 years old when he fathered Mahalalel. ¹³ Kenan lived 840 years after he fathered Mahalalel, and he fathered other sons and daughters. ¹⁴ So Kenan's life lasted 910 years; then he died.

¹⁵ Mahalalel was 65 years old when he fathered Jared. ¹⁶ Mahalalel lived 830 years after he fathered Jared, and he fathered other sons and daughters. ¹⁷ So Mahalalel's life lasted 895 years; then he died.

¹⁸ Jared was 162 years old when he fathered Enoch. ¹⁹ Jared lived 800 years after he fathered Enoch, and he fathered other sons and daughters. ²⁰ So Jared's life lasted 962 years; then he died.

²¹ Enoch was 65 years old when he fathered Methuselah. ²² And after he fathered Methuselah, Enoch walked with God 300 years and fathered other sons and daughters. ²³ So Enoch's life lasted 365 years. ²⁴ Enoch walked with God; then he was not there because God took him.

25 Methuselah was 187 years old when he fathered Lamech. 26 Methuselah lived 782 years after he fathered Lamech, and he fathered other sons and daughters. 27 So Methuselah's life lasted 969 years; then he died.

28 Lamech was 182 years old when he fathered a son. 29 And he named him Noah, saying, "This one will bring us relief from the agonizing labor of our hands, caused by the ground the LORD has cursed." 30 Lamech lived 595 years after he fathered Noah, and he fathered other sons and daughters. 31 So Lamech's life lasted 777 years; then he died.

32 Noah was 500 years old, and he fathered Shem, Ham, and Japheth. (Genesis 5 CSB)

IN WHOSE IMAGE?

In the first paragraph of this passage, we see the affirmation that mankind had originally been made in the image of God. However, when we are introduced to Seth, a distinction is made. The Scriptures specifically state that Adam did not have a son in the likeness of God, but in his own likeness and in his own image. Now, in just a few chapters, we will see the Bible affirms that mankind still does bear the image of God. However, this image had been marred by Adam's sin. There was now a second image and likeness that was present in addition to the original image of God—the likeness of sinful man.

There is no record of any children being born prior to Adam's sin. Thus every child who has ever come in the world has been born in this manner, bearing both the image of God and the image of sinful man.

There are, of course, some who believe that every child is born in innocence and only later learns to do things that are wrong. One problem with this idea is that there is never a child who does not choose to do wrong at some point. If every child were born without sin, we would expect at least one would remain that way, yet this never occurs.

You and I experience this choice every day in our own lives in a very practical sense. In any circumstance, we know there is a right thing to do, a nobler path, a higher way. There is something deep inside of us that wants to do that. We truly desire to be that kind of person. Yet there is also a part of us that just wants to do what is beneficial to our own selves, even if it is selfish and to the detriment of others.

Thus we are at war with ourselves. We have competing desires between doing what is right and doing what is wrong, and our lives become the product of those choices. Reality dictates that we are not what we desire to be but rather what we choose to be.

THE MAN WHO WALKED WITH GOD

Did you see it? In the recounting of the lives of these men, the common thread is the mention of when they were born, how old they were when they became the father of a particular son, the fact that they had other sons and daughters, and how old they were when they died. These are all just basic details. Nothing very interesting is included—nothing, that is, except for one man.

Enoch was different. He didn't just live and die and have children. There was something special about him. This was of such immense significance that God pauses in the genealogy to make special mention of it. Enoch, too, did have sons and daughters, but that wasn't the most important thing about him.

He walked with God.

Of course, the fact that he never died is quite amazing as well. Yet the emphasis is not on that but rather on his special relationship with God. He truly experienced heaven on earth as he walked deeply in God's presence. I like to think that every step of his life led him deeper and deeper into the presence of God until it was eventually necessary for him to leave this world altogether. Regardless of the details of his departure, the life of Enoch is one to be greatly admired—and imitated.

THE REIGN OF DEATH

Aside from the person of Enoch, there is something else very significant about this chapter. It is easy to miss because it is so common that it escapes our attention. The account does seem like just a list of a bunch of names, but there is one thread that runs through it all—aside from Enoch. That one thing is *death.* Every one of them dies.

God had warned Adam and Eve that death would surely be the result of their sin. Satan had contradicted this. However, the reign of death recorded in this chapter through ten generations confirms that God was telling the truth.

It has been well said that death is mankind's greatest enemy. Every one of us must fight a battle with it, but every one of us will eventually lose that battle. It is a sobering truth. Our hearts cry out at the agony of it all. *This isn't the way it should be,* we protest. *Why does death have to always be the end?* Yet despite our protests and questions, death continues its march throughout time and history.

However, God has promised one day to crush the power of Satan, and He will most assuredly conquer death itself. Its victories are only temporary. It will win only some minor battles. In the end, God wins the war. Both death and Satan will be completely defeated forever!

A HIDDEN PROMISE

We have already seen in Adam and Eve that names in the Bible can have very significant meaning. That is also true for those that appear in this chapter. For instance, *Noah* means "comfort" or "relief." As we just read, his father, Lamech, specifically named him this as a prophecy that he would "bring us relief from the agonizing labor of our hands, caused by the ground the LORD has cursed" (Genesis 5:29 CSB). Note that the Lamech spoken of here is not the same person we met in the previous chapter, as he is in the line of Seth—not Cain.

Yet what is so intriguing about this passage is not the meaning of any one name but the meaning of all ten names when they are put together in their order of appearance:

- Adam   Man
- Seth   Appointed
- Enosh   Mortal
- Kenan   Sorrow
- Mahalalel   The blessed God
- Jared   Shall come down
- Enoch   Teaching
- Methuselah   His death shall bring
- Lamech   The despairing
- Noah   Rest or comfort

If we were to read the names as a sentence, this is what we would see:

Man (is) appointed mortal sorrow.
The blessed God shall come down teaching.
His death shall bring, (to) the despairing, comfort.

This is precisely what we have already seen in the Garden of Eden. Man became mortal as a result of sin. This was accompanied by much sorrow and pain. Yet God promised a Savior who would defeat both Satan and the power of death. Later on God reveals that it is

He Himself—the blessed God—who is that Savior who would come down. In doing so, He would bring comfort and restoration to sinful man.

JUDGMENT DECREED

GENESIS 6

There had been ten generations from Adam to Noah in a span of over fifteen hundred years. For each of the men in the genealogy, a specific son was named. After that, there is the mention of other sons and daughters for each of them.

The first named son was Seth. He was not Adam's firstborn son, since he was born after the death of Abel. It is reasonable, then, to assume that this was likely true of many others in the list as well. After all, the purpose of the account was to trace the line of Noah—not the line of Adam.

Thus it seems that it was normal for a man to father more than one son and more than one daughter *after* becoming the father of one particular named son, who may not have been his firstborn. Remember that lifespans were quite long at this point in history.

So families at that time were probably quite large as well, at least by today's standards. Mankind was exceedingly fruitful, increasing vastly in numbers, and filling the earth quite rapidly. Perhaps there were even as many people on the earth then as there are today. We can't know for sure, but that is certainly possible.

We might suspect that God was quite pleased with this. After all, wasn't that what God had wanted from the very beginning—that mankind would be fruitful and multiply and fill the earth? Well, that was certainly part of His desire, but that wasn't all of it. We will see in this next passage that something crucial was missing.

The Descent of Man

¹ *When mankind began to multiply on the earth and daughters were born to them, ² the sons of God saw that the daughters of mankind were*

beautiful, and they took any they chose as wives for themselves. ³ *And the* LORD *said, "My Spirit will not remain with mankind forever, because they are corrupt. Their days will be 120 years."* ⁴ *The Nephilim were on the earth both in those days and afterward, when the sons of God came to the daughters of mankind, who bore children to them. They were the powerful men of old, the famous men.*

Judgment Pronounced

⁵ *When the* LORD *saw that human wickedness was widespread on the earth and that every inclination of the human mind was nothing but evil all the time,* ⁶ *the Lord regretted that he had made man on the earth, and he was deeply grieved.* ⁷ *Then the* LORD *said, "I will wipe mankind, whom I created, off the face of the earth, together with the animals, creatures that crawl, and birds of the sky—for I regret that I made them."* ⁸ *Noah, however, found favor with the* LORD.

The Account of Noah

⁹ *These are the family records of Noah. Noah was a righteous man, blameless among his contemporaries; Noah walked with God.* ¹⁰ *And Noah fathered three sons: Shem, Ham, and Japheth.*

¹¹ *Now the earth was corrupt in God's sight, and the earth was filled with wickedness.* ¹² *God saw how corrupt the earth was, for every creature had corrupted its way on the earth.* ¹³ *Then God said to Noah, "I have decided to put an end to every creature, for the earth is filled with wickedness because of them; therefore I am going to destroy them along with the earth.*

¹⁴ *"Make yourself an ark of gopher wood. Make rooms in the ark, and cover it with pitch inside and outside.* ¹⁵ *This is how you are to make it: The ark will be 450 feet long, 75 feet wide, and 45 feet high.* ¹⁶ *You are to make a roof, finishing the sides of the ark to within eighteen inches of the roof. You are to put a door in the side of the ark. Make it with lower, middle, and upper decks.*

¹⁷ *"Understand that I am bringing a flood—floodwaters on the earth to destroy every creature under heaven with the breath of life in it. Everything on earth will perish.* ¹⁸ *But I will establish my covenant with you, and you will enter the ark with your sons, your wife, and your sons' wives.* ¹⁹ *You are also to bring into the ark two of all the living creatures, male and female, to keep them alive with you.* ²⁰ *Two of*

everything—from the birds according to their kinds, from the livestock according to their kinds, and from the animals that crawl on the ground according to their kinds—will come to you so that you can keep them alive. [21] Take with you every kind of food that is eaten; gather it as food for you and for them." [22] And Noah did this. He did everything that God had commanded him. (Genesis 6 CSB)

THE DESCENT OF MANKIND

God wasn't pleased at all with how much mankind had populated the earth. But why wasn't He? God was not merely interested in numbers and geography. He was interested in people. God had made mankind in His own image. After sin entered the world, mankind also bore the image of sinful man. Yet God's desire was for mankind to still reflect *His* image, to live a righteous life, and to walk with Him—to live a life like Enoch. That did not happen.

Instead, mankind became so corrupt that *"Every* inclination of the human mind was *nothing but evil all the time"* (Genesis 6:5 CSB, emphasis added). It would be hard to imagine a worse description. Mankind had descended into complete darkness. The image of God had all but vanished.

So what was God's reaction to this? He was grieved, and His heart was filled with pain.

We have already discussed the personhood of God—that He has a mind, a will, and emotions. This passage affirms that. God is not an impersonal force. His emotions are real. He grieves and experiences true emotional pain. This does not mean He is weak. It just means He is real and personal and relatable.

We ourselves have deep emotions because He has deep emotions. We are not greater than God in this matter—far from it. Rather, in this we are a reflection of His image. We should not suppose, then, that His emotions are any less than ours. They are most definitely far greater.

THE MAN OF FAVOR

Even though the world was full of evil at this time, all was not lost. There was still one man who had not corrupted his ways. That man's name was Noah, the grandson of Enoch—the man who had walked with God like no other.

God described Noah as "a righteous man, blameless among his contemporaries" and one who, like his grandfather, "walked with God" (Genesis 6:9 CSB). This was the kind of person God wanted—and still wants today—to fill the whole earth. Thus this is not merely the account of God's judgment on sinful man. It is the account of a righteous man named Noah, whom God rescued from judgment.

JUDGMENT DECREED

In response to the great wickedness of mankind, God pronounced His judgment on the world. It would come in the form of a global flood. All life on earth would be destroyed. This may seem like an extreme punishment, but we must remember that the wickedness of mankind was quite extreme as well. Perhaps, the world had just reached a point of no return, and the only way to restore what God had intended was to start over.

Even though Noah found favor in the eyes of God, it is significant to see that this did not prevent the judgment from coming. God did, however, provide a way of escape in the midst of His judgment—a way of salvation. This would not be the last time God would allow judgment to come but rescue the righteous from it.

THE ARK

God's particular method of salvation in this case was for Noah to build a very large boat. This would serve to preserve not only the lives of his family but the lives of animals as well.

You're probably wondering if it was even possible for one boat to hold so many animals, and that's a great question. When the specifics are carefully considered, it was actually very possible. However, to understand this, there are a few things to keep in mind. First, it wasn't necessary to take every breed of dog, but just one pair of the generic dog *kind*. Breeds are produced by selecting and isolating certain genetic qualities that already exist in the genetic pool. The actual number of different kinds of animals in the world is surprisingly few, even though the number of breeds is quite large.

Secondly, the vast majority of animals are pretty small, but what about the large ones? Well, Noah would not have needed to take full-grown adults. If fact, it would have been very wise to take ones that were still too young to reproduce. This would minimize food consumption and minimize the amount of supplies needed. This would also minimize the amount of "clean up" that would have been required.

Finally, the ark was enormous. It totaled ten thousand square feet (one thousand square meters). The Ark Encounter in eastern Kentucky, by Answers in Genesis, is a replica of what the ark may have looked like. I had the privilege of touring this with my parents shortly after it opened. We made the mistake of walking to the wrong end of the boat initially, so we first had to walk back all the way to the entrance on the other side.

Then we had to walk almost halfway back to get to the stairs to reach the ark itself. After going around the entire first floor, going up the stairs to the second floor, walking around the entire second floor, walking up the stairs to the third floor, and finally walking around the entire third floor, we were absolutely exhausted and found a place to sit for a while. Then, to our collective dismay, we realized how far we would still have to walk to get out. It's really, really, really big!

It was a truly wonderful experience, though. The entire construction is in a sense a feasibility study, showing in great detail how the biblical account of the flood and the ark was entirely plausible. In fact, all of the animals could have easily fit inside it with plenty of room to spare.

It's also interesting to note that the dimensions prescribed for the ark had a six to one ratio of length to width. This just happens to be recognized even today as ideal proportions for such a vessel.

In the last verse, we see a simple description of Noah's response—he "did everything that God had commanded him" (Genesis 6:22 CSB). This demonstrates that Noah was, indeed, a righteous man who walked with God—precisely the kind of person God wanted.

JUDGMENT COMES
GENESIS 7

While the previous chapter described the judgment that was to come, this chapter describes the actual coming of that judgment. God provides a few more details about the numbers of animals to be taken into the ark, specifically that the "clean" animals should number more than the "unclean."

The concept of "clean" animals is described in much greater detail a bit later on in the Bible, but it apparently existed in the time of Noah as well. "Clean" animals refer to those that were appropriate for human consumption, while the "unclean" animals were not. Obviously, more of the "clean" animals would be needed to fulfill the needs of Noah and his family.

Be sure to take note of the specific details that are given in this account, including dates. Such details again demonstrate that these are not merely fanciful stories but accurate accounts of real events that occurred in real places at real times in human history.

¹ Then the L<small>ORD</small> said to Noah, "Enter the ark, you and all your household, for I have seen that you alone are righteous before me in this generation. ² You are to take with you seven pairs, a male and its female, of all the clean animals, and two of the animals that are not clean, a male and its female, ³ and seven pairs, male and female, of the birds of the sky—in order to keep offspring alive throughout the earth. ⁴ Seven days from now I will make it rain on the earth forty days and forty nights, and every living thing I have made I will wipe off the face of the earth." ⁵ And Noah did everything that the L<small>ORD</small> commanded him.

⁶ Noah was six hundred years old when the flood came and water covered the earth. ⁷ So Noah, his sons, his wife, and his sons' wives entered the ark because of the floodwaters. ⁸ From the animals that are clean, and from the animals that are not clean, and from the birds and every creature that crawls on the ground, ⁹ two of each, male and female, came to Noah and entered the ark, just as God had commanded him. ¹⁰ Seven days later the floodwaters came on the earth.

The Flood

¹¹ In the six hundredth year of Noah's life, in the second month, on the seventeenth day of the month, on that day all the sources of the vast watery depths burst open, the floodgates of the sky were opened, ¹² and the rain fell on the earth forty days and forty nights. ¹³ On that same day Noah and his three sons, Shem, Ham, and Japheth, entered the ark, along with Noah's wife and his three sons' wives. ¹⁴ They entered it with all the wildlife according to their kinds, all livestock according to their kinds, all the creatures that crawl on the earth according to their kinds, every flying creature—all the birds and every winged creature—according to their kinds. ¹⁵ Two of every creature that has the breath of life in it came to Noah and entered the ark. ¹⁶ Those that entered, male and female of every creature, entered just as God had commanded him. Then the L<small>ORD</small> shut him in.

¹⁷ The flood continued for forty days on the earth; the water increased and lifted up the ark so that it rose above the earth. ¹⁸ The water surged and increased greatly on the earth, and the ark floated on the surface of the water. ¹⁹ Then the water surged even higher on the earth, and all the high mountains under the whole sky were covered. ²⁰ The mountains were covered as the water surged above them more than twenty feet. ²¹ Every creature perished—those that crawl on the earth, birds, livestock, wildlife, and those that swarm on the earth, as well as all mankind. ²² Everything with the breath of the spirit of life in its nostrils—everything on dry land died. ²³ He wiped out every living thing that was on the face of the earth, from mankind to livestock, to creatures that crawl, to the birds of the sky, and they were wiped off the earth. Only Noah was left, and those that were with him in the ark. ²⁴ And the water surged on the earth 150 days. (Genesis 7 CSB)

THE DOOR

In the previous chapter, God specifically instructed Noah to make a door in the side of the ark. It appears there was only one of these. This, then, was the only way of escape from the judgment of God. It was open for a specified amount of time, but not forever. There was one moment in time when the opportunity to enter through that door came to an end. When the rain started to fall, it was too late.

After Noah and his family had entered into God's salvation (the ark), the Bible records that the LORD shut him in. Thus it was not Noah who determined when the opportunity for salvation had passed. It was God Himself.

When God told Noah to enter the ark, He also gave the reason for it. It was because God had found him righteous. Even though Noah bore the image of sinful man just like we do today, God declared that he was "a righteous man, blameless among his contemporaries," and someone who "walked with God" (Genesis 6:9 CSB). He also trusted in God's plan of salvation. It was only the righteous who could enter through the door of the ark and escape God's judgment.

THE DOOR TODAY

Just as in the days of Noah, God has pronounced judgment on all mankind today because of our sinfulness. As we have discussed previously, this judgment is not merely a physical one but a spiritual one as well. However, just like in the days of Noah, God has also provided a way of salvation—a way of escape from that judgment. Just as there was one door into the ark, there is also only one way to escape God's ultimate judgment for our sin.

Jesus is that way.

Later on, we will see that Jesus specifically identifies Himself as "the gate" (John 10:7-9 CSB) and the only way to God (John 14:6). He is *the door.* That door has been open now for two thousand years. Anyone can enter through it, but no one is forced to do so. By our faith in Jesus and His death on the cross, which paid the penalty for our sins, we can be made righteous—and only the righteous will escape the judgment of God.

However, this way of escape will not remain open forever. Just like it was in the days of Noah, a time will come when God will close that door as well. It could happen very soon for some of us, for no one knows the day of his death.

May I suggest to you, then, that you enter through that door today before the rain comes and it is too late?

GOD REMEMBERED

GENESIS 8

In Genesis 6, God commanded Noah to build the ark. In Genesis 7, God commanded him to go into the ark. In Genesis 8, God commands him to come out of the ark. God's judgment comes to an end. The rain stops, and the water recedes.

From the dates given, it appears that Noah and his family had spent about one year on the ark. It must have been quite sobering for them to realize that the entire world had perished under the judgment of God and that they alone had been spared. Once again, death reigned. However, they didn't stay in the ark forever. God remembered Noah!

As you read this passage, be sure to take note of how Noah demonstrates his gratitude to God immediately after coming out of the ark and then how God responds.

> *¹ God remembered Noah, as well as all the wildlife and all the livestock that were with him in the ark. God caused a wind to pass over the earth, and the water began to subside. ² The sources of the watery depths and the floodgates of the sky were closed, and the rain from the sky stopped. ³ The water steadily receded from the earth, and by the end of 150 days the water had decreased significantly. ⁴ The ark came to rest in the seventh month, on the seventeenth day of the month, on the mountains of Ararat.*
>
> *⁵ The water continued to recede until the tenth month; in the tenth month, on the first day of the month, the tops of the mountains were visible. ⁶ After forty days Noah opened the window of the ark that he had made, ⁷ and he sent out a raven. It went back and forth until*

the water had dried up from the earth. [8] Then he sent out a dove to see whether the water on the earth's surface had gone down, [9] but the dove found no resting place for its foot. It returned to him in the ark because water covered the surface of the whole earth. He reached out and brought it into the ark to himself. [10] So Noah waited seven more days and sent out the dove from the ark again. [11] When the dove came to him at evening, there was a plucked olive leaf in its beak. So Noah knew that the water on the earth's surface had gone down. [12] After he had waited another seven days, he sent out the dove, but it did not return to him again. [13] In the six hundred first year, in the first month, on the first day of the month, the water that had covered the earth was dried up. Then Noah removed the ark's cover and saw that the surface of the ground was drying. [14] By the twenty-seventh day of the second month, the earth was dry.

[15] Then God spoke to Noah, [16] "Come out of the ark, you, your wife, your sons, and your sons' wives with you. [17] Bring out all the living creatures that are with you—birds, livestock, those that crawl on the earth—and they will spread over the earth and be fruitful and multiply on the earth." [18] So Noah, along with his sons, his wife, and his sons' wives, came out. [19] All the animals, all the creatures that crawl, and all the flying creatures—everything that moves on the earth—came out of the ark by their families.

[20] Then Noah built an altar to the LORD. He took some of every kind of clean animal and every kind of clean bird and offered burnt offerings on the altar. [21] When the LORD smelled the pleasing aroma, he said to himself, "I will never again curse the ground because of human beings, even though the inclination of the human heart is evil from youth onward. And I will never again strike down every living thing as I have done.

[22] As long as the earth endures,
seedtime and harvest, cold and heat,
summer and winter, and day and night
will not cease." (Genesis 8 CSB)

A LOCAL FLOOD?

So, did this really happen? Was there actually a global flood around forty-four hundred years ago? Couldn't it have been just a local flood that was exaggerated?

76

The suggestion of a local flood is quite common, but it makes the account of Noah completely absurd. Think about it for a moment. If it were merely a local flood, then why would God have told him to build such an enormous boat? Why not just tell him to seek higher ground or, better yet, take a much-deserved vacation in the Swiss Alps? Furthermore, what would have been the point of gathering so many animals? If the flood were local, then there would be no need to preserve the animals in that small area. There would have been many more elsewhere. Even if he had wanted to save the animals, he could have just guided them away instead of putting them all on a boat.

So again, the idea that the flood was local makes the entire account absurd on multiple levels. The Bible specifically states that it was global with waters rising above even the highest mountains.

EVIDENCE OF THE FLOOD

There is actually a great deal of evidence that supports the occurrence of a global flood. For one thing, the remains of marine animals have been found of the tops of mountains all over the world. How does that happen? Well, if those mountains were once covered with water from the global flood, then that is exactly what we would expect. Without a global flood, though, this would be quite a mystery with no real explanation.

There is also the reality of fossilization. We know that fossils don't form very often. When something dies, it is typically eaten by various carnivores, and the bones are scattered. Fossils only form when something is buried rapidly immediately after it dies. But when does this ever happen? We don't observe animals burying their own dead, so what possible mechanism can account for this?

A global flood certainly would do this on a very large scale. In fact, it probably accounts for the vast majority of the fossils we find today. Incidentally, this would mean that the fossil record may largely be a snapshot in time rather than a prolonged history of life.

These are just a few points in a sea of evidence for the flood (pun intended), yet a complete discussion of this evidence is beyond the scope of this book. Suffice it to say, though, that the world we see today corresponds precisely with what we would expect if there had been a global flood in the recent past. If you're interested in pursuing this topic further, please check out the appendix.

THE GRATITUDE OF NOAH

Before we move on, it is important to note the gratitude of Noah. As soon as he and his family come out of the ark, he offers a sacrifice to God. The judgment had ended, and he and his family had been spared. Thus it was a most fitting time for worship, and God is pleased by it.

GOD'S COVENANT WITH NOAH
GENESIS 9

A s the next chapter begins, God's judgment has just come to an end. Noah and his family have come out of the ark, along with all the animals.

God's initial blessing to mankind back in the very first chapter was that they "be fruitful and increase in number; [and] fill the earth and subdue it" (Genesis 1:28 NIV). Now, everything outside the ark that lived on land had perished. God was starting over with a man who was righteous and walked with Him.

In this new world, just as in the old, God gives (1) a blessing, (2) a provision, (3) a command, and (4) a covenant. As you read, consider how these are both similar and different from those given to Adam and Eve in the Garden.

God's Blessing

¹ God blessed Noah and his sons and said to them, "Be fruitful and multiply and fill the earth.

God's Provision

² "The fear and terror of you will be in every living creature on the earth, every bird of the sky, every creature that crawls on the ground, and all the fish of the sea. They are placed under your authority. ³ Every creature that lives and moves will be food for you; as I gave the green plants, I have given you everything.

God's Command

[4] "However, you must not eat meat with its lifeblood in it. [5] And I will require a penalty for your lifeblood; I will require it from any animal and from any human; if someone murders a fellow human, I will require that person's life.

[6] "Whoever sheds human blood,
by humans his blood will be shed,
for God made humans in his image.

[7] "But you, be fruitful and multiply; spread out over the earth and multiply on it."

God's Covenant with Noah

[8] Then God said to Noah and his sons with him, [9] "Understand that I am establishing my covenant with you and your descendants after you, [10] and with every living creature that is with you—birds, livestock, and all wildlife of the earth that are with you—all the animals of the earth that came out of the ark. [11] I establish my covenant with you that never again will every creature be wiped out by floodwaters; there will never again be a flood to destroy the earth."

[12] And God said, "This is the sign of the covenant I am making between me and you and every living creature with you, a covenant for all future generations: [13] I have placed my bow in the clouds, and it will be a sign of the covenant between me and the earth. [14] Whenever I form clouds over the earth and the bow appears in the clouds, [15] I will remember my covenant between me and you and all the living creatures: water will never again become a flood to destroy every creature. [16] The bow will be in the clouds, and I will look at it and remember the permanent covenant between God and all the living creatures on earth." [17] God said to Noah, "This is the sign of the covenant that I have established between me and every creature on earth."

Ham's Shameful Act

[18] Noah's sons who came out of the ark were Shem, Ham, and Japheth. Ham was the father of Canaan. [19] These three were Noah's sons, and from them the whole earth was populated.

> [20] *Noah, as a man of the soil, began by planting a vineyard.* [21] *He drank some of the wine, became drunk, and uncovered himself inside his tent.* [22] *Ham, the father of Canaan, saw his father naked and told his two brothers outside.* [23] *Then Shem and Japheth took a cloak and placed it over both their shoulders, and walking backward, they covered their father's nakedness. Their faces were turned away, and they did not see their father naked.*
>
> [24] *When Noah awoke from his drinking and learned what his youngest son had done to him,* [25] *he said:*
>
> *Canaan is cursed.*
> *He will be the lowest of slaves to his brothers.*
> [26] *He also said:*
> *Blessed be the LORD, the God of Shem;*
> *Let Canaan be Shem's slave.*
> [27] *Let God extend Japheth;*
> *let Japheth dwell in the tents of Shem;*
> *let Canaan be Shem's slave.*
> [28] *Now Noah lived 350 years after the flood.* [29] *So Noah's life lasted 950 years; then he died. (Genesis 9 CSB)*

THE HEARTBEAT OF GOD

God's new blessing to Noah is virtually identical to the one He gave to Adam and Eve, and we will see this continue throughout the Bible. God's heartbeat is to see men and women filling the entire earth—men and women who reflect His image and who walk with Him. His vision for the world never changes.

GOD'S PROVISION

In God's initial provision of food to mankind, He had given only plants to Adam and Eve for consumption. Remember that there was no death on the earth at that time, so eating meat would have been impossible.

God's new provision does include meat from animals. Since the idea of clean and unclean animals was present at the time of the flood, it seems possible that meat was already eaten before then. However, God explicitly authorizes it after the flood.

GOD'S COMMAND

God gave two specific commands to Noah. The first command just concerned how meat was to be eaten—without blood in it. The second command concerned what we refer to as *capital punishment*. God endowed mankind with both the responsibility and the obligation to take the life of one who takes the life of another. It appears this may not have been practiced prior to the flood. Both Cain and Lamech murdered other men. However, neither of them forfeited their lives on account of that, even though it was God Himself who judged them.

Yet what was the outcome of such a society where murder had minimal consequences? The world became so violent that God chose to completely destroy it. It is possible, then, that God instituted capital punishment as a means to restrain violence in society and to protect the world from reaching the level of depravity to which it had descended before the flood.

We must note, though, that what God instituted was justice—not vengeance. Justice requires that the offender is the one who is punished, and the punishment is in proportion to the crime. It would be an eye for an eye, not a life for an eye. Vengeance is disproportionate and often encompasses many innocent people. God does not condone this.

GOD'S COVENANT: THE RAINBOW

After the judgment of the flood ended, God established His third covenant with mankind. In this covenant, man had no obligation. It was purely a promise from God to us, specifically that there will never again be a flood that would destroy the whole earth. God did not promise that He will never judge the world again. He most certainly will, and He has promised to do so. We just need not fear that His judgment will come as a global flood.

God designated the rainbow to be the specific sign of this covenant. Thus it is a reminder that there will never be another global flood. It is also a reminder that God *did* judge the world for its wickedness in the past. Therefore, it is also a warning that God does not leave sin unpunished. He didn't leave sin before the flood unpunished, and He certainly will not leave sin today unpunished. Yet He provided a way of escape then, and He does so today as well.

HAM'S SHAME

Although Noah was a righteous man, he certainly wasn't perfect. This is seen in Noah's drunkenness at the end of this chapter.

After the flood, the new world was drastically different from the old. Some have suggested that this may have included the fermentation process. As a result, the potency of the wine may have caught Noah unaware, but we don't know for sure.

We aren't given a complete picture of what exactly it was that Ham did. It seems that he may have not merely seen his father but had done something else disgraceful as well. As a result, when Noah learns about it later, he is enraged. He curses the descendants of Ham but blesses those of his other two sons.

THE TABLE OF NATIONS

GENESIS 10

Our next chapter reveals details about the immediate family line of Noah through each of his three sons, Shem, Ham, and Japheth.

We are only given two additional generations for the sons of Japheth and three generations of Ham. However, for the sons of Shem, five additional generations are provided. The reason for this will become apparent in chapter 12, when a particular descendent of Shem becomes the primary means through which God interacts with mankind and continues His ultimate plan of restoration.

We also see the first mention of languages (plural) in this chapter. In the very next chapter, the Bible affirms that there was just one language spoken by the whole world at this time (Genesis 11:1). This makes sense. Adam and Eve would have surely spoken the same language, and everyone descended from them. Of course, immediately after the flood the world was reduced to a population of just eight people, so it would certainly make sense that there was only one language spoken among them. The next chapter will detail the origin of many more languages.

[1] *These are the family records of Noah's sons, Shem, Ham, and Japheth. They also had sons after the flood.*

The Sons of Japheth

[2] *Japheth's sons: Gomer, Magog, Madai, Javan, Tubal, Meshech, and Tiras.* [3] *Gomer's sons: Ashkenaz, Riphath, and Togarmah.* [4] *And Javan's sons: Elishah, Tarshish, Kittim, and Dodanim.* [5] *From these descendants, the peoples of the coasts and islands spread out into their lands according to their clans in their nations, each with its own language.*

The Sons of Ham

[6] *Ham's sons: Cush, Mizraim, Put, and Canaan.* [7] *Cush's sons: Seba, Havilah, Sabtah, Raamah, and Sabteca. And Raamah's sons: Sheba and Dedan.*

[8] *Cush fathered Nimrod, who began to be powerful in the land.* [9] *He was a powerful hunter in the sight of the LORD. That is why it is said, "Like Nimrod, a powerful hunter in the sight of the LORD."* [10] *His kingdom started with Babylon, Erech, Accad, and Calneh, in the land of Shinar.* [11] *From that land he went to Assyria and built Nineveh, Rehoboth-ir, Calah,* [12] *and Resen, between Nineveh and the great city Calah.*

[13] *Mizraim fathered the people of Lud, Anam, Lehab, Naphtuh,* [14] *Pathrus, Casluh (the Philistines came from them), and Caphtor.*

[15] *Canaan fathered Sidon his firstborn and Heth,* [16] *as well as the Jebusites, the Amorites, the Girgashites,* [17] *the Hivites, the Arkites, the Sinites,* [18] *the Arvadites, the Zemarites, and the Hamathites. Afterward the Canaanite clans scattered.* [19] *The Canaanite border went from Sidon going toward Gerar as far as Gaza, and going toward Sodom, Gomorrah, Admah, and Zeboiim as far as Lasha.*

[20] *These are Ham's sons by their clans, according to their languages, in their lands and their nations.*

The Sons of Shem

[21] *And Shem, Japheth's older brother, also had sons. Shem was the father of all the sons of Eber.* [22] *Shem's sons were Elam, Asshur, Arpachshad, Lud, and Aram.*

83

[23] *Aram's sons: Uz, Hul, Gether, and Mash.*

[24] *Arpachshad fathered Shelah, and Shelah fathered Eber.* *[25]* *Eber had two sons. One was named Peleg, for during his days the earth was divided; his brother was named Joktan.* *[26]* *And Joktan fathered Almodad, Sheleph, Hazarmaveth, Jerah,* *[27]* *Hadoram, Uzal, Diklah,* *[28]* *Obal, Abimael, Sheba,* *[29]* *Ophir, Havilah, and Jobab. All these were Joktan's sons.* *[30]* *Their settlements extended from Mesha to Sephar, the eastern hill country.*

[31] *These are Shem's sons by their clans, according to their languages, in their lands and their nations.*

[32] *These are the clans of Noah's sons, according to their family records, in their nations. The nations on earth spread out from these after the flood. (Genesis 10 CSB)*

THE SONS OF SHEM

As previously noted, God's focus will soon move to a particular descendant of Shem whose name was Abram. God would later change his name to Abraham. God's plan of restoration will go through the descendants of this man and particularly through his son Isaac and then through Isaac's son Jacob. Jacob would later be renamed Israel. He becomes the father of twelve sons, and these become the heads of the twelve tribes of Israel.

The term *antisemitism* refers to hatred and hostility toward the Israelites (or Jewish people). This word comes from the name of Abraham's ancestor Shem, the son of Noah. So, one who is hostile toward the Jewish people is "anti-Shem."

Eber is also mentioned as a descendent of Shem. We will see in the next chapter that he is in the line of Abraham as well. The native language of the Jewish people is known as Hebrew. This is very similar to "Eber" and may derive from it. The words *Jewish* and *Jews* come from one specific son of Jacob named Judah.

Knowing this will hopefully avoid some confusion going forward. You will see many references to Abraham, Isaac, Jacob, Israel, Judah, the Hebrews, the Israelites, and the Jews. While there are subtle reasons why one name is used in a particular context over another, they are all referring to the descendants of Abraham through his grandson Jacob.

THE TOWER OF BABEL
GENESIS 11

I n the previous chapter, you may have noticed a peculiar reference to one of the descendants of Shem named Peleg, who was one of the sons of Eber. The record specifically states that the reason he was named Peleg was that in his time the earth was divided. *Peleg* means "division." This division of the earth likely refers to the events recorded in this chapter. Remember that I encouraged you to take note of the references to languages in the previous passage as families spread out over the earth. We will now see the explanation for how this occurred.

Again, the Bible affirms in this chapter that there was originally only one language in the world. Today there are thousands of different languages. So where did they all come from? This chapter is the answer to that question. As you read this chapter, be sure to remember the specific blessing that God made to Noah's family after the flood. He blessed them and said, "Be fruitful and multiply [and] spread out over the earth" (Genesis 9:7 CSB). A very important part of that blessing was the command to spread out over the earth. God's desire for mankind was not to remain in a single location, but to inhabit all of the earth.

There is one last thing to take note of as well. The latter part of this chapter gives the family line of Noah to Abram. You will recall that the ages given in the previous genealogy from Adam to Noah were exceedingly large. I mentioned then that the ages would fall rapidly after the flood. This is where that occurs.

The Tower of Babel

¹ The whole earth had the same language and vocabulary. ² As people migrated from the east, they found a valley in the land of Shinar and settled there. ³ They said to each other, "Come, let's make oven-fired bricks." (They used brick for stone and asphalt for mortar.) ⁴ And they said, "Come, let's build ourselves a city and a tower with its top in the sky. Let's make a name for ourselves; otherwise, we will be scattered throughout the earth."

⁵ Then the LORD came down to look over the city and the tower that the humans were building. ⁶ The LORD said, "If they have begun to do this as one people all having the same language, then nothing they plan to do will be impossible for them. [7] Come, let's go down there and confuse their language so that they will not understand one another's speech." [8] So from there the LORD scattered them throughout the earth, and they stopped building the city. [9] Therefore it is called Babylon, for there the LORD confused the language of the whole earth, and from there the LORD scattered them throughout the earth.

The Line of Abram

[10] These are the family records of Shem. Shem lived 100 years and fathered Arpachshad two years after the flood. [11] After he fathered Arpachshad, Shem lived 500 years and fathered other sons and daughters. [12] Arpachshad lived 35 years and fathered Shelah. [13] After he fathered Shelah, Arpachshad lived 403 years and fathered other sons and daughters. [14] Shelah lived 30 years and fathered Eber. [15] After he fathered Eber, Shelah lived 403 years and fathered other sons and daughters. [16] Eber lived 34 years and fathered Peleg. [17] After he fathered Peleg, Eber lived 430 years and fathered other sons and daughters. [18] Peleg lived 30 years and fathered Reu. [19] After he fathered Reu, Peleg lived 209 years and fathered other sons and daughters. [20] Reu lived 32 years and fathered Serug. [21] After he fathered Serug, Reu lived 207 years and fathered other sons and daughters. [22] Serug lived 30 years and fathered Nahor. [23] After he fathered Nahor, Serug lived 200 years and fathered other sons and daughters. [24] Nahor lived 29 years and fathered Terah. [25] After he fathered Terah, Nahor lived 119 years and fathered other sons and daughters. [26] Terah lived 70 years and fathered Abram, Nahor, and Haran.

[27] These are the family records of Terah. Terah fathered Abram, Nahor, and Haran, and Haran fathered Lot. [28] Haran died in his native land, in Ur of the Chaldeans, during his father Terah's lifetime. [29] Abram and Nahor took wives: Abram's wife was named Sarai, and Nahor's wife was named Milcah. She was the daughter of Haran, the father of both Milcah and Iscah. [30] Sarai was unable to conceive; she did not have a child.

[31] Terah took his son Abram, his grandson Lot (Haran's son), and his daughter-in-law Sarai, his son Abram's wife, and they set out together from Ur of the Chaldeans to go to the land of Canaan. But when they came to Haran, they settled there. [32] Terah lived 205 years and died in Haran. (Genesis 11 CSB)

THE CONFUSION OF LANGUAGES

God's command to Noah had been very specific. Mankind was told to be fruitful and multiply and fill the earth. So what did they do? The exact opposite. They wanted to build a city with a tower, and their purpose for doing this was to not be scattered throughout the earth.

Adam and Eve had been the first to reject the commandment of God. After that, the world, almost in its entirety, had become so evil that God destroyed everything, sparing only Noah and his family. Just a few generations after that, mankind once again joined together in their rebellion against Him.

It is notable, though, to see the great mercy God exhibits in His response in this case. We see that there is no death resulting from His judgment—no new worldwide calamity. Instead, He merely acts in such a way that compels mankind to fulfill His purpose and plan. He does this by dividing the people into different languages. By referring back to the previous chapter, it seems evident that these languages were given to specific families to keep them together. God Himself created families, and He is committed to keeping them together.

However, with the ability to communicate between families now lost, the people of the day had no choice but to abandon their rebellious plans and spread out over the earth, just as God had commanded them.

GOD'S ULTIMATE PLAN

God's purpose for mankind was to fill the entire earth with people who bear His image and likeness and who walk in relationship with Him.

Prior to the flood, the earth was quite populated, but not with people who walked with God. Now, the world would once again become filled with people scattered over the face of the whole earth. Yet these people would be those who had again rejected God.

So what was God to do now? His heart's desire had not changed. How could He still accomplish His purpose? Mankind seemed wholly unable or unwilling to walk with Him and keep His commands. They seemed so prone to fall into the deceitfulness of sin.

Despite mankind's continued rebellion, God's ultimate plan continued to unfold. He was not caught off guard in the least. His plan will continue to be revealed in the next chapter.

THE GREAT DISPERSION

You might be wondering just how many languages were created at this time and where each of those families went. Perhaps the best estimate is that there were around seventy original languages. Over time these languages changed, just like they do today, until each of them became families of languages. Each language within a family has similarities, yet each is distinctive enough to be considered unique.

The location of Babel was probably near modern-day Iraq, which in ancient times was referred to as Babylon. The similarity of *Babylon* to *Babel* is quite obvious. Even in the English language today, the verb *babel* refers to the making of sounds that cannot be understood, just as the people of that day could not understand each other.

From Babel, it appears that most of the descendants of Japheth migrated north into Europe. The descendants of Ham seem to have migrated mostly south into Africa. The descendants of Shem probably moved mostly to the east. Please note, though, that this merely identifies migrations in general. There were probably many exceptions as well.

WORLDWIDE FLOOD STORIES

We have seen that God divided the descendants of Noah into different languages. These divisions then scattered over the face of the whole earth. Although each of these groups had a unique language, they still shared a common oral history, passed down from Noah and his sons. This would have likely included the details of the global flood, as that would have been fairly recent history at the time.

We might wonder, then, if there are any corroborating stories of a global flood from any other cultures in the world. If there are, then that would serve as evidence to the truthfulness of the biblical account. In fact, we *do* find such accounts, and there aren't just a few of them. There aren't just dozens of them either. There are literally hundreds of them from all over the world.

Indeed, some of the details in these accounts differ significantly, but this is certainly no surprise. It would actually be more surprising if each of the accounts retained absolute consistency through thousands of years of oral transmission. Even so, in many of the accounts, specific details are, indeed, retained that are completely consistent with the biblical account. Thus there is much corroborating evidence for the global flood in cultures all around the world. For more resources on this topic, please refer to the appendix.

ONE BLOOD

We understand that all of the cultures across the world trace their lineage back to Noah and his three sons and then back to Adam. Therefore, in every sense of the word, we are one human *family*.

Paul affirmed this in his address to the people of Athens, which we read earlier. He specifically stated that it was "from one man" that God had made all the nations of the world (Acts 17:26 NIV). The word translated as "man" is actually the word for "blood." Thus we are all blood relatives in every sense of the term. There is really only one human race, of which we are all a part. We are all of one blood.

THE CHINESE LANGUAGE

Over the past decade, I have had the privilege of interacting with many different people from both China and Taiwan. During this time, I have been able to listen in as they speak to each other in their native language, and it is truly fascinating. The Chinese language, as you may know, is a tonal language. The same word, pronounced with different tones, has completely different meanings. Perhaps the most fascinating thing about the language is the Chinese script. Unlike many other languages, they do not use an alphabet. Instead, they have individual characters for each word. These are essentially pictographs or word pictures.

As I understand it, there is a subset of simpler characters. These simple characters are then combined to form other words. Thus one word is often represented as a combination of several other characters. Essentially, each character is a picture or story of what it represents.

What does this all have to do with the Bible? Well, it is quite interesting to look at these characters in light of what we have read in Genesis thus far. Remember that the people who first spoke the Chinese language (or its root language) and created the Chinese script would have possessed at least an oral history of the events that occurred in the first eleven chapters of the Bible. The question then becomes whether or not we find any correlation between Chinese characters and the biblical account.

We most certainly do! Genesis 6–9 was the story of a very large boat that only had a total of eight people in it—Noah, his three sons, and each of their wives. The Chinese word for a large boat is the combination of three characters—*eight, person,* and *vessel* (see **Table 2: Chinese Character Summary**). So, in essence, the Chinese word picture of a large boat is an *eight-person vessel*. It is not a twelve-person vessel or a twenty-person vessel. It's an eight-person vessel. It literally tells the story of Noah! The correlation is quite precise, but this is just the beginning.

The character for *flood* combines two specific characters—*total* and *water*. However, the word for *total* is itself comprised of three characters—

together, earth, and again the number *eight.* So the flood is depicted as *total water,* or *water* when all *eight* (people) on *earth* were *together.*

Genesis 3 records the account of the temptation of mankind. You will recall that there were two named trees in this story—the tree of life and the tree of death (the tree of the knowledge of good and evil). The temptation begins with Satan talking to the woman, who then desires or covets the forbidden fruit. The Chinese character for *covet* is the combination of three characters—(1) one *tree,* (2) another *tree,* and (3) *a woman.*

The character for the word *forbidden* is similar in that it contains two *trees* and the character for *command.* Another word is the symbol indicating *negative,* apparently as it refers to the outcome of something. This character combines two *trees* and *a serpent.* The word for *restrain* combines one *tree* and the symbol for *mouth.*

Genesis 11 is the story of how people with one language made bricks with clay and grass to build a tower. The Chinese character for *tower* comes from a total of five symbols—*grass, clay, mankind, one,* and *mouth* (or language). A *tower,* then, is what was built with *grass* and *clay* by *mankind* when they spoke *one language.*

These are just a small sample of the many Chinese characters that show a striking correlation to the Genesis account. For more information on this, please see the appendix.

One last character I want to mention is my favorite one of all. It is the character for the word *righteousness.* We have already seen the concept of the substitute, where the sacrifice of the innocent covers over the shame of the guilty. Adam and Eve were guilty, but it was the death of an innocent animal that provided clothing suitable to cover their shame. The offering that Abel made followed this pattern as well and was acceptable to God. Noah also, immediately after coming out of the ark, sacrificed an animal on an altar to the Lord.

This all came from the idea of the substitute. Because of our sin, we cannot stand before God as righteous. Our sin demands a penalty, and that penalty must be paid. However, that penalty may be paid by a substitute. The offering of animals pointed directly to this. Over time, it was the lamb that became the animal most closely identified with these sacrificial offerings.

So what comprises the Chinese character for *righteousness?* It comes from just two symbols, arranged on top of one another. The one on the bottom is the character for *me* or *us,* and the character on top is the word for *lamb* or *sheep*. Thus righteousness is represented as *a lamb that covers me!*[2]

This is, in essence, the gospel in the Chinese language. We are only righteous when our sin is covered over by the sacrifice of Jesus, the Lamb of God!

Large Ship	eight + person + vessel
Total	together + earth + eight
Flood	total + water
Covet	tree + tree + woman
Forbidden	tree + tree + command
Negative	tree + tree + serpent
Restrain	tree + mouth
Tower	grass + clay + mankind + one + mouth/language
Righteousness	lamb (over) me

Table 2: Chinese Character Summary

2. The majority of this information comes from C. H. Kang and Ethel R. Nelson, *The Discovery of Genesis: How the Truths of Genesis Were Found Hidden in the Chinese Language.*

PART II

THE PROMISE OF PARADISE RESTORED: THE PATRIARCHS

GOD'S COVENANT WITH ABRAM

GENESIS 12:1-8

U p until now, we have read the entirety of each chapter in Genesis, from the first verse of chapter 1 to the last verse of chapter 11. This was important, as these passages are foundational to understanding the Bible as a whole. From this point on, however, we will look at smaller portions of key passages whenever possible. These will highlight the continued unfolding of God's ultimate plan of restoration throughout history.

At this point in time, the people of the world were continuing to scatter over the face of the whole earth in different language groups. Sadly, these people had rejected God along with His purpose and plan. Still, God had not given up on His desire to have a world full of people who walk with Him and reflect His image.

But what would He do now? How could He still accomplish His purpose now that the whole world had rejected Him and didn't even speak the same language anymore? How could He restore what was lost?

We find the answers to these questions in this next chapter. As we have already mentioned, the answers concern a man named Abram, a descendant of Shem, the son of Noah. God had already made covenants with mankind, first in the Garden of Eden, second with Adam after the fall, and then with Noah. God now makes a fourth covenant, this time with Abram. Be sure to pay close attention to what God says to him at the outset of the story and how it concerns the scattered people of the world.

¹ The LORD said to Abram:
Go from your land,
your relatives,
and your father's house
to the land that I will show you.
² I will make you into a great nation,
I will bless you,
I will make your name great,
and you will be a blessing.
³ I will bless those who bless you,
I will curse anyone who treats you with contempt,
and all the peoples on earth
will be blessed through you.

⁴ So Abram went, as the LORD had told him, and Lot went with him. Abram was seventy-five years old when he left Haran. ⁵ He took his wife, Sarai, his nephew Lot, all the possessions they had accumulated, and the people they had acquired in Haran, and they set out for the land of Canaan. When they came to the land of Canaan, ⁶ Abram passed through the land to the site of Shechem, at the oak of Moreh. (At that time the Canaanites were in the land.) ⁷ The LORD appeared to Abram and said, "To your offspring I will give this land." So he built an altar there to the LORD who had appeared to him. ⁸ From there he moved on to the hill country east of Bethel and pitched his tent, with Bethel on the west and Ai on the east. He built an altar to the LORD there, and he called on the name of the LORD. ⁹ Then Abram journeyed by stages to the Negev. (Genesis 12:1-8 CSB)

A BLESSING FOR ALL PEOPLE

God's promise to Abram is of immense importance in His plan of restoration. He promises that He would personally bless Abram, make him into a great nation, and make his name great. A great nation would need a place to live, and God promises that as well.

God then declares that He would deal with the other people of the world based on how they treated Abram and his descendants. If nations blessed Abram, then God would bless them. If they cursed Abram, then God would curse them as well. This is a remarkable promise, indeed, but God didn't stop there. The final promise God makes to Abram is that all the peoples on earth would be blessed through him.

So what does God mean by this? How would He fulfill this amazing promise? As the story unfolds, God Himself answers this question for us. He speaks of a specific descendant of Abram through whom this blessing will come. In the judgment of Satan in the Garden, God had spoken of the Offspring of the woman.

Later it will be revealed that the descendant of Abram and the Offspring of the woman are one and the same person. His name would be Jesus. He is the One through whom God would bring a blessing to all the people of the world.

THE PROMISED LAND

After Abram began his journey to the land God would show him, an additional promise is given to him, specifically that God would give that land to the descendants of Abraham. Although Abraham would be merely a visitor there, his descendants would take possession of it. Thus this land became known as the Promised Land. This is where the Jewish people lived for two thousand years up until shortly after the resurrection of Jesus. After being driven out of the land for nearly nineteen hundred years, God gave their land back to them in 1948 in fulfillment of prophecy.

THE MAN OF FAITH
GENESIS 15:1-6

I n the previous chapter, we saw God's first interaction with Abram and the establishment of God's covenant with him. We now pick up the story several years later. Abram had become quite wealthy. Perhaps he saw this as a partial fulfillment of God's promise to bless him. However, God's greatest blessings are never merely financial. They're far greater than that.

God had promised to give the land of Canaan to Abram's descendants. However, his wife was still barren at this time, and they had no children. So what was Abram to think of God's promise? Would God really keep His covenant? Was it even possible for that to happen now, as both he and his wife had grown older?

As the years passed by, surely doubt began to creep in. Nonetheless, God returned to reaffirm His covenant. Pay careful attention to Abram's response.

> [1] After this, the word of the LORD came to Abram in a vision:
> "Do not be afraid, Abram.
> I am your shield,
> your very great reward."

> [2] But Abram said, "Sovereign LORD, what can you give me since I remain childless and the one who will inherit my estate is Eliezer of Damascus?" [3] And Abram said, "You have given me no children; so a servant in my household will be my heir."

> [4] Then the word of the LORD came to him: "This man will not be your heir, but a son who is your own flesh and blood will be your heir." [5] He

took him outside and said, "Look up at the sky and count the stars—
if indeed you can count them." Then he said to him, "So shall your
offspring be."

⁶ Abram believed the LORD, and he credited it to him as righteousness.
(Genesis 15:1-6 NIV)

RIGHTEOUSNESS BY FAITH

God credited Abram with righteousness. This is an enormously important statement in understanding the whole of Scripture. It suggests that previous to this, Abram was *not* righteous. If he had already been righteous, God could not have credited it to him. Even God cannot give someone what he already possesses. This, then, is a profound reality. God declares someone who is unrighteous to be righteous. But how could God do this? If Abram was unrighteous, then the penalty for his sins would surely need to be paid.

Again, the concept of the substitute comes in. As previously stated, the Substitute would eventually be revealed to be Jesus, a descendant of Abram. He would pay the penalty for Abram's sin along with the sins of the whole world. This is sometimes referred to as "The Great Exchange." Jesus, as our Substitute, not only takes our sin onto Himself, but also transfers His righteousness onto us.

Thus the righteousness with which Abram was credited was not his own. He didn't have any. The righteousness with which Abram was credited could only be the righteousness of Jesus Himself, for God alone is righteous.

So how exactly was Abram declared righteous? What did he do to obtain it? How did he come to acquire it? Did he diligently follow a long list of dos and don'ts given to him by God? Did he offer thousands of sacrifices? Did he undergo some religious ritual or ceremony? Did he give away his wealth and take a vow of poverty? Did he just live "a good life" that was "better than most"?

No. He did none of those things. So how then did he come to possess it? Abram believed God, and it was credited to him as righteousness.

The clothing that Adam and Eve had made for themselves was insufficient. When Cain offered to God the work of his own hands, it was rejected. Man cannot make himself righteous by his own efforts. He can only receive it as a gift from God. God gives His righteousness to those who respond to Him in faith.

FAITH TESTED
GENESIS 22:1-19

M any years would pass after this remarkable reaffirmation of God's covenant with Abram. However, Abram and Sarai grew even older and still had no children. Sarai gave up hope, and so she suggested that Abram have a child through her servant, a woman named Hagar. Abram agreed, and a son named Ishmael was born. Abram was already eighty-six years of age at this time.

However, this was not God's purpose or plan, and it resulted in a lot of problems. Sarai became jealous of Hagar, as anyone could have predicted, and she mistreated her because of it. The animosity has continued down through the generations between the descendants of Isaac, who are the Jewish people, and the descendants of Ishmael, which include the Arabic nations.

After this, God again reaffirmed His covenant with Abram, changing his name from Abram, meaning "exalted father," to Abraham, meaning "father of many." It must have been awkward enough to bear the name of "exalted father" for so many years when he had no children. Then, when he finally had become the father of one son, God changed his name to "father of many" for some reason. Thus the awkwardness continued. Yet inherent in that new name was a promise from God that He wasn't done with Abraham yet.

God specifically promised this time that it would be through Abraham's wife Sarai that a son would come. To emphasize this, God changed her name to Sarah. *Sarai* could be translated "my princess," whereas *Sarah* indicates "princess" in general. Thus the new name defines not merely her relationship to her father or husband but to her descendants as well.

Finally, God institutes circumcision as a sign of His covenant with Abraham. He commands that this should be done to all baby boys from that time on throughout all the generations of Abraham.

Sometime later, God reaffirmed His promise again by telling Abraham that he will yet have a son through Sarah. Sarah overheard God saying this, and her reaction was to laugh at the absurdity of the idea, as she was well past the age of childbearing by then. God's response was to simply ask, "Is anything too hard for the LORD?" (Genesis 18:14 CSB).

Of course, the answer to that question is an emphatic, "No!" The God who made the world and everything in it and who commanded mankind to be fruitful and multiply could surely make procreation possible, even in the lives of an elderly couple. He was, and still is, the Author of life.

At last, when Sarah had reached the age of ninety years old and Abraham was one hundred, she gave birth to a son, just as God had promised. She named him Isaac. Intriguingly enough, Isaac means "laughter." While both Abraham and Sarah had each previously laughed at the thought of having a son in their old age, the laughter they experienced at the birth of Isaac did not come from the absurdity of the idea but from the pure joy of the fact that it had happened!

After the birth of Isaac, Abraham must have truly felt like the most blessed person on the face of the earth. Everything God had promised him had come true, and his life was filled with unimaginable joy. The next chapter in the story, however, threatens to shatter everything, as God tests the faith of Abraham.

As you read through the passage, you will no doubt wonder what kind of God would ever put anyone through such a thing. In fact, the thought occurred to me to just skip this story altogether. It certainly would have been easier to do so. However, if the difficulties of the account are at least answered in part, then we can also see the great significance of the story and the remarkable foreshadowing it contains. Again, it's all about Jesus.

So we pick up our story several years after the birth of Isaac, though we aren't sure exactly how many years it is. The best guesses put the age of Isaac somewhere between twelve and twenty-five years of age.

¹ After these things God tested Abraham and said to him, "Abraham!"

"Here I am," he answered.

² "Take your son," he said, "your only son Isaac, whom you love, go to the land of Moriah, and offer him there as a burnt offering on one of the mountains I will tell you about."

³ So Abraham got up early in the morning, saddled his donkey, and took with him two of his young men and his son Isaac. He split wood for a burnt offering and set out to go to the place God had told him about. ⁴ On the third day Abraham looked up and saw the place in the distance. ⁵ Then Abraham said to his young men, "Stay here with the donkey. The boy and I will go over there to worship; then we'll come back to you." ⁶ Abraham took the wood for the burnt offering and laid it on his son Isaac. In his hand he took the fire and the knife, and the two of them walked on together.

⁷ Then Isaac spoke to his father Abraham and said, "My father."

And he replied, "Here I am, my son."

Isaac said, "The fire and the wood are here, but where is the lamb for the burnt offering?"

⁸ Abraham answered, "God himself will provide the lamb for the burnt offering, my son." Then the two of them walked on together.

⁹ When they arrived at the place that God had told him about, Abraham built the altar there and arranged the wood. He bound his son Isaac and placed him on the altar on top of the wood. ¹⁰ Then Abraham reached out and took the knife to slaughter his son.

¹¹ But the angel of the LORD called to him from heaven and said, "Abraham, Abraham!"

He replied, "Here I am."

¹² Then he said, "Do not lay a hand on the boy or do anything to him. For now I know that you fear God, since you have not withheld your only son from me." ¹³ Abraham looked up and saw a ram caught in the thicket by its horns. So Abraham went and took the ram and offered it as a burnt offering in place of his son. ¹⁴ And Abraham named that place The LORD Will Provide, so today it is said, "It will be provided on the LORD's mountain."

¹⁵ Then the angel of the LORD called to Abraham a second time from heaven ¹⁶ and said, "By myself I have sworn," this is the LORD's declaration: "Because you have done this thing and have not withheld your only son, ¹⁷ I will indeed bless you and make your offspring as numerous as the stars of the sky and the sand on the seashore. Your offspring will possess the city gates of their enemies. ¹⁸ And all the nations of the earth will be blessed by your offspring because you have obeyed my command."

19 Abraham went back to his young men, and they got up and went together to Beer-sheba. And Abraham settled in Beer-sheba. (Genesis 22:1-19 CSB)

HUMAN SACRIFICE?

Now you see what makes this passage so difficult. How could a holy God ask a father to kill his own son—and to do that as an act of worship no less? Does God desire human sacrifice? Does God ordain the killing of the innocent? Does He promote senseless murder? What is going on here?

First of all, we need to recognize that God did *not* allow Abraham to kill Isaac. If God really desired human sacrifice, then He surely would not have intervened. But then what was the point?

Isaac was an enormous blessing of God to Abraham and Sarah. He was born miraculously as the fulfillment of God's wonderful covenant, and it was through Isaac that God had promised to bless all the people of the earth.

At the time God commanded Abraham to offer Isaac as a sacrifice, Isaac was as yet unmarried and had no children. This presented a big problem. How could God bless the world through the descendants of Isaac if he died before having children?

The writer of the book of Hebrews in the New Testament answers that question for us, indicating that Abraham believed God would raise Isaac from the dead in order to keep His promise (Hebrews 11:17-19). We observe a hint of that suspicion in Abraham when he tells his servants specifically, "The boy and I will go over there to worship; then *we'll* come back to you" (Genesis 22:5 CSB, emphasis added). This certainly indicates a great deal of faith on behalf of Abraham, but of course, Abraham's faith had grown quite strong through the years as He had seen God provide wonderful things in his life, including the birth of Isaac. After all, is anything too hard for the LORD?

Still, we have to answer the question of what this was all about. The answer is in the very first sentence of the passage. God was testing Abraham—testing his faith.

The Bible presents God as being omniscient—that He has always known and always will know everything. So the outcome of this test was not in doubt in any way, at least from God's perspective. He already knew that Abraham would not hold back, and He already knew that He Himself would intervene. Thus the purpose of the test was not for

God's sake but for Abraham's. In this testing, Abraham exercised his faith in God, and it was strengthened even more as a result.

The blessing of God—Isaac—was not to become an idol in Abraham's life. Some have suggested that when we receive God's blessings, we must do so with open hands. God may give and God may take away according to His infinite wisdom. We must hold on to His blessings with open hands—not with closed fists. In the physical sense, this is impossible, but it captures the idea in the emotional and spiritual sense. We deeply enjoy the blessings of God when He gives them, but we must not claim them as an eternal right of possession. We must be willing for God to take them away as well, all the while being grateful for the time we were allowed to enjoy them.

Finally, as we look back on this story with Jesus' death and resurrection in mind, we are able to see the shadow of a much grander picture.

THE GOSPEL ACCORDING TO ABRAHAM

God had already given us the first gospel in the promise of the Offspring of the woman. We saw the second gospel in the sacrifice of the innocent that clothed the shame of Adam and Eve. We then noted that the door in the ark which provided an escape from the flood foreshadowed Jesus as the only escape from God's ultimate judgment. Now we see yet another picture of God's ultimate plan of salvation in Abraham's offering of Isaac. Before that will become clear, though, allow me to recount the details of that story.

We note that God described Isaac as Abraham's son, his only son, whom he loved. We already know that Abraham had one other son named Ishmael. Yet there was something unique about Isaac. He was the son of the covenant, the son of the promise, the result of a miraculous birth.

We also note that Abraham was commanded to offer him as a sacrifice in a very specific place that God would show him. Next, we observe that it was Isaac in particular who carried the wood for the offering up the hill, to which he was later bound. On their journey, Isaac asked where the lamb for the offering was. Everything else was in place, but hadn't they forgotten the most important thing? Abraham's response was that God Himself would provide a lamb.

It is also Abraham, as the father of Isaac, who raised the knife to make the offering, before God intervened. Just in time, a substitute was made. Isaac was spared, and God provided a ram to die in his place. The ram had been caught in a thicket, which may have consisted of thorns or thistles. This reminds us of the curse of the ground which resulted from Adam's sin.

These are the details of what happened in the account of Abraham and Isaac. Now let us look at what that foreshadowed two thousand years later, in the life of Jesus.

When Jesus began His earthly ministry at the age of about thirty, He was proclaimed, "The Lamb of God" (John 1:29 CSB). Although Abraham had assured Isaac that God would provide a lamb for the sacrifice, no lamb was provided on that day. Instead, a ram was given. God's provision of a Lamb did not come until the birth of Jesus Christ. The birth of Isaac had been miraculous, in that Sarah was past the age of childbearing when she conceived. The birth of Jesus would be miraculous, too, but to a far greater degree, as He was born of a virgin!

When Jesus was sentenced to die, He Himself—God's one and only Son, whom the Father loved—carried the wood, just like Isaac had done. This time, though, it was in the shape of a cross. He carried that cross up perhaps the very same hill that Isaac had climbed. We can't be sure, but we do know it was in the same region. So it certainly could have been the very same hill.

Jesus was then bound to that wood when He was nailed to the cross, just like Isaac was bound to the wood he had carried. Jesus also had a crown of thorns around His head, just as the ram's horns had been caught in the thicket.

On that day, however, there would be no one to hold back death, and there would be no other substitute provided. Jesus Himself was the Substitute for you and me. Thus the account of Genesis 22 is the story of a man offering up his own beloved son because of his love for God. The entirety of the Bible is the story of God Himself offering up His own beloved Son because of His love for man.

ISRAEL'S HISTORY: ABRAHAM TO MOSES

ACTS 7:2-50

S ometime after this, Abraham's wife, Sarah, died. Abraham remarried and had five other sons. Thus Abraham became not only the father of two nations but the father of many nations, just as God had promised.

Abraham's son Isaac had twin sons named Jacob and Esau. God declared that it would specifically be through the line of Jacob, the younger of the two, that His covenant would be fulfilled. Jacob would later be renamed Israel. From that time on his descendants were commonly referred to as the Israelites or the children of Israel. Jacob became the father of a total of twelve sons and one daughter. The twelve sons became the heads of the twelve tribes of Israel.

One of these sons was named Joseph. He is of particular significance because his entire life story foreshadows the life of Jesus. He was the firstborn son of Jacob's wife, Rachel, and was the beloved of his father. Jesus is also identified as the firstborn of God and His beloved. Joseph was betrayed by his own brothers who were jealous of him. In this betrayal, he was cast down into a pit and then later brought out of it. Jesus was also betrayed by His own people. The casting down into a pit and being brought back up foreshadows His death and resurrection. Later, through Joseph, God rescues not only the descendants of Abraham but all of Egypt as well from a great famine. Through Jesus, God brings salvation, not to just the Jewish people but to the whole world.

Another son of Jacob was named Judah. His descendants would eventually include the line of kings through a man named David. He was the second and greatest earthly king of Israel. God revealed to David that the promise given to Abraham, Isaac, and Jacob would be fulfilled specifically through one of his descendants.

Finally, another son of Jacob was named Levi. His descendants eventually became the line of the priests through a man named Aaron. Aaron's brother Moses is one of the most important characters in the Old Testament. He is credited as being the author of the first five books of the Bible, which includes everything we have read so far from Genesis.

To fill in the rest of the story from Abraham to Moses, we turn once again to the book of Acts. You may recall that we used a different passage from this book earlier to serve as our map for understanding the Bible as a whole. The story picks up shortly after the resurrection of Jesus from the dead. There was a man named Stephen, who was a devout believer in Jesus. He had been falsely accused of blasphemy, which in the Jewish culture was punishable by death.

In his defense, he gives his own summary of the history of Israel. You will see a retelling of much of what we have already covered as well as a summary of some of the things we will see very soon.

² "Brothers and fathers," he replied, "listen: The God of glory appeared to our father Abraham when he was in Mesopotamia, before he settled in Haran, ³ and said to him: Leave your country and relatives, and come to the land that I will show you.

⁴ "Then he left the land of the Chaldeans and settled in Haran. From there, after his father died, God had him move to this land in which you are now living. ⁵ He didn't give him an inheritance in it—not even a foot of ground—but he promised to give it to him as a possession, and to his descendants after him, even though he was childless. ⁶ God spoke in this way: His descendants would be strangers in a foreign country, and they would enslave and oppress them for four hundred years. ⁷ I will judge the nation that they will serve as slaves, God said. After this, they will come out and worship me in this place. ⁸ And so he gave Abraham the covenant of circumcision. After this, he fathered Isaac and circumcised him on the eighth day. Isaac became the father of Jacob, and Jacob became the father of the twelve patriarchs.

The Patriarchs in Egypt

⁹ "The patriarchs became jealous of Joseph and sold him into Egypt, but God was with him ¹⁰ and rescued him out of all his troubles. He gave him favor and wisdom in the sight of Pharaoh, king of Egypt, who appointed him ruler over Egypt and over his whole household. ¹¹ Now a famine and great suffering came over all of Egypt and Canaan, and our ancestors could find no food. ¹² When Jacob heard there was grain in Egypt, he sent our ancestors there the first time. ¹³ The second time, Joseph revealed himself to his brothers, and Joseph's family became known to Pharaoh. ¹⁴ Joseph invited his father Jacob and all his relatives, seventy-five people in all, ¹⁵ and Jacob went down to Egypt. He and our ancestors died there, ¹⁶ were carried back to Shechem, and were placed in the tomb that Abraham had bought for a sum of silver from the sons of Hamor in Shechem.

Moses, a Rejected Savior

¹⁷ "As the time was approaching to fulfill the promise that God had made to Abraham, the people flourished and multiplied in Egypt ¹⁸ until a different king who did not know Joseph ruled over Egypt. ¹⁹ He dealt deceitfully with our race and oppressed our ancestors by making them abandon their infants outside so that they wouldn't survive. ²⁰ At this time Moses was born, and he was beautiful in God's sight. He was cared for in his father's home for three months. ²¹ When he was put outside, Pharaoh's daughter adopted and raised him as her own son. ²² So Moses was educated in all the wisdom of the Egyptians and was powerful in his speech and actions.

[23] "When he was forty years old, he decided to visit his own people, the Israelites. [24] When he saw one of them being mistreated, he came to his rescue and avenged the oppressed man by striking down the Egyptian. [25] He assumed his people would understand that God would give them deliverance through him, but they did not understand. [26] The next day he showed up while they were fighting and tried to reconcile them peacefully, saying, 'Men, you are brothers. Why are you mistreating each other?'

[27] "But the one who was mistreating his neighbor pushed Moses aside, saying: Who appointed you a ruler and a judge over us? [28] Do you want to kill me, the same way you killed the Egyptian yesterday?

[29] "When he heard this, Moses fled and became an exile in the land of Midian, where he became the father of two sons. [30] After forty years had passed, an angel appeared to him in the wilderness of Mount Sinai, in the flame of a burning bush. [31] When Moses saw it, he was amazed at the sight. As he was approaching to look at it, the voice of the Lord came: [32] I am the God of your ancestors—the God of Abraham, of Isaac, and of Jacob. Moses began to tremble and did not dare to look.

[33] "The Lord said to him: Take off the sandals from your feet, because the place where you are standing is holy ground. [34] I have certainly seen the oppression of my people in Egypt; I have heard their groaning and have come down to set them free. And now, come, I will send you to Egypt.

[35] "This Moses, whom they rejected when they said, Who appointed you a ruler and a judge?—this one God sent as a ruler and a deliverer through the angel who appeared to him in the bush. [36] This man led them out and performed wonders and signs in the land of Egypt, at the Red Sea, and in the wilderness for forty years.

Israel's Rebellion against God

[37] "This is the Moses who said to the Israelites: God will raise up for you a prophet like me from among your brothers. [38] He is the one who was in the assembly in the wilderness, with the angel who spoke to him on Mount Sinai, and with our ancestors. He received living oracles to

give to us. ³⁹ Our ancestors were unwilling to obey him. Instead, they pushed him aside, and in their hearts turned back to Egypt. ⁴⁰ They told Aaron: Make us gods who will go before us. As for this Moses who brought us out of the land of Egypt, we don't know what's happened to him. ⁴¹ They even made a calf in those days, offered sacrifice to the idol, and were celebrating what their hands had made. ⁴² God turned away and gave them up to worship the stars of heaven, as it is written in the book of the prophets:

House of Israel, did you bring me offerings and sacrifices for forty years in the wilderness?
⁴³ You took up the tent of Moloch and the star of your god Rephan, the images that you made to worship. So I will send you into exile beyond Babylon.

God's Real Tabernacle

⁴⁴ "Our ancestors had the tabernacle of the testimony in the wilderness, just as he who spoke to Moses commanded him to make it according to the pattern he had seen. ⁴⁵ Our ancestors in turn received it and with Joshua brought it in when they dispossessed the nations that God drove out before them, until the days of David. ⁴⁶ He found favor in God's sight and asked that he might provide a dwelling place for the God of Jacob. ⁴⁷ It was Solomon, rather, who built him a house, ⁴⁸ but the Most High does not dwell in sanctuaries made with hands, as the prophet says:

⁴⁹ Heaven is my throne, and the earth my footstool. What sort of house will you build for me? says the Lord, or what will be my resting place? ⁵⁰ Did not my hand make all these things?" (Acts 7:2-50 CSB)

A PROPHET LIKE MOSES

In Stephen's account of Israel's history, he reminded his accusers of a prophecy that Moses had given them long before. Specifically, he had told them that God would one day "raise up for you a prophet like me from among your own brothers" (Deuteronomy 18:15 CSB). So when was this prophecy fulfilled? Who was the prophet like Moses that God sent?

To answer this question, it is necessary to take a closer look at the life of Moses. This will allow us to identify to whom he was referring when we find someone who matches that pattern. We haven't covered most of this yet, and we actually won't cover everything listed here, as the entire account of the life of Moses would take far too much time. Nonetheless, the following is a brief overview of the life of Moses:

> Moses was born to a Jewish family after four hundred years of silence from God. At the time of Moses' birth, the Israelites were ruled by a foreign nation, and the king ordered the killing of all the baby boys—yet he was spared. He spent time as a child in the country of Egypt.

> In adulthood, he gave up life as a ruler and became a shepherd. He heard the actual voice of God and was called to rescue his people from slavery. He fasted for forty days in communion with God. He also performed miracles, which included the miraculous provision of bread.

> During his ministry, he was rejected by his own people and criticized by his own family. Still, he offered to give his own life to God in exchange for his people, even though God did not accept his offer to do so.

So who in history could be this "prophet like Moses"? There is really only one person who even comes close, and it probably comes as no surprise by now that this person is, in fact, Jesus.

> Jesus was born after four hundred years of silence from God, which was the time between the last prophet of the Old Testament and the time of Jesus. At the time of His birth, Rome ruled over Israel, and King Herod ordered the killing of all the baby boys in Bethlehem—yet He was spared. His parents escaped with Him to Egypt, where they lived for a few years of His childhood.

> Although He was the Lord of heaven from eternity past, He gave that up to come to earth as Shepherd of His people, Israel. He would later identify Himself as the Good Shepherd who would lead and protect His people. When He began His

ministry, He heard the actual voice of God the Father. He had come to bring His people out of slavery—not out of slavery to Rome but out of slavery to sin. He fasted for forty days in communion with God. He also performed miracles, including a miraculous provision of bread. Yet He Himself was the true Bread from heaven.

He was rejected by His own people and criticized by His own family, yet He offered His own life to God for the sake of the world. However, unlike Moses, God the Father *did* accept His offer.

There are actually even more similarities than this, but suffice it to say that Jesus is the prophet like Moses whom God promised would one day come.

THE CALL OF MOSES
EXODUS 3

We pick up the story as God appears to Moses for the very first time. He does so in quite a remarkable way. We already saw an overview of this in the previous chapter. This was a very significant part of God's unfolding purpose and plan, so it's worth looking at the full account.

As we just mentioned, God had been silent for four hundred years at this time, having last spoken to Jacob (Israel). The Israelites were now slaves in Egypt, and life was very hard. Had God forgotten about them? Had He failed to remember the covenant He had made with Abraham? Did He not see their misery? These questions must have filled their hearts and minds in the midst of this great struggle.

Moses had previously been in a position of influence where he might have been able to intervene on behalf of his people, but that influence had ended. He had become a fugitive after killing an Egyptian man forty years earlier. Surely God couldn't still use him for anything now. Or could He? Is anything too hard for the LORD? Well, God's strength is certainly much greater than our weakness, and God was not done with Moses yet. In the course of time, when all hope seemed lost, God came down.

As you read the account, be sure to take note of God's great heart for His people and His deep concern for them. Pay close attention to how Moses responds to God, as we will discuss this in more detail afterward. Also note that the word *pharaoh* is the word used for the king of Egypt.

> [1] *Meanwhile, Moses was shepherding the flock of his father-in-law Jethro, the priest of Midian. He led the flock to the far side of the wilderness and came to Horeb, the mountain of God.* [2] *Then the angel of the* LORD *appeared to him in a flame of fire within a bush. As Moses looked, he saw that the bush was on fire but was not consumed.* [3] *So Moses thought, "I must go over and look at this remarkable sight. Why isn't the bush burning up?"*

> [4] *When the* LORD *saw that he had gone over to look, God called out to him from the bush, "Moses, Moses!"*

> *"Here I am," he answered.*

> [5] *"Do not come closer," he said. "Remove the sandals from your feet, for the place where you are standing is holy ground."* [6] *Then he continued, "I am the God of your father, the God of Abraham, the God of Isaac, and the God of Jacob." Moses hid his face because he was afraid to look at God.*

> [7] *Then the* LORD *said, "I have observed the misery of my people in Egypt, and have heard them crying out because of their oppressors. I know about their sufferings,* [8] *and I have come down to rescue them from the power of the Egyptians and to bring them from that land to a good and spacious land, a land flowing with milk and honey—the territory of the Canaanites, Hethites, Amorites, Perizzites, Hivites, and Jebusites.* [9] *So because the Israelites' cry for help has come to me, and I have also seen the way the Egyptians are oppressing them,* [10] *therefore, go. I am sending you to Pharaoh so that you may lead my people, the Israelites, out of Egypt."*

> [11] *But Moses asked God, "Who am I that I should go to Pharaoh and that I should bring the Israelites out of Egypt?"*

[12] *He answered, "I will certainly be with you, and this will be the sign to you that I am the one who sent you: when you bring the people out of Egypt, you will all worship God at this mountain."*

[13] *Then Moses asked God, "If I go to the Israelites and say to them, 'The God of your ancestors has sent me to you,' and they ask me, 'What is his name?' what should I tell them?"*

[14] *God replied to Moses, "I AM WHO I AM. This is what you are to say to the Israelites: I AM has sent me to you."* *[15]* *God also said to Moses, "Say this to the Israelites: The LORD, the God of your ancestors, the God of Abraham, the God of Isaac, and the God of Jacob, has sent me to you. This is my name forever; this is how I am to be remembered in every generation.*

[16] *"Go and assemble the elders of Israel and say to them: The LORD, the God of your ancestors, the God of Abraham, Isaac, and Jacob, has appeared to me and said: I have paid close attention to you and to what has been done to you in Egypt.* *[17]* *And I have promised you that I will bring you up from the misery of Egypt to the land of the Canaanites, Hethites, Amorites, Perizzites, Hivites, and Jebusites—a land flowing with milk and honey.* *[18]* *They will listen to what you say. Then you, along with the elders of Israel, must go to the king of Egypt and say to him: The LORD, the God of the Hebrews, has met with us. Now please let us go on a three-day trip into the wilderness so that we may sacrifice to the LORD our God.*

[19] *"However, I know that the king of Egypt will not allow you to go, even under force from a strong hand.* *[20]* *But when I stretch out my hand and strike Egypt with all my miracles that I will perform in it, after that, he will let you go.* *[21]* *And I will give these people such favor with the Egyptians that when you go, you will not go empty-handed.* *[22]* *Each woman will ask her neighbor and any woman staying in her house for silver and gold jewelry, and clothing, and you will put them on your sons and daughters. So you will plunder the Egyptians." (Exodus 3 CSB)*

THE GOD OF ABRAHAM, ISAAC, AND JACOB

God introduces Himself to Moses as "the God of Abraham, the God of Isaac, and the God of Jacob" (Exodus 3:5 CSB). This is important for at least two reasons. First, He was not a new god. The Israelites were living in the land of Egypt, the people of whom worshiped a myriad of false gods. This was not one of them. This was the same God who created the heavens and the earth, who made Adam and Eve in His own image, who rescued Noah in the Ark, who divided the people into various languages, and who had appeared to His forefather Abraham.

Secondly, God had not forgotten them. God affirmed that He would surely keep His covenant to make the descendants of Abraham into a great nation, to give them the land of the Canaanites, and to bless the whole world through them. God keeps His promises.

WHO AM I?

When God appeared to Moses and revealed His plan, Moses responded with a simple question. "Who am I?" Long after this world has passed away and all of human history is complete, this may well rank as the most irrelevant question ever asked of God. To be sure, the question of our identity is important, but it had absolutely nothing to do with what God was going to accomplish.

Look again at what God had said and particularly pay attention to the pronouns He uses: "*I* have observed the misery of *my* people. . . . and have heard them crying out. . . . *I* know about their sufferings. . . . *I* have come down to rescue them . . ." (Exodus 3:7-8 CSB, emphasis added). God Himself was concerned about His own people, and He was going to rescue them—not Moses. So it didn't matter who Moses was.

It is interesting to note, though, how God responds to his question. He really doesn't answer it at all. He doesn't tell Moses who *Moses* is. He doesn't give him a pep talk about believing in himself or giving it his best effort. He simply responds by saying, "I will certainly be with you"(Exodus 3:12 CSB). Again, it didn't matter who Moses was. It mattered who God is. God promised to be with Moses, and that was all that would be necessary. After all, is anything too hard for the LORD?

The answer to that question was still, "No!" Nothing was too hard for God when Sarah gave birth to Isaac. Nothing was too hard for God when He spoke to Moses, and nothing is too hard for God still today.

WHO ARE YOU?

After God answered Moses' first question with the promise that He Himself would be with him, Moses then asked a different question, essentially asking, "Who are You?" Moses specifically asked for God's name. This is a pretty remarkable request, as God had never revealed this to anyone before.

God honored this great request and revealed that His name was "I AM." In many languages, names have obvious meanings, but this is fairly uncommon in English. So when we see "I AM," it really doesn't look like a name to us. It certainly did for Moses, though.

Now, we must clarify that God is actually known by many different names, each of which captures something unique about Him. These include such names, when translated into English, as "God, My Provider," "The God Who Sees Me," "Lord God Almighty," and many, many more. Nonetheless, the name "I AM" is extremely important, as it is seen as God's covenant name with Israel. The name itself indicates self-existence. God *is*. He *exists* apart from everything else. He is the Creator of the physical universe of time, space, and matter, but He exists outside of all of that.

As He is eternally perfect in His being, He does not change. He is who He is. He has been, He is, and He will always be the same. There is no one like God. Centuries later, Jesus would identify Himself with this same name.

THE PASSOVER LAMB
EXODUS 12:1-42

After he had received the call of God—and after asking a few more questions and protesting a bit—Moses returned to Egypt to lead the Israelites out of slavery. God had warned Moses that Pharaoh would strongly oppose this. God foretold that He would have to perform many wonders before the Israelites would be set free. This is exactly what happened.

These wonders of which God had spoken are known as the plagues of Egypt. Remember that the Egyptians had abandoned the truth about God and were worshipping many false gods in the form of idols. There were gods and goddesses associated with the Nile River, frogs, fertility, the sky, the sun, healing, locusts, cattle, and many other things.

God's desire throughout history is that all mankind would know Him and live in relationship with Him. That desire did not in any way exclude the Egyptians of that day, regardless of how much they dishonored Him with their worship of idols. Though they did not know

Him, God desired to reveal Himself to them. He did so through the plagues that He brought upon them.

It was almost as if God was saying to the Egyptians, *You have a god of the Nile River? Well, actually I am the God of the Nile River. You have a god of the sky? I am the God of the sky. A god of the sun? A goddess of healing? I am the God over everything.* This continued on for a total of nine different plagues. God showed the Egyptians in an unmistakable way that there was no God but Him and Him alone. All their idols were false gods that could do nothing for them. He desperately wanted them to know Him. Nonetheless, Pharaoh refused to acknowledge the one true God, and his heart was hardened.

The Egyptians worshiped their pharaohs as gods as well. They believed that each pharaoh was the son of Ra, their sun god, and that their rule was absolute. It was perhaps necessary, then, for God to demonstrate once and for all that Pharaoh himself was a false god. The last plague of Egypt accomplished that very thing. We refer to it as the Passover.

By now you have seen that many of the events in the Bible foreshadow something far greater. As you read the account below, be sure to remember this and to consider what the larger meaning might be.

> [1] *The LORD said to Moses and Aaron in the land of Egypt,* [2] *"This month is to be the beginning of months for you; it is the first month of your year.* [3] *Tell the whole community of Israel that on the tenth day of this month they must each select an animal of the flock according to their fathers' families, one animal per family.* [4] *If the household is too small for a whole animal, that person and the neighbor nearest his house are to select one based on the combined number of people; you should apportion the animal according to what each will eat.* [5] *You must have an unblemished animal, a year-old male; you may take it from either the sheep or the goats.* [6] *You are to keep it until the fourteenth day of this month; then the whole assembly of the community of Israel will slaughter the animals at twilight.* [7] *They must take some of the blood and put it on the two doorposts and the lintel of the houses where they eat them.* [8] *They are to eat the meat that night; they should eat it, roasted over the fire along with unleavened bread and bitter herbs.* [9] *Do not eat any of it raw or cooked in boiling water, but only roasted over fire—its head as well as its legs and inner organs.* [10] *You must not leave any of it until morning; any part of it left until morning you must burn.* [11] *Here is how you must eat it: You must be dressed for travel, your sandals on your feet, and your staff in your hand. You are to eat it in a hurry; it is the LORD's Passover.*

¹² "I will pass through the land of Egypt on that night and strike every firstborn male in the land of Egypt, both people and animals. I am the LORD; I will execute judgments against all the gods of Egypt. ¹³ The blood on the houses where you are staying will be a distinguishing mark for you; when I see the blood, I will pass over you. No plague will be among you to destroy you when I strike the land of Egypt.

¹⁴ "This day is to be a memorial for you, and you must celebrate it as a festival to the LORD. You are to celebrate it throughout your generations as a permanent statute. ¹⁵ You must eat unleavened bread for seven days. On the first day you must remove yeast from your houses. Whoever eats what is leavened from the first day through the seventh day must be cut off from Israel. ¹⁶ You are to hold a sacred assembly on the first day and another sacred assembly on the seventh day. No work may be done on those days except for preparing what people need to eat—you may do only that.

¹⁷ "You are to observe the Festival of Unleavened Bread because on this very day I brought your military divisions out of the land of Egypt. You must observe this day throughout your generations as a permanent statute. ¹⁸ You are to eat unleavened bread in the first month, from the evening of the fourteenth day of the month until the evening of the twenty-first day. ¹⁹ Yeast must not be found in your houses for seven days. If anyone eats something leavened, that person, whether a resident alien or native of the land, must be cut off from the community of Israel. ²⁰ Do not eat anything leavened; eat unleavened bread in all your homes."

²¹ Then Moses summoned all the elders of Israel and said to them, "Go, select an animal from the flock according to your families, and slaughter the Passover animal. ²² Take a cluster of hyssop, dip it in the blood that is in the basin, and brush the lintel and the two doorposts with some of the blood in the basin. None of you may go out the door of his house until morning. ²³ When the LORD passes through to strike Egypt and sees the blood on the lintel and the two doorposts, he will pass over the door and not let the destroyer enter your houses to strike you.

²⁴ "Keep this command permanently as a statute for you and your descendants. ²⁵ When you enter the land that the LORD will give you as he promised, you are to observe this ceremony. ²⁶ When your children ask you, 'What does this ceremony mean to you?' ²⁷ you are to reply, 'It is the Passover sacrifice to the LORD, for he passed over the houses of the

Israelites in Egypt when he struck the Egyptians, and he spared our homes.'" So the people knelt low and worshiped. ²⁸ Then the Israelites went and did this; they did just as the LORD had commanded Moses and Aaron.

The Exodus

²⁹ Now at midnight the LORD struck every firstborn male in the land of Egypt, from the firstborn of Pharaoh who sat on his throne to the firstborn of the prisoner who was in the dungeon, and every firstborn of the livestock. ³⁰ During the night Pharaoh got up, he along with all his officials and all the Egyptians, and there was a loud wailing throughout Egypt because there wasn't a house without someone dead. ³¹ He summoned Moses and Aaron during the night and said, "Get out immediately from among my people, both you and the Israelites, and go, worship the LORD as you have said. ³² Take even your flocks and your herds as you asked and leave, and also bless me."

³³ Now the Egyptians pressured the people in order to send them quickly out of the country, for they said, "We're all going to die!" ³⁴ So the people took their dough before it was leavened, with their kneading bowls wrapped up in their clothes on their shoulders.

³⁵ The Israelites acted on Moses's word and asked the Egyptians for silver and gold items and for clothing. ³⁶ And the LORD gave the people such favor with the Egyptians that they gave them what they requested. In this way they plundered the Egyptians.

³⁷ The Israelites traveled from Rameses to Succoth, about six hundred thousand able-bodied men on foot, besides their families. ³⁸ A mixed crowd also went up with them, along with a huge number of livestock, both flocks and herds. ³⁹ The people baked the dough they had brought out of Egypt into unleavened loaves, since it had no yeast; for when they were driven out of Egypt, they could not delay and had not prepared provisions for themselves.

⁴⁰ The time that the Israelites lived in Egypt was 430 years. ⁴¹ At the end of 430 years, on that same day, all the LORD's military divisions went out from the land of Egypt. ⁴² It was a night of vigil in honor of the LORD, because he would bring them out of the land of Egypt. This same night is in honor of the LORD, a night vigil for all the Israelites throughout their generations. (Exodus 12:1-42 CSB)

THE BLOOD OF THE LAMB

Pharaoh's heart had remained hard. He had refused to acknowledge that God was the one true God, and all of Egypt joined him in his idolatry. So God pronounced judgment. The firstborn of both men and animals would die on the same night. However, as He always does, God also provided a way of escape. Although this way of escape was available to everyone, it wasn't forced upon anyone. It was only received by those who demonstrated their faith in God for salvation by following His instructions. These instructions were very specific.

Each family had to take a lamb and keep it for exactly four days. It had to be a pure and spotless lamb with no defect. At the end of the four days, the lamb was to be killed. The blood of the lamb was to be applied to the doors of their homes. They were to eat all of the meat that night and do so dressed in a particular way—they had to be ready to leave. They were slaves in Egypt, but after this, they would be free! They would embark on a journey to a distant land that God had prepared for them.

Yet it was not those who lived *good lives* who escaped the judgment, and it wasn't those who lived *bad lives* who suffered under it. The most virtuous family in all the land would have experienced the judgment *without* the blood of the Passover lamb, and the least virtuous family would have escaped it *through* the blood of the Passover lamb.

So what was the point of all these detailed instructions? The full meaning would only become evident some sixteen hundred years later, once again, in the Person of Jesus Christ. God has pronounced judgment on the entire world. Ever since the time of Adam, all mankind has sinned against God and deserves His punishment. Yet God provides a way of escape that was foreshadowed in the Passover lamb.

When Jesus first began His ministry, He was called the Lamb of God. Three years later, He would enter Jerusalem. Exactly four days later, He would be arrested. When He was on trial, the Roman governor himself proclaimed Jesus to be innocent—a pure and spotless Lamb. Nevertheless, He was handed over to be crucified. The day on which this took place was the very same day that the Jewish people were celebrating the Passover! So, while thousands of Passover lambs were being killed, Jesus Himself hung on the Cross, giving His own life as the Lamb of God. It was His death that paid the penalty for our sins and makes it possible for us to escape God's judgment.

Even though this is available to everyone, it is not forced upon anyone. What, then, must we do to escape the judgment of God for our own sin? It will not be those who have lived *good lives* who escape the judgment of sin, and it won't be those who have lived *bad lives* who will suffer under it. The most virtuous person in the world will experience God's judgment *without* the blood of the Lamb of God, and the least virtuous person will escape the judgment *through* the blood of the Lamb of God. Just like the Israelites, the only thing that matters is whether or not we personally apply the blood of Jesus, the Lamb of God, not to the doors of our homes but to the doors of our hearts. When we put our faith in His death and resurrection, we escape His judgment and are set free from our sin. Finally, we begin our journey to a very distant country—heaven—where God has prepared a place for us.

THE PASSOVER TODAY

The Jewish people today still celebrate the Passover every year. I've had the immense privilege of attending some of these celebrations myself. The meal typically lasts a few hours and is most often observed in a house overflowing with family and friends. As a Christian, it is truly wonderful to see how everything in the ceremony points directly to Jesus. Tragically, most Jewish people don't notice this at all.

Part of the ceremony involves unleavened bread, or bread made without yeast. Yeast symbolizes sin in the Bible, so the unleavened bread symbolizes a life without sin. There is also a special white cloth that has three separate pockets. One piece of unleavened bread is placed in each of them. At one point during the meal, the middle piece of bread is taken out, broken, wrapped in a white napkin, and hidden away in a secret place. Later on, all of the children in attendance are encouraged to search the house to find the missing piece of bread. The one who finds it is rewarded with a special prize.

It is important to understand that the specific details of the ceremony are not set forth anywhere in the Bible. It all comes from traditions that have been handed down for over thirty-five hundred years. This makes it all the more amazing how the ceremony itself is such an amazing picture of Jesus Christ.

We have already introduced the fact that God is a Trinity. Jesus is the Son and is referred to specifically as the Second Person of the Trinity. (The Father is the first, and the Spirit is the third.) In the Passover ceremony, the cloth with three pockets symbolizes this truth. The middle (or second) piece of bread represents Jesus, who would one day refer to Himself as the Bread of Life. His own body would be broken in death, then wrapped in a burial cloth and hidden away. Three days later, His followers went to the tomb in search of the body, but it wasn't there.

Anyone who seeks and finds Jesus today receives a truly great reward.

MANY OTHER PEOPLE

God's purpose in bringing the plagues upon Egypt was, in part, so that the Egyptians would know Him. We might wonder whether or not that was successful. Had any of these Egyptians, who saw all the wonders that God had displayed with their own eyes, come to believe in Him? We are given the answer to that question at the end of the passage. It specifically states that the Israelites traveled with six hundred thousand men, not counting women and children, so there were probably well over a million people total. Then it says, "A mixed crowd also went up with them…" (Exodus 12:38 CSB). This "mixed crowd" was not counted as part of the Israelites, because they weren't a part of them. Thus they must have been from some other nation. The most likely conclusion is that many of these people were, in fact, Egyptians. God's purpose had been fulfilled.

I find it strange, though, that so many Egyptians stayed behind and continued to worship their false gods. Hadn't they seen more than enough evidence that proved there was only one God, and it wasn't any of the ones they were worshipping? Hadn't their own gods proven to be weak and incapable of defending them? Why wouldn't all of them acknowledge this obvious truth and worship the one true God who had revealed Himself to them in such a powerful way?

The reality is that people still today do not always follow where the evidence leads. The heart, mind, and will are all involved in our beliefs. Evidence appeals to the mind but not the heart of man, nor his will. Perhaps that is the reason why there are so many still today who, despite all the evidence in the world, refuse to accept the truth and choose to believe a lie instead. This is not all that different from Adam and Eve in the Garden, who rejected the truth spoken by God and believed the lies of Satan.

THE BREAD FROM HEAVEN
EXODUS 16

After the observance of the Passover, Pharaoh finally let the people of Israel go. As they began their journey, God appeared to them as a cloud by day and a pillar of fire by night. This was not only a constant reminder of God's presence but also a means of guiding them on their journey through the desert.

However, it didn't take long for Pharaoh to change his mind. After all, Egypt had just lost a large amount of slave labor, which they had likely used to build the great pyramids that we still see today. So Pharaoh decided to send his entire army after them. As they drew near, the Israelites found themselves trapped against the banks of the Red Sea.

Remember that this was just days after God had stretched out His mighty arm to free them from the misery of slavery. Nonetheless, the Israelites abandoned all faith in Him. They grumbled against God and even accused Him of bringing them out into the desert to die. They feared the feeble strength of men instead of trusting in the infinite strength of God.

The similarity between the Israelites here and Adam and Eve in the Garden is intriguing. Adam and Eve also charged God with evil intent. Neither they nor the Israelites recognized God as holy and righteous and good. Nonetheless, God did not punish Israel for their grumbling and accusations against Him this time but simply rescued them in a miraculous way. He parted the waters of the Red Sea, and the people walked through on dry ground.

After they had all reached the other side, the Egyptians followed them. Once the entire army was in the midst of the sea, God caused the waters to flow back together, and the entire Egyptian army drowned. Never again would the armies of Pharaoh be a threat to the Israelites. Never again would they suffer under the yoke of slavery in Egypt. The threat had been completely removed. The enemy was completely destroyed. They were finally free—*truly* free.

God had been their Protector and Provider. Never again would they need to fear an army of men, for God had proven that He was mighty to save and worthy of their complete trust. Nevertheless, it wouldn't take long for them to fall back into distrust and grumbling. In fact, just three days later they were once again asking if God had brought them out into the desert to die. God was patient with them again and provided for their needs. This pattern would be repeated time and time again.

We pick up the story shortly after this when they faced another test. Again, they had the choice to either trust God for His provision or to grumble against Him and accuse Him of evil. Can you guess which one they chose?

¹ The entire Israelite community departed from Elim and came to the Wilderness of Sin, which is between Elim and Sinai, on the fifteenth day of the second month after they had left the land of Egypt. ² The entire Israelite community grumbled against Moses and Aaron in the wilderness. ³ The Israelites said to them, "If only we had died by the LORD's hand in the land of Egypt, when we sat by pots of meat and ate all the bread we wanted. Instead, you brought us into this wilderness to make this whole assembly die of hunger!"

⁴ Then the LORD said to Moses, "I am going to rain bread from heaven for you. The people are to go out each day and gather enough for that day. This way I will test them to see whether or not they will follow my instructions. ⁵ On the sixth day, when they prepare what they bring in, it will be twice as much as they gather on other days."

⁶ So Moses and Aaron said to all the Israelites, "This evening you will know that it was the LORD who brought you out of the land of Egypt, ⁷ and in the morning you will see the LORD's glory because he has heard your complaints about him. For who are we that you complain about us?" ⁸ Moses continued, "The LORD will give you meat to eat this evening and all the bread you want in the morning, for he has heard the complaints that you are raising against him. Who are we? Your complaints are not against us but against the LORD."

⁹ Then Moses told Aaron, "Say to the entire Israelite community, 'Come before the LORD, for he has heard your complaints.'" ¹⁰ As Aaron was speaking to the entire Israelite community, they turned toward the wilderness, and there in a cloud the LORD's glory appeared.

¹¹ The LORD spoke to Moses, ¹² "I have heard the complaints of the Israelites. Tell them: At twilight you will eat meat, and in the morning you will eat bread until you are full. Then you will know that I am the LORD your God."

¹³ So at evening quail came and covered the camp. In the morning there was a layer of dew all around the camp. ¹⁴ When the layer of dew evaporated, there were fine flakes on the desert surface, as fine as frost on the ground. ¹⁵ When the Israelites saw it, they asked one another, "What is it?" because they didn't know what it was.

Moses told them, "It is the bread the LORD has given you to eat. ¹⁶ This is what the LORD has commanded: 'Gather as much of it as each person needs to eat. You may take two quarts per individual, according to the number of people each of you has in his tent.'"

[17] So the Israelites did this. Some gathered a lot, some a little. [18] When they measured it by quarts, the person who gathered a lot had no surplus, and the person who gathered a little had no shortage. Each gathered as much as he needed to eat. [19] Moses said to them, "No one is to let any of it remain until morning." [20] But they didn't listen to Moses; some people left part of it until morning, and it bred worms and stank. Therefore Moses was angry with them.

[21] They gathered it every morning. Each gathered as much as he needed to eat, but when the sun grew hot, it melted. [22] On the sixth day they gathered twice as much food, four quarts apiece, and all the leaders of the community came and reported this to Moses. [23] He told them, "This is what the LORD has said: Tomorrow is a day of complete rest, a holy Sabbath to the LORD. Bake what you want to bake, and boil what you want to boil, and set aside everything left over to be kept until morning.'"

[24] So they set it aside until morning as Moses commanded, and it didn't stink or have maggots in it. [25] "Eat it today," Moses said, "because today is a Sabbath to the LORD. Today you won't find any in the field. [26] For six days you will gather it, but on the seventh day, the Sabbath, there will be none."

[27] Yet on the seventh day some of the people went out to gather, but they did not find any. [28] Then the LORD said to Moses, "How long will you refuse to keep my commands and instructions? [29] Understand that the LORD has given you the Sabbath; therefore on the sixth day he will give you two days' worth of bread. Each of you stay where you are; no one is to leave his place on the seventh day." [30] So the people rested on the seventh day.

[31] The house of Israel named the substance manna. It resembled coriander seed, was white, and tasted like wafers made with honey. [32] Moses said, "This is what the LORD has commanded: Two quarts of it are to be preserved throughout your generations, so that they may see the bread I fed you in the wilderness when I brought you out of the land of Egypt.'"

[33] Moses told Aaron, "Take a container and put two quarts of manna in it. Then place it before the LORD to be preserved throughout your

generations." [34] *As the* LORD *commanded Moses, Aaron placed it before the testimony to be preserved.*

[35] *The Israelites ate manna for forty years, until they came to an inhabited land. They ate manna until they reached the border of the land of Canaan.* [36] *(They used a measure called an omer, which held two quarts.) (Exodus 16 CSB)*

A STIFF-NECKED PEOPLE

Along their journey from Egypt to the Promised Land, God would allow the Israelites to encounter many different trials. In each case, He was ready to show His mighty power and meet their needs in miraculous ways—if they would only trust Him. Yet time and time again, they grumbled and complained against God, charged Him with evil intent, and refused to look to Him for their salvation.

In this story alone, we see them in the very real crisis of being without food. They immediately accuse God of bringing them there in order to starve them to death. God responds with great patience, miraculously providing food for well over a million people in a desert. He specifically commands them to take only enough for a single day.

But why does He do this? He desperately wanted them to learn to trust in Him and in His goodness—to believe that He would provide for them again the next day. But what did they do? They refused to trust Him and instead gathered more than what they needed, so God caused the food to spoil. Then He commanded them to gather twice as much on the sixth day so that they could observe the seventh day as a day of rest just as He had commanded back in the Garden of Eden. God promised to prevent the extra food from spoiling when it was gathered on the sixth day. So what did they do? They went out to gather food on the seventh day. None was to be found.

God continued to demonstrate in powerful ways that they could trust Him, to prove to them that He was their God, their Protector and Provider, and that He was good. Yet the people rejected Him time and time again. So great was their continued rebellion that God would refer to them as "a stiff-necked people" (Exodus 32:9 CSB).

It is quite fascinating that *these people* were God's chosen ones. Out of all the people on the earth, He chose to bless them and reveal Himself to them in truly miraculous ways. Still, we might wonder why God would choose such a rebellious people who were so slow to trust Him.

One possibility is that God chose them to extravagantly demonstrate His infinite love and patience and mercy. Even though they were the most rebellious and stubborn people imaginable, He still loved them. Because of this, everyone in the world can look at the Jewish people and say, "If God can love them, He can love me too."

This is not to malign the Jewish people in any way. On the contrary, God chose them for His special purpose. Nearly the entire Bible was written by Jews. Jesus Himself was a Jew, lived in the land of the Jewish people, and observed all the Jewish customs. All of the first Christians were Jewish, and Christianity began in Jerusalem, the capital city of Israel.

Recall also that God promised to bless those who bless Abraham (and His descendants) and to curse those who curse him. True Christians love the Jewish people dearly, along with all the other people of the world. So, again, this is in no way intended to malign the Jewish people but to merely recognize that the history of Israel is full of rebellion against God and a slowness to trust Him.

Indeed, God doesn't merely love those who love Him—He even loves those who continually reject Him. No one is beyond the love of God.

FORTY YEARS IN THE DESERT

The Jewish people would spend a total of forty years in the desert on their journey from Egypt to the Promised Land. It doesn't actually take that long to get there, even on foot. However, when they first reached the Promised Land, they saw that the people living in the land were larger than they were. Once again, they feared man more than they trusted God. They also charged Him with evil intent again.

In His judgment, God delayed the blessings He had promised from the entire generation of those who had rejected Him. They would not be allowed to enter the Promised Land. His blessing would still come, but He would save it for the next generation.

During that entire forty years, the Jewish people would go outside the camp every day, six days a week, and receive God's miraculous provision of food. Perhaps this would finally teach them that they really could trust God, that He really was their Protector and Provider, and that He really was good.

Before we move on, it will be important to remember this story when we get to the life of Jesus. He will one day refer to Himself as the true Bread that came down from heaven, not in a physical sense but in a spiritual one. We all experience physical hunger, but we are not merely physical beings. We are also spiritual beings with a spiritual hunger for God. Jesus will assert that He alone can satisfy our spiritual hunger.

THE WATER FROM THE ROCK

EXODUS 17:1-7

I n the previous chapter, we saw that the people were in desperate need of food. In this chapter, they are in desperate need of water. To be sure, this is a very real need. Without water, they would surely die.

Remember, though, that God's miraculous provision of food was still showing up every day (except the Sabbath) and would continue to do so for many years to come. This would seem to be overwhelming evidence that God was truly their Protector and Provider and that they just needed to trust Him. Surely they had learned this lesson by now. Or had they?

¹ The entire Israelite community left the Wilderness of Sin, moving from one place to the next according to the LORD's command. They camped at Rephidim, but there was no water for the people to drink. ² So the people complained to Moses, "Give us water to drink."

"Why are you complaining to me?" Moses replied to them. "Why are you testing the LORD?"

³ But the people thirsted there for water and grumbled against Moses. They said, "Why did you ever bring us up from Egypt to kill us and our children and our livestock with thirst?"

⁴ Then Moses cried out to the LORD, "What should I do with these people? In a little while they will stone me!"

⁵ The LORD answered Moses, "Go on ahead of the people and take some of the elders of Israel with you. Take the staff you struck the Nile with in your hand and go. ⁶ I am going to stand there in front of you on the rock at Horeb; when you hit the rock, water will come out of it and the people will drink." Moses did this in the sight of the elders of Israel. ⁷ He named the place Massah and Meribah because the Israelites complained, and because they tested the LORD, saying, "Is the LORD among us or not?" (Exodus 17:1-7 CSB)

JESUS, THE ROCK

Yes, once again, the people of Israel refused to trust God, and they even resorted to the same accusation they had used before—God had brought them out into the desert to die. Their lack of faith would become increasingly absurd, as time and time again God miraculously met all of their needs.

The particular manner of God's provision here is significant, as it often is. Moses was commanded to strike the rock, and he did so. The water gushed out, and the people were able to satisfy their thirst and live. Later on their journey, they would face the very same situation— they needed water again. After all, they were in a desert. Yet God would prescribe a different method to Moses this time. He would command him to merely *speak* to the rock. However, as Moses was frustrated with the continued complaints of the people, he neglected God's command and *struck* the rock again.

God was not pleased at all, and as a result, He declared that Moses would not be permitted to enter the Promised Land. He would be able to lead the people up to it, but he himself would never be able to enter into it.

This certainly seems like a harsh punishment for a seemingly minor offense, but once again there is a bigger picture. The rock is symbolic of Jesus (1 Corinthians 10:4). He would be struck only once when He died on the Cross. After that, there would be no need for Him to ever suffer again. His death would be a payment in full for sins once for all. It would release the springs of living water to satisfy the spiritual thirst of all mankind. He would be struck once, and after that, all that remains is for us to speak to Him to satisfy our spiritual thirst.

THE LAW OF GOD
EXODUS 20:1-17

We come now to a truly monumental event in the history of Israel. It is typically referred to as the "Giving of the Law," as this is when God gave the people of Israel a set of laws that would be the basis on which their society would be governed. It is commonly referred to as "The Law of Moses," since Moses was the one who received it. However, it really is "The Law of God," as He was the One who gave it.

This all took place three months after the Israelites had left Egypt on their journey to the Promised Land when they arrived at the base of Mt. Sinai. It was on this mountain that the LORD God came down and called Moses to come up. The law would become a part of God's special covenant with Israel. Their responsibility was to obey His Law. In return, God promised to be their God and bless them beyond measure. However, whenever they broke His Law, He also promised to punish them for it until they repented.

The first five books of the Bible are ascribed to Moses and are referred to as the Torah. These formed the foundation of Jewish life and culture, and they typically were held with greater importance than the other books. Within these first five books, the Jewish people actually enumerated a total of 613 commandments in all. These are typically divided into three categories—the moral, the ceremonial, and the civil law.

The moral law defined morality once and for all. While every one of us has a conscience, it is not left to us to define what is right and wrong—that is God's prerogative alone. Mankind is only left to learn, understand, and apply God's law.

The ceremonial law was specific to the nation of Israel for a particular time in history. It was primarily concerned with worship and included instructions about various ceremonies that they were required to observe. The Passover Feast was one of these.

The civil law was focused on life in general for the people of Israel. These laws were much like the laws of any nation in the world today. They addressed punishment for various crimes as well as property rights and such.

Now, before you start to get worried, let me assure you that we are not going to read all 613 commandments here—only ten of them. These ten are known as "The Ten Commandments," which are the basis of the moral law. These are what most often come to mind when we talk about the Law of Moses because they are foundational to the Law as a whole.

For your convenience, I have enumerated the commandments in the passage, but please note that the numbers are not actually part of the original text. Admittedly, different traditions vary slightly on a few of the commandments, yet this ordering seems to align best with the text itself. The first four commandments focus on mankind's relationship with God, while the last six concern our relationships with each other.

¹ Then God spoke all these words:

² I am the LORD your God, who brought you out of the land of Egypt, out of the place of slavery.

[1] ³ Do not have other gods besides me.

[2] ⁴ Do not make an idol for yourself, whether in the shape of anything in the heavens above or on the earth below or in the waters under the earth. ⁵ Do not bow in worship to them, and do not serve them; for I, the LORD your God, am a jealous God, bringing the consequences of the fathers' iniquity on the children to the third and fourth generations of those who hate me, ⁶ but showing faithful love to a thousand generations of those who love me and keep my commands.

[3] ⁷ Do not misuse the name of the LORD your God, because the LORD will not leave anyone unpunished who misuses his name.

[4] ⁸ Remember the Sabbath day, to keep it holy: ⁹ You are to labor six days and do all your work, ¹⁰ but the seventh day is a Sabbath to the LORD your God. You must not do any work—you, your son or daughter, your male or female servant, your livestock, or the resident alien who is within your city gates. ¹¹ For the LORD made the heavens and the earth, the sea, and everything in them in six days; then he rested on the seventh day. Therefore the LORD blessed the Sabbath day and declared it holy.

[5] ¹² Honor your father and your mother so that you may have a long life in the land that the LORD your God is giving you.

[6] ¹³ Do not murder.

[7] ¹⁴ Do not commit adultery.

[8] ¹⁵ Do not steal.

[9] ¹⁶ Do not give false testimony against your neighbor.

[10] ¹⁷ Do not covet your neighbor's house. Do not covet your neighbor's wife, his male or female servant, his ox or donkey, or anything that belongs to your neighbor. (Exodus 20:1-17 CSB)

A CLOSER LOOK AT THE LAW

As mentioned before, the first four commandments have to do with *worship*. God does not share His matchless glory with anyone or anything else. The Israelites were to worship God and God alone. They were to respect His glory by not making any idol to represent Him. They were to honor His name and His day. So the first four commandments can be summarized as, (1) God, (2) God's image, (3) God's name, and (4) God's day.

As for the other six commandments regarding relationships between mankind, it is certainly interesting that honoring one's parents is placed first. Furthermore, this was one of only two of the laws that was *prescriptive* rather than *prohibitive*. It did not identify something they were to *avoid doing* but something they were to *do*. (The other prescriptive law was the previous one, which commanded them to remember the Sabbath day.)

Most of the other laws seem pretty fundamental. Almost no one would argue that murder, lying, stealing, and adultery are wrong. Still, the last commandment is intriguing. It speaks not of something we shouldn't *do* but of something we shouldn't *feel*.

Morality, then, is not merely a matter of what we do or don't do. It is also a matter of the heart. Indeed, I would suggest that morality encompasses the entirety of our beings—our hearts and our minds and our wills.

GUILTY ON ALL CHARGES

So how do you and I measure up before God's moral law? A typical person in the world today refers to himself or herself as "a *good* person," perhaps better than most or at least a little above average. Many people have the idea that there is an enormous chart with a point plotted for every person in the world, and they assume that they are perhaps in the top twenty-five percent or better. Yet God does not measure a person's morality in relation to anyone else—His scale is absolute.

This is also true of our own justice systems. If I live my entire life and never commit a crime but then get angry and steal something, what will happen to me? Will the judge consider how many crimes I have committed relative to the societal average and let me go free? Of course not! At least not if he is a good judge. Even if I tell him how many good things I have done in my life, that is irrelevant. The bottom line is that what I did was wrong, and the person I stole from has a right to be compensated for his loss. The scale is absolute. I am either innocent or guilty. It's the same concerning God's Law, and it doesn't take too long to figure out whether I'm innocent or guilty in His eyes.

The first commandment says to never have any other gods before God. This is the sin of blasphemy. For the Jewish people at the time the Law was given, the primary application was to forbid them from worshipping any of the gods of the nations around them. Remember that God had just demonstrated that all the gods of Egypt were false gods and powerless against Him. Today, the primary application for us is to put God first in our lives above all else. Admittedly, I do not always live that way, so I am guilty of breaking this commandment.

The second commandment has to do with idols. The New Testament identifies greed as the same thing as idolatry (Colossians 3:5). Now I have never bowed down to an actual idol, but I have certainly been greedy. So I am also guilty of breaking this law.

The third commandment has to do with honoring God's name, and I have dishonored it in times past. I haven't always honored God's day either, nor have I always honored my parents. So I'm guilty of breaking commandments three, four, and five also. I'm not doing very well at all!

In the New Testament, Jesus equates murder with hatred and adultery with lust. This makes me guilty of breaking commandments six and seven too. The last three commandments have to do with stealing, lying, and coveting, and I have failed in each of these. This was mostly when I was much younger, but I'm still guilty all the same.

So I don't know about you, but I myself am actually guilty of breaking all of the ten commandments in some way at some point in my life. Thus if I were to stand before God and He were to judge me according to His Law, I would be declared guilty on all counts, and I would be subject to His punishment.

My guess is that you would be too.

HOPE REMAINS

Nonetheless, there is still hope. How so? Well, let me put it this way. Let's assume that I didn't just steal something but rather did something far worse that cost someone a lot of money. If I were found guilty, the judge could order me to repay the damages. However, what if the damages were far too much for me to pay? What could I do? What hope would there be for me?

The answer is that someone else could pay the damages on my behalf. If my father or brother were very wealthy and had compassion on me, they could pay my debt. As soon as it was paid, I would be free. The person who suffered the damages would be fully compensated.

That person would have no more legal basis for any action against me because the debt would have been paid in full. Therefore, though I made no payment of my own for the crime I committed, I would be a free man. I would have no need to fear any future punishment. It would be as if I had never committed the crime at all.

This is our only hope before God as well. We are guilty and subject to punishment for our sins. Yet Jesus Christ Himself paid that penalty on our behalf when He died on the Cross. The penalty for sin is death, and that is why He had to die. He was our Substitute. At the moment I accept His payment for my sin, my debt is paid in full and I am free. Justice is satisfied. I can never be held responsible for my sin again. The fact that I paid none of it and that Jesus paid all of it is completely irrelevant. The only thing that matters is that the debt has been paid in full.

A SNAKE IN THE DESERT

NUMBERS 21:4-9

The next stop on our journey takes us thirty-eight years into the future. As mentioned before, Israel had reached the Promised Land long before only to turn back in fear of man and a lack of trust in God. As a result, God had made them wander in the desert ever since. The generation that had seen so many amazing miracles simply refused to trust God. Consequently, they were not permitted to enter the Promised Land. That privilege would be left to the next generation. They would only have to wait another two years for that to happen.

Their wandering continued as it had begun—as a journey of faithlessness and grumbling against God. Still, they continued to receive His miraculous provision of food every single day of their lives.

In the majority of times when Israel refused to trust God, He responded with grace and mercy along with provision for their needs. However, from time to time, He did bring judgment upon them. The following account is one example of when He brought judgment. The details of the account may seem peculiar at first, but as we shall see, there is once again great significance in them.

⁴ They traveled from Mount Hor along the route to the Red Sea, to go around Edom. But the people grew impatient on the way; ⁵ they spoke against God and against Moses, and said, "Why have you brought us up out of Egypt to die in the wilderness? There is no bread! There is no water! And we detest this miserable food!"

⁶ Then the LORD sent venomous snakes among them; they bit the people and many Israelites died. ⁷ The people came to Moses and said, "We sinned when we spoke against the LORD and against you. Pray that the LORD will take the snakes away from us." So Moses prayed for the people.

⁸ The LORD said to Moses, "Make a snake and put it up on a pole; anyone who is bitten can look at it and live." ⁹ So Moses made a bronze snake and put it up on a pole. Then when anyone was bitten by a snake and looked at the bronze snake, they lived. (Numbers 21:4-9 NIV)

A STRANGE WAY OF ESCAPE

It seemed that absolutely nothing could ever convince the Israelites that God was faithful to them and would be their Protector and Provider. So God brought His judgment against them this time. This judgment came in the form of poisonous snakes that bit some of the people and caused them to die. The Israelites, to their credit, were quick to repent. They went to Moses, confessed their sins, and then made a very specific request—that God would take the snakes away.

However, God did not grant them their request. His judgment had been pronounced, and it would remain in place. Nevertheless, just as we have seen before, He did provide a way of escape from the judgment to those who would trust Him. It would again be available to everyone but not forced upon anyone.

In this case, the way of salvation admittedly seems a bit odd. Moses was told to make a snake and put it up on a pole. Then, anyone who was bitten was supposed to go look at it. If they did so, they would live.

So why would God give them such a strange method of healing? The fact that the snake was lifted up on a pole makes sense, as it would then be easier to see from farther away. Recall that there were over a million people who left Egypt, so that amount of people would certainly take up quite a large area. But why would God say they had to go and *look* at this snake? Of all the things He could have prescribed for them, why did He choose this particular response?

Imagine for a moment that you were among the people of Israel at this time and that you had been bitten by a snake. You have seen other people die from these bites already, so you are terrified that you, too, will die very shortly. You are panicked and distraught, and you cry out in agony. Someone hears you and runs up to you and says, "Haven't you heard? God has made a way for you to be healed! Moses made a snake and put it up on a pole, and God promised that anyone who looked at it would be cured! Come on! Let's go, so you can be healed!" What would you do? What would you think? Would you go?

I have shared this passage with many people throughout the years, and nearly every one of them has affirmed that they would, in fact, go look at the snake if they had been in that situation. And I would too. After all, what would anyone have to lose? There was no other way to be healed—only one. So going to look at the snake would certainly be worth the risk. All who did go to look at the snake were healed. All who did not go were not healed and died.

Do you see what the point of it all was now? In order to be healed, they had to put their trust in God. They had to believe in His provision of healing. They had to believe that He really was their Provider and Protector. They had to take an actual step of faith. That was what God wanted them to do all along. In order to be healed, they didn't have to have great faith or even average faith. The weakest faith in the world would have resulted in healing if it brought the dying person close enough to look at the snake on the pole. Thus it wasn't the *strength* of a person's faith but the *object* of that faith.

THE SYMBOL OF MEDICINE

If you go by a hospital in practically any city today, you might notice a strange sort of symbol there, usually on the main sign out front. You will also notice it if an ambulance happens to pass by. The same symbol appears on the logo for the World Health Organization, the American Medical Association, the Chinese Medical Association, and just about every other association connected in any way to health or medicine. It is the symbol of a snake lifted up on a pole!

Why is this? How did a snake on a pole come to be the universal symbol of healing? May I suggest it came from this story from the Bible, where the lifting up of a snake on a pole brought healing to those who were dying?

JESUS, THE ONE LIFTED UP

Perhaps you have already suspected that this story might have a larger meaning. You might have also suspected that it just might have everything to do with Jesus. If so, you were right. John 3:16 is one of the most well-known verses in the Bible. It states, "For God loved the world in this way: He gave his one and only Son, so that everyone who believes in him will not perish but have eternal life" (John 3:16 CSB). Most people, however, are unaware of the verses that come just before that famous text. These verses are as follows: "Just as *Moses lifted up the snake in the wilderness*, so the Son of Man must be lifted up, so that everyone who believes in him may have eternal life" (John 3:14-15 CSB, emphasis added). And now the deeper meaning is revealed!

You and I, along with the whole world, have been bitten by a snake—though not a literal one. We read about this back in the Garden of Eden. Satan had taken the form of a snake when he tempted Adam and Eve, who then sinned against God. It is the bite of this snake that has poisoned every one of us. This poison, though, is not physical in nature, but spiritual, bringing spiritual death to all of us because of our sin. Nonetheless, God has provided a way of salvation—an antidote. Yet there is only one of them.

Jesus paid the penalty of death by being *lifted up* on a Cross and dying there, just as Moses had *lifted up* the snake on a pole. Yet just because He died doesn't mean that everyone is automatically healed. An act of faith is required from each of us. The antidote must be taken.

So how do we do that? How do we apply the antidote? How can we be healed? Those who were bitten by the snake in the desert had to go and look upon that snake on the pole, trusting in God to save them. So, too, you and I must go and look upon Jesus who was lifted up on the Cross. We must put our faith completely in God's power to heal us based on the death of Jesus Christ. If we do that, then we will surely be healed. If we don't, we will surely die and be separated from God forever.

The choice is given to both you and me. If you had been among the Israelites who had been bitten by a snake in the desert, would you have gone to look at that snake on the pole? I'm sure I would have, and I'm reasonably certain that most people would have done so as well. After all, there was no other antidote. No other medicine. No other hope. Why wouldn't we at least give it a chance?

And what about the Cross of Jesus? You, too, are one who has been bitten by the serpent and are dying spiritually. Will you not come to the Cross and look upon Jesus, trusting in God to heal you spiritually? You need not have great faith—only enough faith to come. There is no other antidote. No other remedy. No other hope. Will you not at least give it a chance? I hope and pray you do.

134

PART III

THE PROMISE OF PARADISE RESTORED: POETS AND PROPHETS

ISRAEL'S HISTORY: ABRAHAM TO DAVID

PSALM 78

T wo years later, the Israelites did finally enter the Promised Land immediately after the death of Moses. Joshua, Moses' long-time assistant, was the one who led the way.

Incidentally, the names *Joshua* and *Jesus* both come from the same Hebrew word *Yeshua*. *Joshua* comes into English directly from Hebrew, and *Jesus* comes from its Greek translation.

It is interesting to note that Moses, who represents the Law, could only bring the Israelites up to the Promised Land. Only Joshua could bring them in. So, too, the Law of God shows us our need for God, but only Jesus can save us (Galatians 3:24).

After Joshua died, there was a period known as the time of the judges, when God used various people to guide and lead them. This lasted for about three hundred fifty years. Then Israel asked God for a king, so they could be like all the other nations. This was quite an insult to God, as He Himself had been their King and Protector and Provider. Why would they want to be like all the other nations who had mere mortals as their kings instead of the one true God? Indeed, it would seem that all the other nations should have wanted to be like them.

Two thousand years later, their rejection of God would go even further. When Jesus was on trial, they claimed to have no king but Caesar, who wasn't even Jewish but was the Roman emperor who believed himself to be a god. Nonetheless, God granted their request for a king and installed a man named Saul. He started out well but soon became corrupted and was then rejected by God.

His successor was a man named David, who is considered the greatest earthly king that Israel ever had. His son, Solomon, succeeded him. After the death of Solomon, the kingdom was divided. The Northern Kingdom, which is sometimes referred to as Ephraim (one of the sons of Joseph), essentially abandoned God at the outset and never returned. As a result, God rejected them as well. The Southern Kingdom, known as Judah, continued the pattern of rebellion and repentance that we have previously observed. God's focus was primarily on this kingdom from that point on.

As we continue our journey, we will leave the historical books behind and look at a few passages from one of the poetic books called the Psalms, which was the songbook of the Jewish people. Although many of these were written by David, the king, the first one we will read was not. However, it does introduce us to David.

This particular psalm provides a summary of Israel's history from Moses all the way down to the time of David. It is a brutally honest account that openly describes the continuous cycle of rebellion and repentance by the people of Israel, which we have already seen.

As stated previously, many people today try to suggest that the Bible is merely a collection of mythical stories that have no true basis in history. Yet this often comes from an inherent bias against the Bible and not from actual evidence or reason.

As we have seen, these accounts are anything but flattering to the people who wrote them, and this is important. Why would people make up stories about themselves that are so embarrassing and that show themselves in such a terrible light? That just doesn't make sense. Even when people recount actual events, they are prone to omit embarrassing details and embellish things to make themselves look better. Thus the very nature of these accounts—that they include the most shameful and embarrassing details about themselves—is very strong evidence for their accuracy and also of their divine origin.

You will notice references to many things we have already read about or mentioned, including the plagues of Egypt, the crossing of the Red Sea, the Passover, the bread from heaven, water from the rock, and the division of Israel into two kingdoms. There will also be a few things that we haven't covered.

¹ My people, hear my instruction;
listen to the words from my mouth.
² I will declare wise sayings;
I will speak mysteries from the past—
³ things we have heard and known
and that our ancestors have passed down to us.
⁴ We will not hide them from their children,
but will tell a future generation
the praiseworthy acts of the LORD,
his might, and the wondrous works
he has performed.
⁵ He established a testimony in Jacob
and set up a law in Israel,
which he commanded our ancestors

to teach to their children
⁶ so that a future generation—
children yet to be born—might know.
They were to rise and tell their children
⁷ so that they might put their confidence in God
and not forget God's works,
but keep his commands.
⁸ Then they would not be like their ancestors,
a stubborn and rebellious generation,
a generation whose heart was not loyal
and whose spirit was not faithful to God.
⁹ The Ephraimite archers turned back
on the day of battle.
¹⁰ They did not keep God's covenant
and refused to live by his law.
¹¹ They forgot what he had done,
the wondrous works he had shown them.
¹² He worked wonders in the sight of their ancestors
in the land of Egypt, the territory of Zoan.
¹³ He split the sea and brought them across;
the water stood firm like a wall.
¹⁴ He led them with a cloud by day
and with a fiery light throughout the night.
¹⁵ He split rocks in the wilderness
and gave them drink as abundant as the depths.
¹⁶ He brought streams out of the stone
and made water flow down like rivers.
¹⁷ But they continued to sin against him,
rebelling in the desert against the Most High.
¹⁸ They deliberately tested God,
demanding the food they craved.
¹⁹ They spoke against God, saying,
"Is God able to provide food in the wilderness?
²⁰ Look! He struck the rock and water gushed out;
torrents overflowed.
But can he also provide bread
or furnish meat for his people?"
²¹ Therefore, the LORD heard and became furious;
then fire broke out against Jacob,
and anger flared up against Israel
²² because they did not believe God

or rely on his salvation.
²³ He gave a command to the clouds above
and opened the doors of heaven.
²⁴ He rained manna for them to eat;
he gave them grain from heaven.
²⁵ People ate the bread of angels.
He sent them an abundant supply of food.
²⁶ He made the east wind blow in the skies
and drove the south wind by his might.
²⁷ He rained meat on them like dust,
and winged birds like the sand of the seas.
²⁸ He made them fall in the camp,
all around the tents.
²⁹ The people ate and were completely satisfied,
for he gave them what they craved.
³⁰ Before they had turned from what they craved,
while the food was still in their mouths,
³¹ God's anger flared up against them,
and he killed some of their best men.
He struck down Israel's fit young men.
³² Despite all this, they kept sinning
and did not believe his wondrous works.
³³ He made their days end in futility,
their years in sudden disaster.
³⁴ When he killed some of them,
the rest began to seek him;
they repented and searched for God.
³⁵ They remembered that God was their rock,
the Most High God, their Redeemer.
³⁶ But they deceived him with their mouths,
they lied to him with their tongues,
³⁷ their hearts were insincere toward him,
and they were unfaithful to his covenant.
³⁸ Yet he was compassionate;
he atoned for their iniquity
and did not destroy them.
He often turned his anger aside
and did not unleash all his wrath.
³⁹ He remembered that they were only flesh,
a wind that passes and does not return.
⁴⁰ How often they rebelled against him

in the wilderness
and grieved him in the desert.
⁴¹ They constantly tested God
and provoked the Holy One of Israel.
⁴² They did not remember his power shown
on the day he redeemed them from the foe,
⁴³ when he performed his miraculous signs in Egypt
and his wonders in the territory of Zoan.
⁴⁴ He turned their rivers into blood,
and they could not drink from their streams.
⁴⁵ He sent among them swarms of flies,
which fed on them,
and frogs, which devastated them.
⁴⁶ He gave their crops to the caterpillar
and the fruit of their labor to the locust.
⁴⁷ He killed their vines with hail
and their sycamore fig trees with a flood.
⁴⁸ He handed over their livestock to hail
and their cattle to lightning bolts.
⁴⁹ He sent his burning anger against them:
fury, indignation, and calamity—
a band of deadly messengers.
⁵⁰ He cleared a path for his anger.
He did not spare them from death
but delivered their lives to the plague.
⁵¹ He struck all the firstborn in Egypt,
the first progeny of the tents of Ham.
⁵² He led his people out like sheep
and guided them like a flock in the wilderness.
⁵³ He led them safely, and they were not afraid;
but the sea covered their enemies.
⁵⁴ He brought them to his holy territory,
to the mountain his right hand acquired.
⁵⁵ He drove out nations before them.
He apportioned their inheritance by lot
and settled the tribes of Israel in their tents.
⁵⁶ But they rebelliously tested the Most High God,
for they did not keep his decrees.
⁵⁷ They treacherously turned away like their ancestors;
they became warped like a faulty bow.
⁵⁸ They enraged him with their high places

and provoked his jealousy with their carved images.
⁵⁹ God heard and became furious;
he completely rejected Israel.
⁶⁰ He abandoned the tabernacle at Shiloh,
the tent where he resided among mankind.
⁶¹ He gave up his strength to captivity
and his splendor to the hand of a foe.
⁶² He surrendered his people to the sword
because he was enraged with his heritage.
⁶³ Fire consumed his chosen young men,
and his young women had no wedding songs.
⁶⁴ His priests fell by the sword,
and the widows could not lament.
⁶⁵ The Lord awoke as if from sleep,
like a warrior from the effects of wine.
⁶⁶ He beat back his foes;
he gave them lasting disgrace.
⁶⁷ He rejected the tent of Joseph
and did not choose the tribe of Ephraim.
⁶⁸ He chose instead the tribe of Judah,
Mount Zion, which he loved.
⁶⁹ He built his sanctuary like the heights,
like the earth that he established forever.
⁷⁰ He chose David his servant
and took him from the sheep pens;
⁷¹ he brought him from tending ewes
to be shepherd over his people Jacob—
over Israel, his inheritance.
⁷² He shepherded them with a pure heart
and guided them with his skillful hands. (Psalm 78 CSB)

DAVID, THE SHEPHERD KING

Israel's history was full of the people refusing to trust God. This psalm affirms that truth quite explicitly. The pattern of rebellion seemed to keep repeating itself again and again. However, the psalm takes an abrupt turn in the last paragraph as it introduces us to David.

So who exactly was this man? David was unquestionably the greatest earthly king that Israel would ever know. When God chose him, He described him as "a man after his own heart" (1 Samuel 13:14 CSB). This was what made David such a great king. In addition to his passion for God, David was just a great man as well. He could truly be described as a *warrior poet*—the same phrase that the movie *Braveheart* used to describe the army of Scots in the final scene. David faced a giant of a man all alone on a battlefield and defeated him, so his position as a warrior is secure. Yet he also wrote music and played the harp!

Oftentimes, masculinity is improperly defined by a single dimension, and the face of a warrior is often the one that is most often used. Yet there is much more to a man than that. A real man is not merely fierce but deeply passionate as well. David was such a man.

He is also known as "the shepherd king." He had a humble beginning, as the youngest of eight sons, and grew up in the small town of Bethlehem, shepherding his father's sheep. Such humble beginnings served well to prepare him to be a great king.

Because of David's great devotion to God, the Lord poured out His blessing upon Him in truly remarkable ways, just as God had promised in His covenant with Israel. He even promised David that one of his very own descendants would sit on the throne of his kingdom forever. Can you guess who that would turn out to be?

Yes, of course, it's Jesus. Jesus was a descendant of David and was even born in Bethlehem, the city of David. Jesus would also be a Shepherd King! In fact, the very charge against Him when He was crucified was that He was the "King of the Jews." So, once again, everything in the Bible, including the story of David, points directly to Jesus. History is truly *His Story!*

WHY HAVE YOU ABANDONED ME?

PSALM 22

P salm 22 is the first of two psalms of David that we will read together. We have already mentioned that he was the second king of Israel, and he succeeded a man named Saul. It is important to understand, though, that David had been anointed as king while Saul was still alive. Remember that God had rejected Saul because his heart had strayed from Him.

As time went on, Saul became more and more envious of David and grew to hate him. He even tried to kill him on multiple occasions. Because of this, several of David's psalms, like this one, are cries of despair to God.

As you read the psalm, understand that this is poetry, so there will be some imagery and symbolism that may seem a bit obscure. Remember, though, that most of the passages we have read so far actually foreshadow something far greater. The same is true of this passage.

¹ My God, my God, why have you abandoned me?
Why are you so far from my deliverance
and from my words of groaning?
² My God, I cry by day, but you do not answer,
by night, yet I have no rest.
³ But you are holy,
enthroned on the praises of Israel.
⁴ Our ancestors trusted in you;
they trusted, and you rescued them.
⁵ They cried to you and were set free;
they trusted in you and were not disgraced.
⁶ But I am a worm and not a man,
scorned by mankind and despised by people.
⁷ Everyone who sees me mocks me;
they sneer and shake their heads:
⁸ "He relies on the LORD;
let him save him;
let the LORD rescue him,
since he takes pleasure in him."
⁹ It was you who brought me out of the womb,
making me secure at my mother's breast.
¹⁰ I was given over to you at birth;
you have been my God from my mother's womb.
¹¹ Don't be far from me, because distress is near
and there's no one to help.
¹² Many bulls surround me;
strong ones of Bashan encircle me.
¹³ They open their mouths against me—
lions, mauling and roaring.
¹⁴ I am poured out like water,
and all my bones are disjointed;
my heart is like wax,
melting within me.

¹⁵ *My strength is dried up like baked clay;*
my tongue sticks to the roof of my mouth.
You put me into the dust of death.
¹⁶ *For dogs have surrounded me;*
a gang of evildoers has closed in on me;
they pierced my hands and my feet.
¹⁷ *I can count all my bones;*
people look and stare at me.
¹⁸ *They divided my garments among themselves,*
and they cast lots for my clothing.
¹⁹ *But you, LORD, don't be far away.*
My strength, come quickly to help me.
²⁰ *Rescue my life from the sword,*
my only life from the power of these dogs.
²¹ *Save me from the lion's mouth,*
from the horns of wild oxen.
You answered me!
²² *I will proclaim your name to my brothers and sisters;*
I will praise you in the assembly.
²³ *You who fear the LORD, praise him!*
All you descendants of Jacob, honor him!
All you descendants of Israel, revere him!
²⁴ *For he has not despised or abhorred*
the torment of the oppressed.
He did not hide his face from him
but listened when he cried to him for help.
²⁵ *I will give praise in the great assembly*
because of you;
I will fulfill my vows
before those who fear you.
²⁶ *The humble will eat and be satisfied;*
those who seek the LORD will praise him.
May your hearts live forever!
²⁷ *All the ends of the earth will remember*
and turn to the LORD.
All the families of the nations
will bow down before you,
²⁸ *for kingship belongs to the LORD;*
he rules the nations.
²⁹ *All who prosper on earth will eat and bow down;*
all those who go down to the dust

will kneel before him—
even the one who cannot preserve his life.
[30] Their descendants will serve him;
the next generation will be told about the Lord.
[31] They will come and declare his righteousness;
to a people yet to be born
they will declare what he has done. (Psalm 22 CSB)

THE SUFFERING OF THE SON OF DAVID

David describes in this psalm a scene of great suffering in the midst of hatred, scorn, and mockery. It is truly horrific. However, there is no record that David himself ever experienced anything quite like this. Thus we are left to wonder what exactly he is describing. Since this never happened to David, the psalm was long considered to be *Messianic* in nature—a psalm that spoke of the Messiah who was to come.

The word *Messiah* is a Hebrew word that literally means "anointed one." In Israel, priests and kings were ceremonially anointed with oil. This essentially identified them as having a special mission from God. However, while there were many anointed ones throughout history, the Bible specifically spoke of a particular Anointed One (Messiah) who would accomplish God's ultimate plan to restore mankind.

You will recall that the New Testament was written in Greek. The Greek word for Messiah is *Christos*, and that is where we get the word *Christ* in English. So whenever you see the word *Messiah* or *Christ*, it is talking about the same Person. Interestingly enough, a thousand years after this psalm was written, Jesus Himself quoted the first verse of it. He did this while He was dying on the Cross.

The first phrase of the United States' national anthem is, "O say, can you see." Now, if I were to quote this in a group of Americans, all of them would be thinking not just of the few words I quoted but of the entire song. It was likely the same for those at the crucifixion of Jesus. When He quoted the first verse of the psalm, they likely recalled the entire song. It was at that moment in history, one thousand years after it was written, the true meaning of this psalm was revealed.

It is a powerful and poetic description of what was taking place at that very moment when Jesus was being crucified. It seems, then, that God gave David a vision of the suffering of the Messiah long before it occurred, and David merely described in poetic form what God had revealed to him. Thus it was not a description of David himself but of the promised Messiah, who would be the Son of David.

THE PROPHECY FULFILLED

Let us now look at just a few of the prophecies of Psalm 22 that were fulfilled in the crucifixion of Jesus.

- *Scorned, despised, and mocked (vv. 6-8).* The psalm records that he was scorned and despised, and peopled mocked him, saying, "He relies on the Lord—let him save him" (Psalm 22:8 CSB). We will see exactly the same thing taking place as Jesus hung on the Cross. In fact, they even used the same words in their mockery of Him, suggesting that if He were really from God, then God would save Him (Matthew 27:43).

- *My tongue sticks to the roof of my mouth (v. 15).* The account of Jesus' crucifixion specifically records Jesus saying He was thirsty, as His tongue stuck to the roof of His mouth (John 19:28).

- *Dogs have surrounded me (v. 16). Dogs* was a term that the Jews would use to describe those who were not Jews. The crucifixion was carried out, not by the Jewish people but by soldiers of Rome. Rome was a world empire at that time, and Israel was a part of their conquest. Thus Jesus was literally surrounded by non-Jewish people when He was being crucified.

- *They pierced my hands and my feet (v. 16).* The manner in which the Jewish people carried out capital punishment was that of stoning. The Romans, however, often used crucifixion, nailing the hands and feet of the condemned to a cross.

  The earliest account of this method of execution seems to have been by King Darius of Persia. This occurred roughly five hundred years *after* the time of David. Yet this is precisely the type of death that David describes. In fact, crucifixion is the only thing that even comes close to this description. Note that crucifixion requires not only the piercing of the hands but also of the feet as well. The psalm identifies both. Thus David described in great detail a method of execution that hadn't even been invented yet, and this was what was used in the execution of Jesus.

- *I can count all my bones (v. 17).* Whenever a person was on a cross, his rib cage would naturally be pushed out as a result of hanging from the nails in his hands. Thus, looking down, Jesus would have quite literally been able to count all of the bones in His rib cage.

- *They divided my garments among themselves and they cast lots for my clothing (v. 18).* Again, the account of Jesus' crucifixion specifically records this taking place, just as the psalm prophesies. When the soldiers began dividing Jesus' garments, they came to one piece of clothing that was larger than the others and in one piece. They decided not to include it among the things they divided up because it presumably wouldn't be fair for one person to get that piece. Thus they decided to cast lots for it. As a result, the Scripture was fulfilled precisely in that the soldiers both divided His garments among themselves and also cast lots for His clothing (John 19:23-24).

This is absolutely amazing! Again, David wrote this a thousand years before Jesus was even born and five hundred years before crucifixion even existed. Yet David, under the inspiration of the Holy Spirit, described the scene of the Cross with astonishing detail.

- *All the ends of the earth will remember and turn to the Lord. All the families of the nations will bow down before you....Their descendants will serve him; the next generation will be told about the Lord. They will come and declare his righteousness; to a people yet to be born they will declare what he has done (vv. 27, 30-31).* The end of the psalm foresees the proclamation of the God of Israel to the entire world throughout the ages.

After the death and resurrection of Jesus, there were about five hundred people who recognized Jesus as the Jewish Messiah, the Christ, and the Son of God. All of these were Jewish people. Today, people from all over the world worship Jesus as God, and every generation proclaims His name to the next.

Indeed, the very fact that you are reading about this today is a fulfillment of this prophecy. From the viewpoint of the crucifixion, *you* belong to the people who were yet *unborn*, and Jesus is being proclaimed to you today in these pages.

THE SHEPHERD'S SHEPHERD

PSALM 23

O ur next psalm, also written by David, the *shepherd king*, will be our last. It is fairly brief but one of the most well-known and most loved of all the psalms.

> *¹ The LORD is my shepherd;*
> *I have what I need.*
> *² He lets me lie down in green pastures;*
> *he leads me beside quiet waters.*
> *³ He renews my life;*
> *he leads me along the right paths*
> *for his name's sake.*
> *⁴ Even when I go through the darkest valley,*
> *I fear no danger,*
> *for you are with me;*
> *your rod and your staff—they comfort me.*
> *⁵ You prepare a table before me*
> *in the presence of my enemies;*
> *you anoint my head with oil;*
> *my cup overflows.*
> *⁶ Only goodness and faithful love will pursue me*
> *all the days of my life,*
> *and I will dwell in the house of the LORD*
> *as long as I live. (Psalm 23 CSB)*

JESUS, THE SHEPHERD'S SHEPHERD

David certainly understood what it was to be a shepherd, having cared for his own father's sheep in his youth. He knew what it was to make sheep lie down in green pastures and to lead them beside still waters. He had protected them with his rod and staff, and his sheep had nothing to fear when he was with them.

But what about David? Was there anyone who would take care of him the way he had taken care of his father's sheep? He had certainly faced much danger at the hands of Saul. He had also fought in Israel's army. Who was there to protect him? Unlike the history of the Jewish people, David trusted God to be His Protector and Provider. Thus God Himself was David's Shepherd. He was the Shepherd's Shepherd.

A thousand years later, Jesus was born as a descendant of David. He would identify Himself as the Good Shepherd who would lay down His life for His sheep. Thus it was Jesus, the Son of God, in particular, who was David's Shepherd. *Jesus* is the Shepherd's Shepherd.

ONE LIKE A SON OF MAN

DANIEL 7

The previous chapter concluded our journey through the poetic books of the Old Testament. Before that, we spent a good portion of time in the historical books. We now come to the final category of books—prophecy. In these books, God reveals future events to prophets who then proclaim these to the people. Oftentimes they were warnings about what God would do if the Jewish people continued in their sin. Other times, they were simply foretelling future events.

This isn't all that the prophetic books contain. A prophet was someone who heard from God and spoke to the people. God had much to say to the people that concerned what was happening at that very moment. Thus the prophetic books contain both the proclamations of God to the people at that moment in time as well as prophecies about what was to come.

Even in the historical books, we saw God giving prophecies, promises, and covenants regarding the future. Some of these prophecies came true very shortly after God gave them. We saw this in the Exodus when God commanded them to eat the Passover in a manner ready to be set free. Other prophecies concerned things that are future still today. However, the most important prophecies concerned the coming of the Messiah, who we already know is Jesus.

The prophecies about the Messiah actually number in the hundreds. These aren't vague illusions about obscure events either. On the contrary, they contain very specific details about times and places and even include predictions of the miraculous. The significance of the large number of prophecies along with their specificity cannot be overstated. The Bible claims to be the actual word of God, and the inclusion of so many predictions makes this claim very easy to test. If the prophecies in the Bible fail to come true, then the Bible is not from God. However, if the prophecies do come true, then how could the Bible *not* be the Word of God?

Indeed, if the Bible is merely the words of men, we certainly would not expect to find any prophecies in it at all. No mere man can predict the future, so why would they include such things that would so easily prove themselves wrong? The answer is that God knows the end from the beginning (Isaiah 46:10), so to tell us what He knows is going to happen in the future is no risk at all for Him. This is strong evidence that the Bible is the true Word of God.

In contrast, the sacred books of other religions seldom if ever dare to predict the future. The Bible is quite unique in this manner.

Daniel is one of the prophetic books in the Bible, named for its author, who lived sometime between 600 and 500 B.C. He was a truly great man of God who was deeply committed to living a holy life in accordance with the Law of God.

The Israelites had been conquered by the Babylonian king, Nebuchadnezzar, at the time. He had ordered that the best of the young men of Israel be brought into his court to serve in his kingdom. Daniel was one of these men. Because of his holy life, God chose to reveal to Daniel some truly amazing things about the future through a series of dreams and visions. The following passage is the record of the first of these dreams. It occurred after Belshazzar had taken over the throne of Babylon from his father, Nebuchadnezzar.

As you read the account, there will be a reference to a being who is called the *Ancient of Days*. This is understood to be a reference to God. And be sure to pay careful attention to the mention of another figure who is identified as *one like a son of man*.

¹ In the first year of Belshazzar king of Babylon, Daniel had a dream, and visions passed through his mind as he was lying in bed. He wrote down the substance of his dream.

² Daniel said: "In my vision at night I looked, and there before me were the four winds of heaven churning up the great sea. ³ Four great beasts, each different from the others, came up out of the sea.

⁴ "The first was like a lion, and it had the wings of an eagle. I watched until its wings were torn off and it was lifted from the ground so that it stood on two feet like a human being, and the mind of a human was given to it.

⁵ "And there before me was a second beast, which looked like a bear. It was raised up on one of its sides, and it had three ribs in its mouth between its teeth. It was told, 'Get up and eat your fill of flesh!'

⁶ "After that, I looked, and there before me was another beast, one that looked like a leopard. And on its back it had four wings like those of a bird. This beast had four heads, and it was given authority to rule.

⁷ "After that, in my vision at night I looked, and there before me was a fourth beast—terrifying and frightening and very powerful. It had large iron teeth; it crushed and devoured its victims and trampled underfoot whatever was left. It was different from all the former beasts, and it had ten horns.

⁸ "While I was thinking about the horns, there before me was another horn, a little one, which came up among them; and three of the first horns were uprooted before it. This horn had eyes like the eyes of a human being and a mouth that spoke boastfully.

⁹ "As I looked,
"thrones were set in place,
* and the Ancient of Days took his seat.*
His clothing was as white as snow;
* the hair of his head was white like wool.*
His throne was flaming with fire,
* and its wheels were all ablaze.*
¹⁰ A river of fire was flowing,
* coming out from before him.*
Thousands upon thousands attended him;
* ten thousand times ten thousand stood before him.*
The court was seated,
* and the books were opened.*

¹¹ "Then I continued to watch because of the boastful words the horn was speaking. I kept looking until the beast was slain and its body destroyed and thrown into the blazing fire. [12] (The other beasts had been stripped of their authority, but were allowed to live for a period of time.)

[13] *"In my vision at night I looked, and there before me was one like a son of man, coming with the clouds of heaven. He approached the Ancient of Days and was led into his presence. [14] He was given authority, glory and sovereign power; all nations and peoples of every language worshiped him. His dominion is an everlasting dominion that will not pass away, and his kingdom is one that will never be destroyed.*

The Interpretation of the Dream

[15] *"I, Daniel, was troubled in spirit, and the visions that passed through my mind disturbed me. [16] I approached one of those standing there and asked him the meaning of all this.*

"So he told me and gave me the interpretation of these things: [17] 'The four great beasts are four kings that will rise from the earth. [18] But the holy people of the Most High will receive the kingdom and will possess it forever—yes, for ever and ever.'

[19] *"Then I wanted to know the meaning of the fourth beast, which was different from all the others and most terrifying, with its iron teeth and bronze claws—the beast that crushed and devoured its victims and trampled underfoot whatever was left. [20] I also wanted to know about the ten horns on its head and about the other horn that came up, before which three of them fell—the horn that looked more imposing than the others and that had eyes and a mouth that spoke boastfully. [21] As I watched, this horn was waging war against the holy people and defeating them, [22] until the Ancient of Days came and pronounced judgment in favor of the holy people of the Most High, and the time came when they possessed the kingdom.*

[23] *"He gave me this explanation: 'The fourth beast is a fourth kingdom that will appear on earth. It will be different from all the other kingdoms and will devour the whole earth, trampling it down and crushing it. [24] The ten horns are ten kings who will come from this kingdom. After them another king will arise, different from the earlier ones; he will subdue three kings. [25] He will speak against the Most High and oppress his holy people and try to change the set times and the laws. The holy people will be delivered into his hands for a time, times and half a time.*

²⁶ *"But the court will sit, and his power will be taken away and completely destroyed forever.* ²⁷ *Then the sovereignty, power and greatness of all the kingdoms under heaven will be handed over to the holy people of the Most High. His kingdom will be an everlasting kingdom, and all rulers will worship and obey him.'*

²⁸ *"This is the end of the matter. I, Daniel, was deeply troubled by my thoughts, and my face turned pale, but I kept the matter to myself."* *(Daniel 7 NIV)*

FOUR KINGDOMS

As was previously mentioned, this particular prophecy was written in the time of King Belshazzar of Babylon. The four kingdoms identified here refer to the four major world empires that would appear. Babylon was the first of these. As history has unfolded, we now know the next kingdom was that of the Medo-Persians, followed by Greece, and then finally Rome.

The details included about these kingdoms are quite extraordinary. For instance, Greece was depicted as a leopard having four wings and four heads. The leopard is quite fast, and this corresponds to the speed of Alexander the Great's conquest. After his death, his kingdom was divided among his four generals.

Remember, though, that this was not written as history after Rome had come to power, but during the time of the Babylonian empire. God is again making known the end from the beginning as only He can.

There are a lot more interesting details about these four kingdoms and how this prophecy matches them perfectly, and I encourage you to investigate that further. However, that is not the reason why we are looking at this passage. We will address this reason in the next section.

ONE LIKE A SON OF MAN

About halfway through the text, we observe a peculiar figure who is referred to as *one like a son of man*. This individual is seen (1) coming with the clouds of heaven, (2) approaching God—the Ancient of Days, (3) being given dominion, glory, and a kingdom, (4) being worshiped by the entire world, and (5) reigning as king forever.

So to whom could this be referring? The title itself indicates that this is a particular human being—*a son of man*. However, this man receives worship from the whole world. The Bible is very clear that only

God, and God alone, is to be worshiped. The first commandment in the Law of God affirmed this. Yet this man receives authority from God and is then worshiped. Furthermore, this man appears to be immortal because he becomes a king who rules forever.

So again, who is this Son of Man who is worshiped as God by all the nations of the world? Of course, it is none other than Jesus Christ. Indeed, who else could it be? From before the beginning of time, Jesus was God the Son. He became a Man two thousand years ago, so He is also the Son of Man. In the future, He will be worshiped by people from every nation, tribe, and language (Revelation 5:9), and He will indeed be King forever because He is everlasting.

Some five hundred years after this, Jesus would be standing before the Jewish religious leaders. They would be desperately searching for some accusation with which to charge Him in order to put Him to death. In His response to them, Jesus would emphatically assert that He was, in fact, this *One like a Son of Man*—the One Daniel saw in the vision Jesus Himself had given him (Matthew 26:64).

THE SUFFERING SERVANT
ISAIAH 52:13–53:12

We now come to one of the most fascinating chapters in the Bible. It was written by the prophet Isaiah who lived around 700 B.C., so a little earlier than Daniel.

This particular passage is a prophecy concerning someone who is simply called "my servant." Isaiah is speaking on behalf of God Himself, so this does not refer to any servant of Isaiah's. Rather, God is referring to this person as *His* servant, meaning this person is acting in service to God Himself. The passage will reveal exactly what this servant would do in service to God.

You will notice that there appears to be a mixture of both future and past tenses in the prophecy. Hebrew verbs are different than those in English, and this seems to be primarily a translation issue between the two. It is commonly understood that the entire passage is not referring to anything in the past, but of events that were, at that time, yet future.

> [13] *See, my servant will act wisely;*
> *he will be raised and lifted up and highly exalted.*
> [14] *Just as there were many who were appalled at him—*
> *his appearance was so disfigured beyond that of any human being*
> *and his form marred beyond human likeness—*
> [15] *so he will sprinkle many nations,*
> *and kings will shut their mouths because of him.*
> *For what they were not told, they will see,*
> *and what they have not heard, they will understand.*
> [53:1] *Who has believed our message*
> *and to whom has the arm of the LORD been revealed?*
> [2] *He grew up before him like a tender shoot,*
> *and like a root out of dry ground.*
> *He had no beauty or majesty to attract us to him,*
> *nothing in his appearance that we should desire him.*
> [3] *He was despised and rejected by mankind,*
> *a man of suffering, and familiar with pain.*
> *Like one from whom people hide their faces*
> *he was despised, and we held him in low esteem.*
> [4] *Surely he took up our pain*
> *and bore our suffering,*
> *yet we considered him punished by God,*
> *stricken by him, and afflicted.*
> [5] *But he was pierced for our transgressions,*
> *he was crushed for our iniquities;*
> *the punishment that brought us peace was on him,*
> *and by his wounds we are healed.*
> [6] *We all, like sheep, have gone astray,*
> *each of us has turned to our own way;*
> *and the LORD has laid on him*
> *the iniquity of us all.*
> [7] *He was oppressed and afflicted,*
> *yet he did not open his mouth;*
> *he was led like a lamb to the slaughter,*
> *and as a sheep before its shearers is silent,*
> *so he did not open his mouth.*
> [8] *By oppression and judgment he was taken away.*
> *Yet who of his generation protested?*
> *For he was cut off from the land of the living;*

for the transgression of my people he was punished.
⁹ He was assigned a grave with the wicked,
  and with the rich in his death,
though he had done no violence,
  nor was any deceit in his mouth.
¹⁰ Yet it was the LORD's will to crush him and cause him to suffer,
  and though the LORD makes his life an offering for sin,
he will see his offspring and prolong his days,
  and the will of the LORD will prosper in his hand.
¹¹ After he has suffered,
  he will see the light of life and be satisfied;
by his knowledge my righteous servant will justify many,
  and he will bear their iniquities.
¹² Therefore I will give him a portion among the great,
  and he will divide the spoils with the strong,
because he poured out his life unto death,
  and was numbered with the transgressors.
For he bore the sin of many,
  and made intercession for the transgressors. (Isaiah 52:13–53:12 NIV)

THE REMARKABLE SUFFERING SERVANT

So who is this suffering servant? Again, we know that this prophecy was given around 700 B.C., so we would need to look in the past twenty-seven hundred years to see if anyone has fulfilled it. To determine if this has happened, we need to look more closely at the details of the prophecy.

It begins by stating that the servant will be *highly exalted.* This is certainly rare for a servant, as their actions are undertaken for the glory of the one they serve and not themselves. Still, this does fit with the story of Joseph, the grandson of Abraham, who we mentioned previously. He was exalted as king *after* he suffered.

The prophecy quickly turns to describe great anguish. The servant is disfigured, a man of sorrows, familiar with pain, rejected, oppressed, and afflicted. Nonetheless, the prophecy declares that *many nations and kings* will be impacted by this servant.

The prophecy then reveals that the circumstances regarding the suffering would be significant. The servant would endure everything, not for any of his own offenses but for those of others. This becomes clearer when we highlight the pronouns in the passage:

He took up *our* pain and bore *our* suffering…
We considered *Him* punished by God…
He was pierced for *our* transgressions…
He was crushed for *our* iniquities…
The punishment that brought *us* peace was on *Him*…
By *His* wounds *we* are healed…
We…have gone astray…
The LORD has laid on *Him* the iniquity of *us* all.

The servant is acting as a *substitute*, bearing the punishment that others deserved.

It goes on to describe the death of this servant, comparing him to a silent lamb being led to the slaughter. This suggests that he is not attempting to escape or defend himself in any way.

His death and burial are associated with two specific sets of people—the wicked and the rich. The death of this servant was not just some random event either, but it happened according to God's set purpose.

Next, the prophecy speaks of a resurrection. Though the servant died, it then speaks of him as being alive once again. "After he has suffered, he will see the light of life" (Isaiah 53:11 NIV). Then the servant is identified with a new title—"my *righteous* servant" (Isaiah 53:11 NIV, emphasis added). This servant has another extraordinary impact on people after his resurrection, as it records that he will justify many (make many righteous). In context, those he is justifying are those that deserved the punishment that he himself suffered. Thus, bearing the sins of others, he makes righteous those who are not righteous.

This is certainly, then, no ordinary servant. His actions are so greatly esteemed that God Himself exalts him and honors him as a champion.

The prophecy concludes by restating his act of bearing the sins of others and also of making intercession on their behalf.

THE SUFFERING SERVANT REVEALED

Who is this suffering servant? Surely by now it is obvious—and no surprise. *Jesus* is the Suffering Servant.

This prophecy has many precise details that are specifically fulfilled in the death, burial, and resurrection of Jesus. It would take too long to go through all of them here, but suffice it to say that this prophecy is overwhelming in its precision and detail of events that would take place seven hundred years later. So while a complete discussion of all of the details would take far too long for our purposes, let us take a look at just a few of them.

- *Despised and rejected (v. 3).* In the New Testament we read that Jesus was, indeed, despised and rejected, particularly by the Jewish leaders of His day who saw Him as a threat to their power (John 1:10-11).

- *He was pierced for our transgressions (v. 5).* Again, we see the prophecy of one being pierced, just as David had written about three hundred years earlier. Yet this prophecy adds that the purpose of the piercing was for the sins (transgressions) of others.

- *He was led like a lamb to the slaughter, and as a sheep before her shearers is silent, so he did not open his mouth (v. 7).* Jesus was proclaimed to be the Lamb of God. When He was on trial for His life, being accused by the religious leaders before the Roman governor, the Scriptures record that He remained silent—just as this prophecy foretold (Matthew 26:63).

- *He was assigned a grave with the wicked, and with the rich in his death (v. 9).* Jesus was crucified with two criminals (the wicked). Yet after He died, a rich man named Joseph of Arimathea provided his own tomb for His burial (Matthew 27:38, 57-60).

- *After he has suffered, he will see the light of life (v. 11).* This is a specific prophecy of the resurrection of Jesus.

- *He bore the sin of many (v. 12).* The New Testament declares that Jesus died specifically to bear the sin of the world (1 Peter 3:18).

- *And made intercession for the transgressors (v. 12).* While He was yet alive on the Cross, He specifically prayed, "Father, forgive them, because they do not know what they are doing" (Luke 23:34 CSB). In doing so, Jesus did make intercession for sinners.

- *My righteous servant will justify many (v. 11).* Jesus is this Righteous Servant, and through His death and resurrection, He makes righteous all those who are unrighteous when they put their trust in Him (2 Corinthians 5:21).

JESUS, THE SUFFERING SERVANT

Now that we have seen that Jesus is, in fact, the Suffering Servant of which Isaiah spoke, let us look at the passage once more in light of this truth.

See, my servant *Jesus* will act wisely; *Jesus* will be raised and lifted up and highly exalted. Just as there were many who were appalled at *Jesus*—the appearance of *Jesus* was so disfigured beyond that of any man and his form marred beyond human likeness—so will *Jesus* sprinkle many nations, and kings will shut their mouths because of *Jesus*....

Jesus grew up before him like a tender shoot, and like a root out of dry ground. *Jesus* had no beauty or majesty to attract us to *Jesus*, nothing in his appearance that we should desire *Jesus*.

Jesus was despised and rejected by men, a man of sorrows, and familiar with suffering. Like one from whom men hide their faces *Jesus* was despised, and we esteemed *Jesus* not.

Surely *Jesus* took up our infirmities and carried our sorrows, yet we considered *Jesus* stricken by God, smitten by him, and afflicted.

But *Jesus* was pierced for our transgressions, *Jesus* was crushed for our iniquities; the punishment that brought us peace was upon *Jesus*, and by the wounds of *Jesus* we are healed.

We all, like sheep, have gone astray, each of us has turned to his own way; and the LORD has laid on *Jesus* the iniquity of us all. *Jesus* was oppressed and afflicted, yet he did not open his mouth; *Jesus* was led like a lamb to the slaughter, and as a sheep before her shearers is silent, so *Jesus* did not open his mouth.

By oppression and judgment *Jesus* was taken away. And who can speak of *Jesus'* descendants? For *Jesus* was cut off from the land of the living; for the transgression of my people *Jesus* was stricken. *Jesus* was assigned a grave with the wicked, and with the rich in his death, though *Jesus* had done no violence, nor was any deceit in his mouth.

Yet it was the LORD's will to crush *Jesus* and cause *Jesus* to suffer, and though the LORD makes his life a guilt offering, *Jesus* will see his offspring and prolong his days, and the will of the LORD will prosper in his hand.

After the suffering of his soul, *Jesus* will see the light of life and be satisfied; by his knowledge my righteous servant *Jesus* will justify many, and *Jesus* will bear their iniquities.

Therefore I will give *Jesus* a portion among the great, and he will divide the spoils with the strong, because *Jesus* poured out his life unto death, and was numbered with the transgressors. For *Jesus* bore the sin of many, and made intercession for the transgressors.

THE FORBIDDEN CHAPTER

The prophecy of Isaiah 53 is simply astounding in its accuracy and precision. It is overwhelming evidence for the claim that Jesus is the promised Jewish Messiah. No other interpretation of the passage is even plausible. Remember, too, that this is from the Old Testament—the part of the Bible that the Jewish people recognize as being from God.

But why, then, do the majority of Jewish people still reject Jesus? The answer, in part, is that most of them have never read this prophecy. It used to be read in Jewish synagogues as part of their scheduled readings. Before the time of Jesus, it was widely considered to be a Messianic prophecy. However, at some point after the time of Jesus, it was removed from the schedule of readings.

So why was this done? Essentially, it is just too obvious that it is talking about Jesus. The Jewish rabbis have largely rejected Jesus as the Messiah. It's almost a part of their culture to do so. So in order to maintain this belief, they had to prevent people from ever reading this clear, amazing prophecy.

Thus Isaiah 53 has come to be known as *the forbidden chapter*.

THE VIRGIN BIRTH

ISAIAH 7:14

We are now quickly nearing the end of our time together in the Old Testament. Thus far, we have looked at a lot of longer passages and a few shorter ones. Now we turn our focus to a few very short passages that are just one or two sentences. They arise almost unexpectedly within larger narratives concerning other things. Yet, although they are short, they are very important.

The first passage comes earlier on in Isaiah than the one we just read. An army is threatening to attack the people of Israel, but God promises that He will protect them. They only need to trust Him. To assure them of this, the prophet Isaiah suggests that the king of Israel ask for a sign from God. For whatever reason, the king declines to do so.

Nonetheless, Isaiah tells the king that God will give him a sign anyway. However, this sign would not come in the immediate future but would speak of a more distant occurrence.

Therefore the Lord himself will give you a sign: The virgin will conceive and give birth to a son, and will call him Immanuel. (Isaiah 7:14 NIV)

WHAT CHILD IS THIS?

The sign that God gives them is certainly a miraculous one. A *virgin*, a woman who has never been with a man, will become pregnant and give birth to a child. This child will be a baby boy.

It is important to note here that this verse is not merely suggesting that a woman who was a virgin will become pregnant on the first night of her marriage and then give birth to a son. On the contrary, the passage clearly states that a virgin will both be pregnant and also give birth. This would make it truly miraculous.

Recall that after the fall of mankind in the Garden of Eden, when God cursed the serpent, He spoke of the Offspring of the woman who would one day crush the head of Satan. A child who would be born of a virgin would uniquely be the offspring of a woman and not the offspring of both a man and a woman. Thus these two prophecies are connected.

We are also told that this child would be called Immanuel. As previously noted, Hebrew names have specific meanings, and this is true of Immanuel as well. It is literally translated as, "God with us." So we have a child who is born miraculously to a virgin. When He is born, people will proclaim that "God is with us." This is not to say, necessarily, that the actual name given to the child would be Immanuel but that the child would be referred to as such. Thus it was more of a descriptive title than an actual name.

What child is this who would be born of a virgin, the Offspring of a woman? Who would be referred to as "God with us"? Once again, it is Jesus who is God the Son from all eternity. He became a Man and entered into the physical universe two thousand years ago, being born of the virgin Mary.

You will recall that God's restoration would unfold in three phases. God the Father had come to be near us. At the moment Jesus was born, God was taking the next step—God had come to be *with* us.

DOES IT REALLY MEAN "VIRGIN"?

There are many skeptics who look at the Bible and seek to undermine everything miraculous within it. If the miracles actually happened, then that would be very strong evidence supporting the truthfulness of the Bible. Thus, to maintain their skepticism or merely to reject Jesus as God on an intellectual basis, it is necessary for them to discount the miraculous.

The tactic most often used by skeptics regarding this particular passage is to suggest that the word translated as *virgin* does not really mean a woman who has never been with a man but merely refers to a young woman. If that were so, then there would certainly be nothing miraculous about it. However, that interpretation would make the passage completely absurd. It would mean that God had told Israel that He was going to give them a great sign from heaven. And what would that great sign from heaven be?

A woman would have a baby!

Well, that is certainly no unique miraculous sign. In fact, my own mother did that too—twice! Pregnancy and birth really are miraculous; however, they are within the natural order of things—not the supernatural. If having a baby was really the miracle God was speaking of, then there would exist in the world today no less than 7.5 billion living proofs of these miraculous signs from heaven.

The only thing that would make the prophecy truly a sign of supernatural involvement would be that the woman having the baby was, indeed, a virgin. We will soon see the fulfillment of this prophecy.

A SON IS GIVEN
ISAIAH 9:6-7

Just a few chapters later we come to another fascinating prophecy in the book of Isaiah, again about a child who is to be born. This time, however, we are given some new information that is also quite intriguing and extraordinary.

> *⁶ For to us a child is born,*
> *to us a son is given,*
> *and the government will be on his shoulders.*
> *And he will be called*
> *Wonderful Counselor, Mighty God,*
> *Everlasting Father, Prince of Peace.*
> *⁷ Of the greatness of his government and peace*
> *there will be no end.*
> *He will reign on David's throne*
> *and over his kingdom,*
> *establishing and upholding it*
> *with justice and righteousness*
> *from that time on and forever.*
> *The zeal of the LORD Almighty*
> *will accomplish this. (Isaiah 9:6-7 NIV)*

A SON IS GIVEN

Previously, we saw that the child was called Immanuel. Here we see that He is called several other things as well—Wonderful Counselor, Mighty God, Everlasting Father, and Prince of Peace. So, just as Immanuel was a descriptive title, these are as well.

The most surprising of these is probably the title of *Mighty God*. How could a mere human child be referred to as God? Of course, being referred to as "Everlasting" is quite significant as well.

The prophecy also speaks of His reign on David's throne. Recall that God had previously promised David that one of his descendants would reign over Israel forever. This prophecy, written three hundred years after David, affirms that this child will be the fulfillment of that promise.

The child would also establish justice and righteousness from that time on and forever. Of the increase of His government there would be no end. Thus this child, like the Son of Man whom Daniel saw in his vision, would reign forever. Death would never bring His reign to an end.

So, to what kind of child could this possibly be referring? Again, Jesus is the One of whom the prophecy could refer. He was the Son of God from before the beginning of time. He was not merely a great man who somehow became a god. Rather, He is God who became a Man.

A MIRACULOUS ENTRY

If the One who created the world and everything in it were, in fact, to enter into His own creation, how would we expect that to happen? That would certainly be a momentous event in the history of the world. Would we expect it to occur in an ordinary way? I don't think so! In fact, if such a child were to be born in an ordinary way, how could he possibly be God? How would anyone know he was anything special?

Thus, in a real way, the virgin birth transforms something beautiful but ordinary into something beautiful and *extraordinary*—just as the child to be born would be extraordinary. A miraculous birth is just what we would expect to see with the entrance of God into the world.

THE BIRTHPLACE OF A KING

MICAH 5:2

We turn now to another intriguing prophecy, this time from a prophet named Micah, who lived during the same time as Isaiah, around 700 B.C. He speaks specifically about the birthplace of a ruler who is to come as well as the origins of that ruler.

> But you, Bethlehem Ephrathah,
> though you are small among the clans of Judah,
> out of you will come for me
> one who will be ruler over Israel,
> whose origins are from of old,
> from ancient times. (Micah 5:2 NIV)

A RULER WHOSE ORIGINS ARE FROM OF OLD

The prophecy concerns a specific town named Bethlehem near Jerusalem. This particular town was known as the city of David. This is significant because of God's promise to David regarding one of his descendants.

It speaks of a ruler who will arise at some point in the future. However, it then describes the peculiar history of this ruler. His origins are "from of old, from ancient times."

So what is this prophecy talking about? How can someone arise as a ruler in the future yet have his origins in the distant past? The only possibility, of course, is that this is referring to Jesus Christ, who existed before the beginning of the world as the eternal Son of God and then entered into our world as a baby born of a virgin in the town of Bethlehem seven hundred years after this prophecy was given.

TWO MESSIAHS?

We have looked at several prophecies now of the coming Messiah. Many of these describe Him as a *suffering* Messiah. Others, like this one, describe Him as a *conquering* or *ruling* Messiah.

So how can these two seemingly contradictory descriptions be understood? How can one who suffers and dies also be one who conquers and rules? The Jewish people themselves struggled to reconcile this. In fact, one proposal was that the prophecies actually spoke of two different Messiahs—one who would suffer and a second who would conquer. These two Messiahs were associated with Joseph and David, whom we have met previously.

Joseph had lived a life of suffering, even though he later became ruler of Egypt. David was Israel's great king and was seen as the conqueror. Still, even David had to endure years of Saul attempting to kill him before he became king.

This was certainly a fascinating way to try to reconcile this dilemma. Nonetheless, we understand today that this was a misunderstanding of the Scriptures. There would be only one Messiah—not two. This Messiah, however, would come on *two separate occasions*—the first time to suffer and the second time to reign forever as King.

We will soon read about His first coming that occurred two thousand years ago. We have yet to experience His second coming, but we will also see His promise of that.

THE NEW COVENANT
JEREMIAH 31:31-34

We come now to the last prophecy in the Old Testament that we will cover together. This one is given to us by a prophet named

Jeremiah, who lived a bit later than Isaiah and Micah, around the time of Daniel in 600 B.C.

At this point in history, Israel has continued their cycle of rebellion against God time and time again. It seemed as if they were wholly incapable of keeping the covenant God had made with them. God always kept His part of it, but they seldom kept theirs. It seemed, then, that this covenant would never work. Mankind was just too prone to sin.

So what was God to do? We find the answer to that question in this prophecy.

> [31] *"The days are coming," declares the LORD,*
> *"when I will make a new covenant*
> *with the people of Israel*
> *and with the people of Judah.*
> [32] *It will not be like the covenant*
> *I made with their ancestors*
> *when I took them by the hand*
> *to lead them out of Egypt,*
> *because they broke my covenant,*
> *though I was a husband to them,"*
> *declares the LORD.*
> [33] *"This is the covenant I will make with the people of Israel*
> *after that time," declares the LORD.*
> *"I will put my law in their minds*
> *and write it on their hearts.*
> *I will be their God,*
> *and they will be my people.*
> [34] *No longer will they teach their neighbor,*
> *or say to one another, 'Know the LORD,'*
> *because they will all know me,*
> *from the least of them to the greatest,"*
> *declares the LORD.*
> *"For I will forgive their wickedness*
> *and will remember their sins no more." (Jeremiah 31:31-34 NIV)*

A NEW COVENANT TO COME

God revealed in this passage for the first time that He would establish a *new covenant* at some point in the future. It would be different than the other covenants and superior to them all. However, oddly enough, no further mention of this wonderful new covenant appears in the remainder of the Old Testament. God continued speaking through

166

prophets for more than one hundred fifty years afterward, but no further details are given about this. After that, there was silence from God for four hundred years.

So when did God keep His word and establish this new covenant? Remember that the majority of Jewish people have rejected Jesus as the promised Messiah. Thus they reject the New Testament in its entirety. As a result, from that perspective, God has been silent for over twenty-four hundred years now. This great New Covenant that God promised has yet to come. It seems that He has all but abandoned His people Israel and also left all the prophecies of the Messiah unfulfilled. The last chapter of history (His story) is left unwritten, and everything is left unresolved. God has abandoned them.

He has abandoned them, that is, only if Jesus is *not* the promised Messiah. But Jesus *is*, indeed, the Messiah. So everything does make sense, and everything has been fulfilled. God has not abandoned His people or failed to keep His promises.

Remember that we can think of the Old Testament as the *Old Covenants* (plural) or *Old Promises*. None of the old covenants have been abandoned by God in any way. The New Testament records the establishment of this new and final covenant. It is the climax of our story, the culmination of all the hopes and expectations of all the ages that came before.

We now turn our attention to this New Testament and the fulfillment of all things.

PART IV

PARADISE RESTORED:
THE BEGINNING

THE WORD MADE FLESH

JOHN 1:1-18

T he New Testament, like the Old, consists of three divisions—historical narratives, the letters, and prophecy. The Old Testament begins with history and ends with prophecy as well. However, whereas the middle section of the Old Testament was *poetry*, the middle section of the New Testament is *the letters*. These letters were written by church leaders to either individuals or congregations in various places.

The historical portion begins with four different eyewitness accounts of the life, death, and resurrection of Jesus. Each has its own unique emphasis and perspective. The final historical book records the growth of Christianity after the resurrection of Jesus. This book is called Acts (the Acts of the Apostles). We have already read two passages from this book.

Our time together in the New Testament will be entirely from the historical books. The first book from which we will read is the fourth eyewitness account of the life of Jesus—the book of John, named for its author, who was one of the three closest disciples of Jesus.

Recall that the Old Testament begins with the statement, "In the beginning God created the heavens and the earth" (Genesis 1:1 NIV). God created the world by merely *speaking* things into existence. Several times in that chapter God said, "Let there be," and various things came into existence. His word is all-powerful.

In this passage, John will introduce us to a being whom he calls *the Word*. This should be understood as a title that describes who He is rather than a name, just as we saw with the title of *Immanuel*. As you read, pay close attention to exactly how *the Word* is described.

Another person is mentioned in this passage who is also named John. However, this is a different person than the author. This John is a prophet sent to announce the coming of the Messiah in fulfillment of yet another prophecy.

> *¹ In the beginning was the Word, and the Word was with God, and the Word was God. ² He was with God in the beginning. ³ Through him all things were made; without him nothing was made that has been*

made. ⁴ In him was life, and that life was the light of all mankind. ⁵ The light shines in the darkness, and the darkness has not overcome it.

⁶ There was a man sent from God whose name was John. ⁷ He came as a witness to testify concerning that light, so that through him all might believe. ⁸ He himself was not the light; he came only as a witness to the light.

⁹ The true light that gives light to everyone was coming into the world. ¹⁰ He was in the world, and though the world was made through him, the world did not recognize him. ¹¹ He came to that which was his own, but his own did not receive him. ¹² Yet to all who did receive him, to those who believed in his name, he gave the right to become children of God— ¹³ children born not of natural descent, nor of human decision or a husband's will, but born of God.

¹⁴ The Word became flesh and made his dwelling among us. We have seen his glory, the glory of the one and only Son, who came from the Father, full of grace and truth.

¹⁵ (John testified concerning him. He cried out, saying, "This is the one I spoke about when I said, 'He who comes after me has surpassed me because he was before me.'") ¹⁶ Out of his fullness we have all received grace in place of grace already given. ¹⁷ For the law was given through Moses; grace and truth came through Jesus Christ. ¹⁸ No one has ever seen God, but the one and only Son, who is himself God and is in closest relationship with the Father, has made him known. (John 1:1-18 NIV)

IN THE BEGINNING

It is quite significant that John begins his book in exactly the same way that the Old Testament does, and this is no doubt intentional. The Jewish people of the day were extremely familiar with the very first verse of the Bible, as it was an absolutely critical part of their culture. The familiarity was likely so great that if anyone ever started quoting that verse and paused, all of the hearers would already be finishing the phrase in their own minds.

There are things like this in American culture as well. If I were to say, "Four score and seven years ago..." and then pause, most Americans would likely be thinking "...our forefathers brought forth upon this continent a new nation." This is a famous speech known as the Gettysburg Address given by Abraham Lincoln during our nation's Civil War.

Thus it is quite interesting what John does here. He begins with exactly the same words that begin the Old Testament: "In the beginning." However, when everyone is expecting to hear the word *God*, he departs from what they were expecting and says something different: "In the beginning *was the Word*" (emphasis added). This would certainly have grabbed everyone's attention. So just who was this *Word* of whom he was speaking?

WHO IS THE WORD?

As the passage unfolds, John reveals more and more about who exactly this is. We first learn that He existed in the beginning. That is certainly important because nothing existed in the beginning except God.

We then learn that the Word was *with* God but also *was* God. This seems like a contradiction at first glance. How can one thing be distinct from something else and yet, at the same time, *be* that something else?

Next, we are told that life itself is *in Him* and that this life gave light to all men. The Word was in the world but unrecognized or unknown by the world. The Word came to His own people, but His own people rejected Him. Furthermore, He also became flesh. He became a man. He was not a man previously, but He became one at a certain point in history. Finally, He came from God the Father.

It's probably not much of a mystery by now that this is talking about Jesus.

As we learned in Genesis, God used the plural pronoun when He spoke of Creation: "Let *us* make mankind in *our* image" (Genesis 1:26 NIV, emphasis added), and we have already discussed the Trinity. So Jesus existed in the beginning as God the Son. He was with the Father and the Spirit, but, at the same time, He was Himself God. He became a man two thousand years ago but was not recognized by the world as God at that time. Even His own people, the nation of Israel, rejected Him.

THE MEANING OF THE WORD

So why, then, did John refer to Him as the Word? First of all, there is an intriguing correlation with the fact that God spoke the universe into existence with His word, so this is likely part of it. Second, when we want to communicate something, we do so through words. The book of Hebrews later in the New Testament contains the following declaration:

¹ In the past God spoke to our ancestors through the prophets at many times and in various ways, ² but in these last days he has spoken to us by his Son, whom he appointed heir of all things, and through whom also he made the universe. (Hebrews 1:1-2 NIV)

God spoke to us by His Son. Jesus Himself is God's ultimate message to mankind, so giving Him the title of the Word is quite appropriate.

Finally, the way we come to know someone is by listening to a person's words. Jesus taught that a man's heart is revealed through his words (Luke 6:45). Jesus is identified as the revelation of the Father, so it is through Jesus—the Word—that we can know the very heart of God.

JESUS, THE WORD MADE FLESH

When we looked at Isaiah's prophecy of the Suffering Servant, it was helpful to read through the passage a second time with the name of Jesus inserted into the references to Him. That strategy will help us understand this passage better as well.

> In the beginning was *Jesus*, and *Jesus* was with God, and *Jesus* was God. *Jesus* was with God in the beginning. Through *Jesus* all things were made; without *Jesus* nothing was made that has been made.

> In *Jesus* was life, and that life was the light of men....

> *Jesus* was in the world, and though the world was made through *Jesus*, the world did not recognize *Jesus*. *Jesus* came to that which was his own, but his own did not receive *Jesus*.

> Yet to all who received *Jesus*, to those who believed in *Jesus'* name, *Jesus* gave the right to become children of God— children born not of natural descent, nor of human decision or a husband's will, but born of God.

> *Jesus* became flesh and made his dwelling among us. We have seen *Jesus'* glory, the glory of the One and Only, who came from the Father, full of grace and truth.

There is no mistaking the fact that the New Testament does not merely present Jesus as a great man. It presents Him as nothing less than *God*.

THE NEW BIRTH

In this passage, John also affirms that, just as Isaiah had prophesied, the world did not recognize Jesus as God. Even the Jewish people themselves rejected Him. He goes on to explain, though, that anyone who does not reject Jesus but receives Him and welcomes Him as God, believing in His Name, will become a child of God. What a wonderful promise!

God is already the Creator of everything, but ever since the Garden of Eden, mankind has been separated from Him because of sin. The promise here is that our relationship with God would be restored. He would no longer be merely our Creator—He would be our Father. Since He is the King over all, that makes believers in Jesus princes and princesses of heaven.

You may have heard the phrase *born again Christian* before. This is the reality to which that phrase refers. Everyone has been born physically, but when we come to faith in Christ, we are born a second time—not physically but spiritually.

So how exactly is someone born into God's family? The passage mentions three specific paths which are not ways of being born as God's children, and we might wonder why John does this.

Remember that the Jewish people identified themselves as God's chosen people, and they certainly were. God had chosen them out of all the nations to be His special people. He had also given them circumcision as a sign of His covenant with them, and He had given them the Law as well. Thus their confidence in God was in (1) their identity as descendants of Abraham, (2) their obedience to the Law, and (3) the sign of circumcision. This is possibly what the passage is referring to when it describes the ways in which we are *not* born into God's family because none of those things can restore our relationship with God.

The only way to become a child of God is through faith in Jesus Christ—to those who believe in Him. If we reject Him and put our faith in other things, like our identity, our good works, or religious ceremonies, we remain separated from God and outside His family.

THE BIRTH OF JESUS ACCORDING TO MATTHEW

MATTHEW 1

W e now turn to the actual birth of Jesus. This is recorded in two of the first four historical books on the life of Jesus—Matthew and Luke. We will look at passages from both of these, as each one includes unique details not mentioned in the other.

Matthew is the very first book of the New Testament. He begins by identifying the ancestry of Jesus back to Abraham. After this, he gives the actual account of Jesus' birth. Be sure to remember the prophecies about the birth of the Messiah that we have already covered, as those will come up here.

¹ An account of the genealogy of Jesus Christ, the Son of David, the Son of Abraham:

From Abraham to David

² Abraham fathered Isaac, Isaac fathered Jacob, Jacob fathered Judah and his brothers,
³ Judah fathered Perez and Zerah by Tamar, Perez fathered Hezron, Hezron fathered Aram,
⁴ Aram fathered Amminadab, Amminadab fathered Nahshon, Nahshon fathered Salmon,
⁵ Salmon fathered Boaz by Rahab, Boaz fathered Obed by Ruth, Obed fathered Jesse,
⁶ and Jesse fathered King David.

From David to the Babylonian Exile

David fathered Solomon by Uriah's wife,
⁷ Solomon fathered Rehoboam, Rehoboam fathered Abijah, Abijah fathered Asa,
⁸ Asa fathered Jehoshaphat, Jehoshaphat fathered Joram, Joram fathered Uzziah,

⁹ *Uzziah fathered Jotham, Jotham fathered Ahaz, Ahaz fathered Hezekiah,*
¹⁰ *Hezekiah fathered Manasseh, Manasseh fathered Amon, Amon fathered Josiah,*
¹¹ *and Josiah fathered Jeconiah and his brothers at the time of the exile to Babylon.*

From the Exile to the Messiah

¹² *After the exile to Babylon Jeconiah fathered Shealtiel, Shealtiel fathered Zerubbabel,*
¹³ *Zerubbabel fathered Abiud, Abiud fathered Eliakim, Eliakim fathered Azor,*
¹⁴ *Azor fathered Zadok, Zadok fathered Achim, Achim fathered Eliud,*
¹⁵ *Eliud fathered Eleazar, Eleazar fathered Matthan, Matthan fathered Jacob,*
¹⁶ *and Jacob fathered Joseph the husband of Mary, who gave birth to Jesus who is called the Messiah.*

¹⁷ *So all the generations from Abraham to David were fourteen generations; and from David until the exile to Babylon, fourteen generations; and from the exile to Babylon until the Messiah, fourteen generations.*

The Birth of the Messiah

¹⁸ *The birth of Jesus Christ came about this way: After his mother Mary had been engaged to Joseph, it was discovered before they came together that she was pregnant from the Holy Spirit.* ¹⁹ *So her husband, Joseph, being a righteous man, and not wanting to disgrace her publicly, decided to divorce her secretly.*

²⁰ *But after he had considered these things, an angel of the Lord appeared to him in a dream, saying, "Joseph, son of David, don't be afraid to take Mary as your wife, because what has been conceived in her is from the Holy Spirit.* ²¹ *She will give birth to a son, and you are to name him Jesus, because he will save his people from their sins."*

²² *Now all this took place to fulfill what was spoken by the Lord through the prophet:*

²³ *See, the virgin will become pregnant*
and give birth to a son,

and they will name him Immanuel,
which is translated "God is with us."

²⁴ *When Joseph woke up, he did as the Lord's angel had commanded him. He married her ²⁵ but did not have sexual relations with her until she gave birth to a son. And he named him Jesus. (Matthew 1 CSB)*

JESUS, SON OF DAVID, SON OF ABRAHAM

The ancestry of Jesus is extremely important. God had chosen Abraham two thousand years before this and promised that through him all the people of the earth would be blessed. He had also made a special promise to David that one of his descendants would reign on his throne forever. Matthew begins his account by identifying Jesus as both the Son of Abraham and the Son of David.

Now, you may have picked up on the fact that this genealogy actually follows the line of Joseph and not Mary. Since Joseph is *not* the biological father of Jesus, what would be the point of this particular ancestry?

Well, both Joseph and Mary were descendants of David, but Joseph was a descendant through the line of the kings, beginning with Solomon. Mary's ancestry came through a different son of David. However, God had cursed the last king of Israel who sat on the throne because of his sin. God declared that no descendant of his would ever sit on the throne again. Nonetheless, the legal right to the throne still continued through his line. So in order to be a king of Israel and sit on David's throne, someone had to be a descendant of David through the line of the kings in order to have the legal right to the throne. Yet in order to avoid God's curse, he couldn't be a descendant of David in the line of the kings. This was a seeming impossible dilemma. But is anything too hard for the Lord?

All this is reconciled in the birth of Jesus. Since Joseph (from the line of kings) married Mary prior to the birth of Jesus and was the husband of Mary at Jesus' birth, the legal right to the throne would have still been passed down to Jesus through Joseph. Joseph was *legally* the father of Jesus. However, Jesus also avoided the judgment of the previous king of Israel in that He was not his actual *biological* son. He was still a biological descendant of David, though, through the ancestry of Mary, which was free of the curse.

God always keeps His promises, and Jesus is the answer to these promises in particular.

The book of Luke actually gives a second genealogy of Jesus, which follows the line of Jesus through Mary. Both of them take different paths, but they both include David. However, instead of ending at Abraham, the genealogy in Luke goes all the way back through Noah on to Adam. After Adam, Luke actually includes God, since Adam was created by Him. Thus, Jesus appears twice in the genealogy—once at the beginning and once at the end. He is God, the Creator of all things, who said, "Let *us* make mankind in *our* image" (Genesis 1:26 NIV, emphasis added). He is also the son of Mary. Thus He is the *first* and the *last*.

The Bible treats all of the people in these genealogies as actual people who lived at various times in history. They are not simply made-up stories about fictitious people. They are all real.

One last thing to note is the Jewishness of the ancestry of Jesus. Many Jewish people have been simply lied to about Christianity and the New Testament. Many of them think it is full of antisemitism or hatred for the Jewish people. Nothing could be further from the truth. It is actually a very Jewish book, written by mostly Jewish people, talking about Jewish culture and events that happened in the Jewish homeland. In fact, it is one of the most Jewish books ever written.

TWO WOMEN

I want to make one last observation on the genealogy of Jesus given here. Early on, there are two specific women mentioned—Rahab and Ruth. This is quite rare for Jewish genealogies as only men are typically mentioned. So who are these women, and why were they mentioned here?

Well, interestingly enough, both of these women were not Jewish by ethnicity. Rahab lived in the city of Jericho when the Israelites finally crossed over the Jordan River to enter the Promised Land. She had heard about the God of Israel and ended up helping two Jewish spies escape. When her city fell, she was spared and joined the Jewish people. She married a man named Salmon and then became the mother of Boaz.

Ruth was a woman from Moab. She married a Jewish man who had come to live in her country with his mother and brother. However, both he and his brother soon died and left her a widow. She then returned with her mother-in-law to the land of Israel. At that time, as a widow, she would have been destitute. However, Boaz, the son of Rahab, married Ruth. It's actually a very beautiful story that is recorded in the Old Testament book of Ruth. Boaz foreshadows Jesus in what is called a *kinsman redeemer*. He has to purchase the property of Ruth's former husband, but in doing so he redeems Ruth as well.

In His infinite wisdom, God decreed that these two non-Jewish women, who both abandoned their false gods and embraced the one true God, would be in the family line of Jesus.

One important truth that comes out of this is that racism has no place in Christianity. From the very beginning, God's heart has been for all the nations. The presence of these two non-Jewish women in the ancestry of Jesus is proof of that.

THE VIRGIN BIRTH

As the account reveals, Joseph was engaged to Mary when she was found to be pregnant. It should be noted that the Jewish culture of this time held to very high morals. It was probably quite normal for both the man and the woman to be virgins on their wedding night. So when Joseph found out that Mary was pregnant, this was quite scandalous. He assumed, of course, that she had been unfaithful to him, and he considered breaking off the engagement. However, an angel appeared to him and told him this was not the case at all. Mary had not been unfaithful but had become pregnant through the Holy Spirit.

It is very important to specify that there was nothing physical between the Holy Spirit and Mary. God exists in the *spiritual* universe, and He created the *physical* universe. He exists completely outside of the physical universe. The Spiritual world is not biological in nature, as biology is exclusively a part of the physical realm. Thus the Holy Spirit, the Third Person of the Trinity, did not have a physical relationship with Mary. For that to have happened, He would have had to enter the physical world Himself, but only the Son ever did that.

When Mary conceived, it was simply a miracle. God had created everything in the universe by merely speaking it into existence, so causing a woman to become pregnant would not require any physical contact on His part—He only had to speak the word.

Joseph was obedient to the angel and took Mary home as his wife, but he did not have any sexual relationship with her until after Jesus was born. Thus the prophecy was fulfilled that the virgin would conceive, and the virgin would give birth to a son.

THE VIRGIN MARY

As a side note, the Scriptures specify that Joseph and Mary had no sexual relationship until after she gave birth to Jesus. It does not state that they *never* had a sexual relationship. In fact, all four accounts of Jesus' life mention Jesus' brothers and sometimes even sisters. Actual names are recorded for four of these brothers—"James, Joseph, Simon, and Judas" (Matthew 13:55 CSB). Thus with four named brothers and the mention of sisters (plural), Jesus was at the very least the oldest of seven.

Initially, it seems that his siblings did not believe in Him as the Son of God. Later, however, at least one of them—his brother James—certainly did (Galatians 1:19). A little-known fact is that the book of James in the New Testament was not written by James, the brother of John. Rather it was written by James, the brother of *Jesus*.

It seems quite apparent from Scripture that Joseph and Mary had a normal marital relationship after the birth of Jesus. Recall that God commanded Adam and Eve to be fruitful and increase in number. They had to have a sexual relationship to fulfill this command. This was good and right and holy. Thus it would be quite strange if God would ask Joseph and Mary to refrain from this.

There is a brief story of Jesus at the age of twelve in the book of Luke that is of interest on this matter as well. Joseph and Mary had taken Jesus with them to Jerusalem to celebrate the Passover. After it was over, they began their journey home. However, at the end of the first day's journey, they realized that Jesus was not with them. They had previously assumed that He was among their relatives. Once they realized He was not with them, they returned to Jerusalem and found Him in the temple.

If Jesus were their only child, this story seems highly implausible. What could have possibly distracted them so much that they didn't notice their only child missing? It is pretty easy to count to one! Yet if, as the Scriptures record, Jesus was the oldest of seven or more children, then this story makes a lot more sense. There may have been the three-month-old in Mary's arms that demanded her constant attention. Add to that a two-year-old that wanted to be carried half the time on Joseph's shoulders. Then there may have been a five-year-old that was constantly running all over the place with Joseph desperately trying to grab his hand and hold on tight. Then there were a few older ones as well. In this scenario, it is easy to imagine how Jesus could have been missed.

THE NAME OF JESUS

God had instructed Joseph to name the child *Jesus* (or *Yeshua* in Hebrew), and this name is quite intriguing. It essentially means "the Lord saves" or "God saves." Recall that the reason the angel gave Joseph for naming Him *Jesus* was because he would save His people from their sins. So He was named *Jesus* or "God saves" because He Himself was God, and He was coming into the world to save His people from their sins. Thus the name of Jesus identifies both *who* He is and *why* He came.

THE BIRTH OF JESUS ACCORDING TO LUKE

LUKE 2:1-20

W e turn now to Luke's account of the birth of Jesus, which reveals some additional details. Luke was not numbered among Jesus' closest disciples during the life of Jesus. He was apparently a doctor by trade who later wrote two of the five historical books of the New Testament—the Gospel of Luke and the book of Acts, from which we have previously read.

The Birth of Jesus

¹ In those days a decree went out from Caesar Augustus that the whole empire should be registered. ² This first registration took place while Quirinius was governing Syria. ³ So everyone went to be registered, each to his own town.

⁴ Joseph also went up from the town of Nazareth in Galilee, to Judea, to the city of David, which is called Bethlehem, because he was of the house and family line of David, ⁵ to be registered along with Mary, who was engaged to him and was pregnant. ⁶ While they were there, the time came for her to give birth. ⁷ Then she gave birth to her firstborn son, and she wrapped him tightly in cloth and laid him in a manger, because there was no guest room available for them.

The Shepherds and the Angels

⁸ In the same region, shepherds were staying out in the fields and keeping watch at night over their flock. ⁹ Then an angel of the Lord stood before them, and the glory of the Lord shone around them, and they were terrified. ¹⁰ But the angel said to them, "Don't be afraid, for look, I proclaim to you good news of great joy that will be for all the people: ¹¹ Today in the city of David a Savior was born for you, who is the Messiah, the Lord. ¹² This will be the sign for you: You will find a baby wrapped tightly in cloth and lying in a manger."

¹³ Suddenly there was a multitude of the heavenly host with the angel, praising God and saying:

[14] *Glory to God in the highest heaven,*
and peace on earth to people he favors!

[15] *When the angels had left them and returned to heaven, the shepherds said to one another, "Let's go straight to Bethlehem and see what has happened, which the Lord has made known to us."*

[16] *They hurried off and found both Mary and Joseph, and the baby who was lying in the manger. [17] After seeing them, they reported the message they were told about this child, [18] and all who heard it were amazed at what the shepherds said to them. [19] But Mary was treasuring up all these things in her heart and meditating on them. [20] The shepherds returned, glorifying and praising God for all the things they had seen and heard, which were just as they had been told. (Luke 2:1-20 CSB)*

THE BIRTHPLACE OF A KING

When Mary conceived, she was living in a city called Nazareth. However, as you will recall, God had revealed through the prophet Micah that the Messiah would be born in Bethlehem. The distance between these two towns is about eighty miles, which was quite a long distance in the days before modern transportation. So Mary was in the wrong place.

Of course, God saw from eternity past that there would be a census of the people at that time. Joseph, being a descendant of David, would have to return to Bethlehem, the city of David, with his pregnant wife. Thus the prophecy was fulfilled just as God had foretold. Jesus, the Messiah, was born in Bethlehem.

The name *Bethlehem* actually means "the house of bread," and this is also of particular interest. In just a few chapters we will see that Jesus identifies Himself as "the Bread of Life," which also ties back to the bread from heaven that God gave the Israelites in the desert. Thus "the Bread of Life" was born in Bethlehem, "the house of bread."

THE SHEPHERD'S SHEPHERD

The first people to be told about the birth of Jesus were humble shepherds tending their flocks nearby. These were likely shepherds who raised sheep specifically for sacrificial offerings in the temple, as they were not far from Jerusalem.

Of all the people in Israel at that time, we might wonder why God would choose to make known the birth of the Messiah to such common laborers. Why not men of power or wealth or strength? The answer is found in the very words of the angel. The birth of Jesus was good news for all the people. Jesus didn't come merely for the noble or the wealthy or the good. He came for everyone, and that included Jews and non-Jews alike. God's promise to Abraham was that through him, *all* people would be blessed. This most extraordinary of announcements was given to the most ordinary of men.

The fact that they were shepherds is also intriguing. After they heard the news, they left their own lambs and went to see Him who would one day be called the Lamb of God. They were shepherds, just as King David had been, but the baby in the manger was the Shepherd's Shepherd.

NO ROOM IN THE INN

It is perhaps surprising that when the Creator of the world entered into His own creation, He did so in such humble circumstances. He was not born in a palace to a family of nobility but to poor peasants of simple means. In fact, He was laid to rest in a feeding trough for animals since there was no place available for them.

This was quite fitting, though. For centuries, the Jewish people had rejected God. They had no place for Him in their hearts. When their God came to live among them, there was still no place for Him. Today, the greatest gift that we can give God is to make sure there is room for Him in our own lives.

THE VISIT OF THE WISE MEN
MATTHEW 2

We now return to the book of Matthew for the next part of our story. This likely took place a year or more after the birth of Jesus. Joseph and Mary were still in Bethlehem at this time when they were visited by a group of people from very far away who were not Jewish.

Be sure to take note of the three gifts that are mentioned in this account, as we will discuss those afterward.

[1] *After Jesus was born in Bethlehem of Judea in the days of King Herod, wise men from the east arrived in Jerusalem,* [2] *saying, "Where*

is he who has been born king of the Jews? For we saw his star at its rising and have come to worship him."

³ When King Herod heard this, he was deeply disturbed, and all Jerusalem with him. ⁴ So he assembled all the chief priests and scribes of the people and asked them where the Messiah would be born.

⁵ "In Bethlehem of Judea," they told him, "because this is what was written by the prophet:

⁶ And you, Bethlehem, in the land of Judah,
are by no means least among the rulers of Judah:
Because out of you will come a ruler
who will shepherd my people Israel."

⁷ Then Herod secretly summoned the wise men and asked them the exact time the star appeared. ⁸ He sent them to Bethlehem and said, "Go and search carefully for the child. When you find him, report back to me so that I too can go and worship him."

⁹ After hearing the king, they went on their way. And there it was—the star they had seen at its rising. It led them until it came and stopped above the place where the child was. ¹⁰ When they saw the star, they were overwhelmed with joy. ¹¹ Entering the house, they saw the child with Mary his mother, and falling to their knees, they worshiped him. Then they opened their treasures and presented him with gifts: gold, frankincense, and myrrh. ¹² And being warned in a dream not to go back to Herod, they returned to their own country by another route.

The Flight into Egypt

¹³ After they were gone, an angel of the Lord appeared to Joseph in a dream, saying, "Get up! Take the child and his mother, flee to Egypt, and stay there until I tell you. For Herod is about to search for the child to kill him." ¹⁴ So he got up, took the child and his mother during the night, and escaped to Egypt. ¹⁵ He stayed there until Herod's death, so that what was spoken by the Lord through the prophet might be fulfilled: Out of Egypt I called my Son.

The Massacre of the Innocents

¹⁶ Then Herod, when he realized that he had been outwitted by the wise men, flew into a rage. He gave orders to massacre all the boys in and around Bethlehem who were two years old and under, in keeping with the time he had learned from the wise men. ¹⁷ Then what was spoken through Jeremiah the prophet was fulfilled:

¹⁸ A voice was heard in Ramah,
weeping, and great mourning,
Rachel weeping for her children;
and she refused to be consoled,
because they are no more.

The Return to Nazareth

¹⁹ After Herod died, an angel of the Lord appeared in a dream to Joseph in Egypt, ²⁰ saying, "Get up, take the child and his mother, and go to the land of Israel, because those who intended to kill the child are dead." ²¹ So he got up, took the child and his mother, and entered the land of Israel. ²² But when he heard that Archelaus was ruling over Judea in place of his father Herod, he was afraid to go there. And being warned in a dream, he withdrew to the region of Galilee. ²³ Then he went and settled in a town called Nazareth to fulfill what was spoken through the prophets, that he would be called a Nazarene. (Matthew 2 CSB)

THE WISE MEN

So who were these *wise men*? It seems that they were probably from the country of Persia. They were well-educated men who were familiar with the patterns of the stars and planets. There also may be a tie to the prophet Daniel since he spent some time there in captivity during the reign of Darius. They may have read some of the prophecies from his writings and perhaps from some other prophets as well.

We actually don't know how many of them there were. Traditionally, they have been portrayed as being three in number, but that merely matches the number of gifts they brought. No number is ever assigned to the wise men themselves.

BORN KING?

"Where is He who is born King of the Jews?" (Matthew 2:2 CSB).

It was a simple question. The wise men seemed to assume that everyone in Israel would have known about this momentous occasion. They couldn't have been more wrong. There already was a king in Israel at that time, and he certainly wasn't thrilled to hear about the existence of another one.

The question of the wise men is interesting for another reason as well. They asked about one who had been *born king*. No one is ever *born* king. The children of kings are born as *princes* or *princesses*—not kings. So again, the question itself was a bit strange. Yet it wasn't inaccurate.

Jesus, as the eternal Son of God, was already the King of the Jews long before He was born into this world. He merely retained this title at birth.

HIS STAR

The wise men mentioned a specific star that they had been following. There is no little speculation about what this might have been. Another Old Testament prophecy (Numbers 24:17) spoke of *a star* coming out of Jacob, so this certainly would be consistent with that.

One possibility is that it was the alignment of two planets and a star, but again we don't know for sure. Whatever the explanation, it was prominent enough to be followed by the wise men and to lead them to Jerusalem.

GOLD, FRANKINCENSE, AND MYRRH

The gifts of the wise men appear to be very symbolic. Gold is associated with royalty, and, since they were looking for Him who had been born *king* of the Jews, gold would have been a most appropriate gift.

Frankincense is associated with priests, who offered sacrifices to God on behalf of the people. Jesus is described as the Great High Priest who would offer Himself once for all as the Lamb of God. Thus frankincense is also a fitting gift for Him.

The last gift, though, seems a bit peculiar. Myrrh was a very expensive perfume, but it was primarily used in the embalming of the dead. So this wasn't something typically associated with birth. However, Jesus was, in every sense, born to die. He had come to save His people from their sins. To accomplish this, He would have to offer Himself up to death as the substitute for the people. Thus myrrh turns out to be a most appropriate gift after all.

There were three significant offices in Jewish culture—the prophets, the priests, and the kings. Jesus fulfilled all three offices, and the gifts symbolized this. In summary, gold recognized Him as King, frankincense recognized Him as Priest, and myrrh recognized Him as Prophet.

The popular Christmas song, "We Three Kings," quite beautifully describes these three gifts and their meaning. The first verse speaks of the journey of the wise men. Then verses two through four speak of the gifts. The final verse speaks of the resurrection of Jesus after his death, which is foreshadowed in the gift of myrrh.

Verse 1

We three kings of Orient are
Bearing gifts we traverse afar
Field and fountain, moor and mountain,
Following yonder star.

Chorus

O Star of Wonder, Star of Night,
Star with Royal Beauty bright,
Westward leading, still proceeding,
Guide us to Thy perfect Light.

Verse 2

Born a King on Bethlehem plain,
Gold I bring to crown Him again,
King for ever, ceasing never,
Over us all to reign.

Verse 3

Frankincense to offer have I,
Incense owns a Deity night,
Prayer and praising all men raising,
Worship Him God on High.

Verse 4

Myrrh is mine; its bitter perfume
Breathes a life of gathering gloom—
Sorrowing, sighing, bleeding, dying,
Sealed in a stone-cold tomb.

Verse 5

Glorious now behold Him arise,
King and God and Sacrifice,
Alleluia, alleluia
Sounds through the earth and skies.

THE SLAUGHTER OF BABIES

You might recall that when Moses was born, the king of Egypt had ordered the slaughter of all the baby boys in the land. Moses had been spared. Later, he would prophecy that God would raise up for the Jewish people a prophet like himself.

Here we see one of the many parallels between the life of Jesus and the life of Moses. When Jesus was born, the king in Jerusalem ordered the very same thing. God intervened, and Jesus was spared, as Mary and Joseph escaped with Him to Egypt.

OUT OF EGYPT

Another prophecy was mentioned that said, "Out of Egypt I called my son" (Hosea 11:1 CSB). The verse has both a near and far meaning, in that it originally referred to the people of Israel, as God had called them His firstborn, but it also refers to something in the future.

God called the nation of Israel out of Egypt when He first appeared to Moses. This is the *near* meaning of the prophecy. The *far* meaning refers to the coming of the Son of God, who was also brought out of Egypt back to the Promised Land.

JESUS, THE LAMB OF GOD
JOHN 1:29-51

Concerning the early years of Jesus' life, we actually know very little, except that He "grew in wisdom and stature and in favor with God and men" (Luke 2:52 NIV). After Mary and Joseph returned to Nazareth from Egypt, there is just one story about Jesus at the age of twelve, and it is quite brief. We aren't given any more information until He begins His ministry around the age of thirty.

As we saw previously, there was a prophet named John whose purpose was to announce the arrival of the Messiah. So who exactly was this prophet?

After Mary had become pregnant through the Holy Spirit and before she had given birth, she visited a relative of hers named Elizabeth, the wife of a man named Zechariah. Elizabeth had been unable to have children and was then past the age of childbearing. However, God had been gracious to them and had answered their prayer by enabling them to conceive. Elizabeth was pregnant with the prophet John when Mary came to visit her. Thus Jesus and John were actually cousins.

This next passage occurs about thirty years after the birth of Jesus. John has already been preparing the Jewish people for the coming of the Messiah by this time, and now He introduces Jesus as that Messiah.

29 The next day John saw Jesus coming toward him and said, "Look, the Lamb of God, who takes away the sin of the world! 30 This is the one I told you about: 'After me comes a man who ranks ahead of me, because he existed before me.' 31 I didn't know him, but I came baptizing with water so that he might be revealed to Israel." 32 And John testified, "I saw the Spirit descending from heaven like a dove, and he rested on him. 33 I didn't know him, but he who sent me to baptize with water told me, 'The one you see the Spirit descending and resting on—he is the one who baptizes with the Holy Spirit.' 34 I have seen and testified that this is the Son of God."

35 The next day, John was standing with two of his disciples. 36 When he saw Jesus passing by, he said, "Look, the Lamb of God!"

37 The two disciples heard him say this and followed Jesus. 38 When Jesus turned and noticed them following him, he asked them, "What are you looking for?"

They said to him, "Rabbi" (which means "Teacher"), "where are you staying?"

39 "Come and you'll see," he replied. So they went and saw where he was staying, and they stayed with him that day. It was about four in the afternoon.

40 Andrew, Simon Peter's brother, was one of the two who heard John and followed him. 41 He first found his own brother Simon and told him, "We have found the Messiah" (which is translated "the Christ"), 42 and he brought Simon to Jesus.

When Jesus saw him, he said, "You are Simon, son of John. You will be called Cephas" (which is translated "Peter").

Philip and Nathanael

⁴³ The next day Jesus decided to leave for Galilee. He found Philip and told him, "Follow me."

⁴⁴ Now Philip was from Bethsaida, the hometown of Andrew and Peter. ⁴⁵ Philip found Nathanael and told him, "We have found the one Moses wrote about in the law (and so did the prophets): Jesus the son of Joseph, from Nazareth."

⁴⁶ "Can anything good come out of Nazareth?" Nathanael asked him.

"Come and see," Philip answered.

⁴⁷ Then Jesus saw Nathanael coming toward him and said about him, "Here truly is an Israelite in whom there is no deceit."

⁴⁸ "How do you know me?" Nathanael asked.

"Before Philip called you, when you were under the fig tree, I saw you," Jesus answered.

⁴⁹ "Rabbi," Nathanael replied, "You are the Son of God; you are the King of Israel!"

⁵⁰ Jesus responded to him, "Do you believe because I told you I saw you under the fig tree? You will see greater things than this." ⁵¹ Then he said, "Truly I tell you, you will see heaven opened and the angels of God ascending and descending on the Son of Man." (John 1:29-51 CSB)

JOHN THE BAPTIST AND LIFE IN THE WOMB

You already know that John was the cousin of Jesus. He was born in answer to the prayers of an elderly couple named Zechariah and Elizabeth, who were past the age of childbearing. Zechariah was a priest who received the high honor of offering a special sacrifice. While he was doing this, an angel appeared to him and told him that his wife would soon conceive. The angel also told him that the son to be born would be a very special prophet who would be "filled with the Holy Spirit while still in his mother's womb" (Luke 1:15 CSB).

After Mary conceived, she traveled to visit her cousin Elizabeth. The angel who had appeared to Mary had revealed Elizabeth's pregnancy to her as well. As Mary struggled with the reality of her own pregnancy as an unmarried woman, it is possible that she thought she may be able to find comfort and wisdom from Elizabeth. Whatever the reason, Mary visited Elizabeth while they were both still pregnant.

The Scriptures record that when Elizabeth first heard Mary's greeting, the baby inside her "leaped for joy" (Luke 1:44 CSB). This is quite intriguing. It wasn't Elizabeth who responded but the baby inside her—the prophet John.

Remember that the angel had said that he would be filled with the Holy Spirit while still in his mother's womb. Mary was pregnant with Jesus, the very Son of God. So you have God the Son in the womb of Mary and God the Holy Spirit filling the prophet John inside the womb of Elizabeth. When the women drew near to each other, John, being filled with the Holy Spirit, sensed the presence of God the Son in the womb of Mary and responded with joy.

The implication is profound. John already had a body, soul, and spirit while he was still in his mother's womb. He was able to sense the presence of God and have an emotional response to it. This is just one of the places in the Scriptures that indicates that life does not begin at birth but at conception. From that moment on, every baby has a body, soul, and spirit. He or she is created in the image of God and is also loved by God.

Christians understand that God Himself is the Moral Lawgiver, and it is He who defines morality. We look to what He says in His Word to discern what is right and wrong. We ourselves do not have a voice in the matter. We only listen to His voice and embrace it. As such, those who follow the teachings of the Bible oppose abortion. The lives of babies in the womb are just as sacred to God as our own.

THE LAMB OF GOD

As we have previously discussed, lambs in Jewish life embodied the concept of sacrificial offerings to God for the sins of the people. You will recall that when Abraham was going to offer Isaac as a sacrifice, he had told his son that God would provide the lamb that was needed.

The Passover feast was celebrated each year with the offering of lambs. Many other offerings for sin used lambs as well.

Yet the death of an animal could never truly pay for the sins of mankind. Every lamb that had ever been offered throughout thousands of years foreshadowed Jesus, the one true Lamb of God. He alone could take away the sins of the world. This is how John introduces Jesus to the world.

THE ONE THE PROPHETS WROTE ABOUT

When Philip met Jesus, he described Him as "the one Moses wrote about in the Law and about whom the Prophets also wrote" (John 1:45 NIV). In this statement, Philip recognized Jesus as the Messiah.

Again, Moses had prophesied that God would raise up for them a prophet like him. Since that time, God had certainly raised up many other prophets, but none of them had risen to the level of which Moses had spoken. Philip saw that Jesus was not just another prophet but something far greater—He was the fulfillment of all the prophecies of the Messiah and, in particular, the prophet like Moses who was to come.

THE SON OF GOD

Both John and Nathanael identify Jesus with the title of *the Son of God*. For a man to be called this was no small thing, as it is an absolute affirmation of His divinity.

Jesus would later identify Himself with this title as well, and the religious leaders would accuse Him of blasphemy because of it. The reason they considered it blasphemy was that by making this assertion, Jesus was making Himself *equal* with God.

THE KING OF ISRAEL

The final title given to Jesus in the passage is that of *the King of Israel*. You will recall that the wise men had come to Jerusalem after the birth of Jesus, searching for the one who had been born King of the Jews.

Remember, too, that in the time of Moses, Israel had no earthly king. God was their king. A few hundred years later, they rejected God and asked for an earthly king so that they could be like the nations around them.

Here we see Jesus, Israel's first King, reclaiming His title once again.

JESUS, THE ONE LIFTED UP

JOHN 3:1-21

The next passage in our journey gives the account of a religious leader named Nicodemus who came to talk with Jesus one night. In Jewish culture, religious leaders were extremely important, powerful, and wealthy.

Nicodemus himself belonged to a group of religious leaders called Pharisees. This group had largely lost sight of God Himself. Instead they focused on meticulously following all 613 commandments in the Law of Moses.

The majority of the religious leaders of the day rejected Jesus completely, but this was not because He didn't fulfill the Messianic prophesies. Rather it was because He was a threat to their authority. He also had not been trained in their schools, so He was a bit of an outsider in that regard.

There were a few religious leaders, however, who still did seek to truly know God, and Nicodemus was one of them. He was particularly curious about *who* Jesus really was, and that is what brought him to see Jesus that night.

As you read this account, it will be important to recall the story of the snake in the desert. You will remember that Moses lifted up a snake on a pole so that everyone who was bitten could look at it in faith and be healed. As a religious leader, Nicodemus would have been quite familiar with that story, and Jesus used that to unveil a greater truth.

¹ There was a man from the Pharisees named Nicodemus, a ruler of the Jews. ² This man came to him at night and said, "Rabbi, we know that you are a teacher who has come from God, for no one could perform these signs you do unless God were with him."

³ Jesus replied, "Truly I tell you, unless someone is born again, he cannot see the kingdom of God."

⁴ "How can anyone be born when he is old?" Nicodemus asked him. "Can he enter his mother's womb a second time and be born?"

[5] Jesus answered, "Truly I tell you, unless someone is born of water and the Spirit, he cannot enter the kingdom of God. [6] Whatever is born of the flesh is flesh, and whatever is born of the Spirit is spirit. [7] Do not be amazed that I told you that you must be born again. [8] The wind blows where it pleases, and you hear its sound, but you don't know where it comes from or where it is going. So it is with everyone born of the Spirit."

[9] "How can these things be?" asked Nicodemus.

[10] "Are you a teacher of Israel and don't know these things?" Jesus replied. [11] "Truly I tell you, we speak what we know and we testify to what we have seen, but you do not accept our testimony. [12] If I have told you about earthly things and you don't believe, how will you believe if I tell you about heavenly things? [13] No one has ascended into heaven except the one who descended from heaven —the Son of Man.

[14] "Just as Moses lifted up the snake in the wilderness, so the Son of Man must be lifted up, [15] so that everyone who believes in him may have eternal life. [16] For God loved the world in this way: He gave his one and only Son, so that everyone who believes in him will not perish but have eternal life. [17] For God did not send his Son into the world to condemn the world, but to save the world through him. [18] Anyone who believes in him is not condemned, but anyone who does not believe is already condemned, because he has not believed in the name of the one and only Son of God.

[19] "This is the judgment: The light has come into the world, and people loved darkness rather than the light because their deeds were evil. [20] For everyone who does evil hates the light and avoids it, so that his deeds may not be exposed. [21] But anyone who lives by the truth comes to the light, so that his works may be shown to be accomplished by God." (John 3:1-21 CSB)

THE NEW BIRTH

Nicodemus opened the conversation with Jesus by acknowledging Him to be a teacher who had come from God. In contrast to how most of the religious leaders felt about Jesus, this was a great show of respect and honor.

Seeing that Nicodemus was seeking truth, Jesus quickly transitioned to the heart of the issue—the new birth—without which no one can see

God. You will recall that we were previously introduced to this *new birth* in the first passage we covered in the New Testament.

Nicodemus was confused by this initially, as he was thinking only about physical realities. From that perspective, what Jesus was saying didn't make any sense. Jesus then explained further that He was speaking of a spiritual reality and a spiritual birth. We have all been born physically (born of water), but only those who believe in Jesus are born of the Spirit.

THE SON OF MAN

Jesus then addressed the question of His own identity. Nicodemus had already acknowledged that Jesus had to have come from God because of the signs (or miracles) He was performing. Jesus builds on that by identifying Himself as the Son of Man.

Nicodemus would have immediately recalled the account of Daniel's dream. When one like a son of man approached the throne of God, he was given dominion and authority and was worshiped by all nations. The fact that Jesus referred to Himself by this title was a clear and unambiguous claim to be that Son of Man—to be *God*.

THE SNAKE IN THE DESERT

We have already discussed the significance of the time when Moses lifted up the snake on the pole and how that foreshadowed Jesus Himself, as the Son of Man, being lifted up on the Cross. Then, anyone could look at Jesus on the Cross, trust completely in Him, and be saved from sin as a result.

Faith, then, is what causes a person to be born again, born from above, and born into God's family. Anyone can receive this new birth that Jesus offers. No one is forbidden, but no one is forced to receive it either.

JESUS, THE BREAD OF LIFE
JOHN 6:1-36

In this next passage it will be important to remember when Moses and the people of Israel had no food in the desert and grumbled against

God. God fed them miraculously with manna, the bread from heaven, for a total of forty years until they entered the Promised Land.

We already discussed that Jesus was the Prophet like Moses, whom God had sent, and there will be another obvious connection in this passage.

Remember also that Nicodemus had been thinking about physical things when Jesus was speaking about spiritual things. That happened quite often during Jesus' ministry, and it comes up here as well.

Jesus Feeds the 5,000

[1] After this, Jesus crossed the Sea of Galilee (or Tiberias). [2] A huge crowd was following him because they saw the signs that he was performing by healing the sick. [3] Jesus went up a mountain and sat down there with his disciples.

[4] Now the Passover, a Jewish festival, was near. [5] So when Jesus looked up and noticed a huge crowd coming toward him, he asked Philip, "Where will we buy bread so that these people can eat?" [6] He asked this to test him, for he himself knew what he was going to do.

[7] Philip answered him, "Two hundred denarii worth of bread wouldn't be enough for each of them to have a little."

[8] One of his disciples, Andrew, Simon Peter's brother, said to him, [9] "There's a boy here who has five barley loaves and two fish—but what are they for so many?"

[10] Jesus said, "Have the people sit down."

There was plenty of grass in that place; so they sat down. The men numbered about five thousand. [11] Then Jesus took the loaves, and after giving thanks he distributed them to those who were seated—so also with the fish, as much as they wanted.

[12] When they were full, he told his disciples, "Collect the leftovers so that nothing is wasted." [13] So they collected them and filled twelve baskets with the pieces from the five barley loaves that were left over by those who had eaten.

[14] When the people saw the sign he had done, they said, "This truly is the Prophet who is to come into the world."

¹⁵ Therefore, when Jesus realized that they were about to come and take him by force to make him king, he withdrew again to the mountain by himself.

Jesus Walks on the Water

¹⁶ When evening came, his disciples went down to the sea, ¹⁷ got into a boat, and started across the sea to Capernaum. Darkness had already set in, but Jesus had not yet come to them. ¹⁸ A high wind arose, and the sea began to churn. ¹⁹ After they had rowed about three or four miles, they saw Jesus walking on the sea. He was coming near the boat, and they were afraid. ²⁰ But he said to them, "It is I. Don't be afraid." ²¹ Then they were willing to take him on board, and at once the boat was at the shore where they were heading.

Jesus, The Bread of Life

²² The next day, the crowd that had stayed on the other side of the sea saw there had been only one boat. They also saw that Jesus had not boarded the boat with his disciples, but that his disciples had gone off alone. ²³ Some boats from Tiberias came near the place where they had eaten the bread after the Lord had given thanks. ²⁴ When the crowd saw that neither Jesus nor his disciples were there, they got into the boats and went to Capernaum looking for Jesus. ²⁵ When they found him on the other side of the sea, they said to him, "Rabbi, when did you get here?"

²⁶ Jesus answered, "Truly I tell you, you are looking for me, not because you saw the signs, but because you ate the loaves and were filled. ²⁷ Don't work for the food that perishes but for the food that lasts for eternal life, which the Son of Man will give you, because God the Father has set his seal of approval on him."

²⁸ "What can we do to perform the works of God?" they asked.

²⁹ Jesus replied, "This is the work of God—that you believe in the one he has sent."

³⁰ "What sign, then, are you going to do so that we may see and believe you?" they asked. "What are you going to perform? ³¹ Our ancestors ate the manna in the wilderness, just as it is written: He gave them bread from heaven to eat."

³² Jesus said to them, "Truly I tell you, Moses didn't give you the bread from heaven, but my Father gives you the true bread from heaven. ³³ For the bread of God is the one who comes down from heaven and gives life to the world."

[34] Then they said, "Sir, give us this bread always."

[35] "I am the bread of life," Jesus told them. "No one who comes to me will ever be hungry, and no one who believes in me will ever be thirsty again. [36] But as I told you, you've seen me, and yet you do not believe." (John 6:1-36 CSB)

WHY DID JESUS WITHDRAW?

Immediately after the crowd realized that Jesus had miraculously fed them, they concluded that He was the Prophet who was to come into the world—the Prophet like Moses.

The connection is fairly obvious. God had provided miraculous food through Moses, and on this day, miraculous food was provided through Jesus.

In response, the people tried to make Jesus king by force. The thought of having another leader like Moses was just too good to pass up—especially if He could miraculously feed them and perform other miracles as well. Of course, they probably had forgotten that their ancestors had constantly grumbled against Moses.

It is quite interesting, though, how Jesus responded to their attempts to make Him king. He left. He was nowhere to be found. He was gone.

Why did He do this? Didn't He want the people to recognize Him as king? Wasn't this what He came for after all? Actually, it really wasn't in this case. You will remember that when He began His ministry, John identified Him as the Lamb of God who takes away the sin of the world.

Jesus didn't come to enjoy the momentary allegiance of the masses in response to what He could give them in the moment. He knew all too well that these people, just like their forefathers, would be loyal one minute and disloyal the next. Jesus hadn't come for any of that.

On the contrary, Jesus came to die and save them from their sins forever. After all, that's what lambs are for. That's why Jesus withdrew. He would one day be crowned as King, but He would first have to die.

WALKING ON WATER

In the midst of this story, another miracle occurred—that of Jesus walking on the water. This seems like a small miracle as far as miracles go. No one was miraculously healed, and not very many people even witnessed it. However, it is interesting that, having just been identified as the Prophet like Moses, Jesus miraculously crossed a large body of water. Moses, too, had led the Israelites through the Red Sea. Perhaps this was a confirmation to the disciples of what the crowd had believed—that Jesus was, indeed, the Prophet like Moses.

THE WORK OF GOD

The next day, the crowds find Jesus once again, and the conversation they have is instructive. Jesus observed that their motivation for seeking Him was merely temporal and physical. He exhorted them to seek for what was eternal and spiritual instead.

They responded by asking what exactly they needed to do in order to do the works God required. Jesus' response was quite profound. He declared that the work God requires is really no work at all. In fact, they had asked the wrong question. God doesn't require *works*. He requires *faith*. Just as Adam and Eve's attempts to cover over their own sin were futile, so our attempts to work our way to heaven are futile as well.

Mankind cannot become righteous in God's sight by his own works. It is only Jesus who can make mankind righteous by His own work of dying on the Cross.

Man's response is faith—not works. Therefore, Jesus declared that the "work" the people must do is to trust in Him—to believe in the One God had sent.

THE BREAD OF LIFE

The crowd then asks Jesus to prove Himself again with even more miraculous signs. They mention that Moses had given the people bread for forty years. Perhaps they hoped for another forty years of free food. However, Jesus didn't give them another miracle, at least not at this point in time. Jesus knew that more evidence was not the issue. After all, had the people in the days of Moses trusted God completely when they saw miracles every day? No, they hadn't, and neither would this crowd put their trust in Jesus if they only saw a few more miracles.

Jesus then corrects their history. It was not Moses but God who had provided the manna in the desert. Moses had no power of his own by which he could do any miracles. He was merely a servant of God.

Jesus then turned the conversation away from physical things to spiritual things. He proclaimed that He Himself was the true Bread of Life that came down from heaven.

Again, we are not merely physical beings with only physical needs. We are spiritual beings with spiritual hunger. In fact, we are not bodies that have spirits—we are spirits that have bodies (and souls).

Jesus did not come to earth to merely meet the physical needs of mankind. His purpose was far greater than that. He came down because mankind desperately needed spiritual food. Only Jesus can satisfy that hunger.

In society today, there are those who have everything the physical world can offer—fame, fortune, and pleasure. Yet many of these people live lives of misery and emptiness. Some of the most famous and wealthy people in the world have even committed suicide.

Why is this? How can so many people, who seem to have so much, be so miserable? May I suggest that it is because only their physical needs have been met. They are starving to death *spiritually*. No amount of anything this world has to offer can satisfy the deepest longings of the human heart for meaning and purpose and belonging. Nothing in this world can bestow true forgiveness and spiritual life. Those can only be found in God.

Jesus alone is the Bread of Life.

JESUS, LIGHT OF THE WORLD, THE I AM
JOHN 8:12-59

The book of John contains several statements that are referred to as the "I Am" statements of Jesus. In his book, John focuses significantly on the question of who Jesus is, and these statements play a significant role in answering that question.

We saw one of these I Am statements in the previous passage where Jesus said, "I Am the Bread of Life." In this next passage, we will see two more of these, one at the very beginning and one at the very end.

In between these two statements, the Pharisees debate with Jesus about who He is and who He claims to be. Jesus, however, turns the conversation around on them, and the Pharisees find themselves on the defensive concerning their own standing before God.

You will recall that the first chapter in the book of John contained the declaration that we become God's children through faith—not ancestry, religious ceremony, or works. We observe here that the Pharisees trusted in those very things.

Finally, the discussion returns to the question of who Jesus was, and this is where Jesus makes the other "I AM" statement. You will notice that the Pharisees react quite strongly to it, and we will discuss the reason for their reaction afterward.

Jesus, the Light of the World

¹² Jesus spoke to them again: "I am the light of the world. Anyone who follows me will never walk in the darkness but will have the light of life."

¹³ So the Pharisees said to him, "You are testifying about yourself. Your testimony is not valid."

¹⁴ "Even if I testify about myself," Jesus replied, "My testimony is true, because I know where I came from and where I'm going. But you don't know where I come from or where I'm going. ¹⁵ You judge by human standards. I judge no one. ¹⁶ And if I do judge, my judgment is true, because it is not I alone who judge, but I and the Father who sent me. ¹⁷ Even in your law it is written that the testimony of two witnesses is true. ¹⁸ I am the one who testifies about myself, and the Father who sent me testifies about me."

¹⁹ Then they asked him, "Where is your Father?"

"You know neither me nor my Father," Jesus answered. "If you knew me, you would also know my Father." ²⁰ He spoke these words by the treasury, while teaching in the temple. But no one seized him, because his hour had not yet come.

Who is Jesus?

²¹ Then he said to them again, "I'm going away; you will look for me, and you will die in your sin. Where I'm going, you cannot come."

²² So the Jews said again, "He won't kill himself, will he, since he says, 'Where I'm going, you cannot come'?"

²³ "You are from below," he told them, "I am from above. You are of this world; I am not of this world. ²⁴ Therefore I told you that you will die in your sins. For if you do not believe that I am he, you will die in your sins."

[25] *"Who are you?" they questioned.*

"Exactly what I've been telling you from the very beginning," Jesus told them. [26] *"I have many things to say and to judge about you, but the one who sent me is true, and what I have heard from him—these things I tell the world."*

[27] *They did not know he was speaking to them about the Father.* [28] *So Jesus said to them, "When you lift up the Son of Man, then you will know that I am he, and that I do nothing on my own. But just as the Father taught me, I say these things.* [29] *The one who sent me is with me. He has not left me alone, because I always do what pleases him."*

[30] *As he was saying these things, many believed in him.*

[31] *Then Jesus said to the Jews who had believed him, "If you continue in my word, you really are my disciples.* [32] *You will know the truth, and the truth will set you free."*

[33] *"We are descendants of Abraham," they answered him, "and we have never been enslaved to anyone. How can you say, 'You will become free'?"*

[34] *Jesus responded, "Truly I tell you, everyone who commits sin is a slave of sin.* [35] *A slave does not remain in the household forever, but a son does remain forever.* [36] *So if the Son sets you free, you really will be free.* [37] *I know you are descendants of Abraham, but you are trying to kill me because my word has no place among you.* [38] *I speak what I have seen in the presence of the Father; so then, you do what you have heard from your father."*

[39] *"Our father is Abraham," they replied.*

"If you were Abraham's children," Jesus told them, "you would do what Abraham did. [40] *But now you are trying to kill me, a man who has told you the truth that I heard from God. Abraham did not do this.* [41] *You're doing what your father does."*

"We weren't born of sexual immorality," they said. "We have one Father—God."

[42] Jesus said to them, "If God were your Father, you would love me, because I came from God and I am here. For I didn't come on my own, but he sent me. [43] Why don't you understand what I say? Because you cannot listen to my word. [44] You are of your father the devil, and you want to carry out your father's desires. He was a murderer from the beginning and does not stand in the truth, because there is no truth in him. When he tells a lie, he speaks from his own nature, because he is a liar and the father of lies. [45] Yet because I tell the truth, you do not believe me. [46] Who among you can convict me of sin? If I am telling the truth, why don't you believe me? [47] The one who is from God listens to God's words. This is why you don't listen, because you are not from God."

Jesus, the I Am

[48] The Jews responded to him, "Aren't we right in saying that you're a Samaritan and have a demon?"

[49] "I do not have a demon," Jesus answered. "On the contrary, I honor my Father and you dishonor me. [50] I do not seek my own glory; there is one who seeks it and judges. [51] Truly I tell you, if anyone keeps my word, he will never see death."

[52] Then the Jews said, "Now we know you have a demon. Abraham died and so did the prophets. You say, 'If anyone keeps my word, he will never taste death.' [53] Are you greater than our father Abraham who died? And the prophets died. Who do you claim to be?"

[54] "If I glorify myself," Jesus answered, "my glory is nothing. My Father—about whom you say, 'He is our God'—he is the one who glorifies me. [55] You do not know him, but I know him. If I were to say I don't know him, I would be a liar like you. But I do know him, and I keep his word. [56] Your father Abraham rejoiced to see my day; he saw it and was glad."

[57] The Jews replied, "You aren't fifty years old yet, and you've seen Abraham?"

[58] Jesus said to them, "Truly I tell you, before Abraham was, I am."

⁵⁹ So they picked up stones to throw at him. But Jesus was hidden and went out of the temple. (John 8:12-59 CSB)

JESUS, THE LIGHT OF THE WORLD

The first I AM statement in this passage is when Jesus claims to be the Light of the World. If you recall, the first mention of light in the Bible comes in the very first chapter of the Old Testament, when God says, "Let there be light" (Genesis 1:3 NIV).

Jesus, as the Second Person of the Trinity, who was in the beginning and through whom all things were created, is God the Son. Thus Jesus is the Creator and the Source of physical light in the world.

Jesus is the Light of the World in the spiritual sense as well. This can be seen in the fulfillment of another prophecy of Isaiah, which again referenced the servant of the Lord, just as we saw in Isaiah 53. This one comes a little earlier in chapter 42.

⁵ This is what God the Lord says—
the Creator of the heavens, who stretches them out,
who spreads out the earth with all that springs from it,
who gives breath to its people,
and life to those who walk on it:
⁶ "I, the Lord, have called you in righteousness;
I will take hold of your hand.
I will keep you and will make you
to be a covenant for the people
and a light for the Gentiles,
⁷ to open eyes that are blind,
to free captives from prison
and to release from the dungeon those who sit in darkness." (Isaiah 42:5-7 NIV)

Jesus is the spiritual Light for not only the people of Israel but for the Gentiles as well. (The word *Gentiles* refers to anyone who is not Jewish.) Jesus is the Light that would lead people from every nation out of spiritual darkness into the light of the knowledge of God.

Isaiah also asserted that He will open the eyes of the blind. This could apply in both a physical and a spiritual sense as well. In other places in the accounts of Jesus' life, He did restore sight to those who were blind.

Yet He also fulfills the prophecy in the spiritual sense, as multitudes of people throughout history have seen their lives transformed after they have encountered Jesus and put their faith in Him. We, who were once spiritually blind, through our faith in Jesus, are now able to see.

THE EVIDENCE OF TRANSFORMED LIVES

People all over the world today are, indeed, enslaved to sin and sitting in darkness. It comes in many different forms. Some have a never-ending thirst for money or power or pleasure. Others are overwhelmed by anger, hatred, and bitterness, and they are unable to let it go. Still others have fallen into slavery of the worst kind—slavery to drugs or alcohol or other addictions.

What hope is there for such people? Is there anything that can replace hatred with love, bitterness with forgiveness, greed with generosity, pride with humility, selfishness with compassion, and immorality with virtue?

There is really only one force that has ever shown that kind of power, and it has been transforming lives for two thousand years— Jesus Christ, the Light of the World. Ever since His feet walked the shores of the Sea of Galilee, Jesus has been transforming lives. In His day, Jesus saw prostitutes become virtuous, the greedy become generous, the broken become whole, the proud become humble, the dishonest become truthful, and the wounded become whole. This transformation continues today all over the world, and it is still as potent and powerful than it ever was. Indeed, it is even more far reaching.

SLANDEROUS ACCUSATIONS AND RACISM

As the conversation continued, the Pharisees seemed to be getting a bit embarrassed. Despite their best efforts, they could not counter Jesus' arguments. Thus they resorted to slander and even racism.

The *slander* came when they accused Him of being demon possessed. Demons, if you recall, are angels who rebelled against God and are now enemies of God. They, like Satan in the Garden, work to deceive people and lead them away from God.

Of course, the life of Jesus was filled with healing people and teaching them to live holy lives, so that accusation was just nonsense. Yet this is a common tactic that we see quite often today. Whenever someone is losing an argument, they often resort to attacking the person, often with baseless accusations.

The *racism* came when they accused Jesus of being a Samaritan. The Samaritans were a remnant of some of the tribes of Israel who had previously been conquered by another nation. This other nation, who worshiped false gods, had intermarried with them. Later, the people had returned to the Jewish religion, but only in part.

Long before, God had commanded that the Jewish people were not to marry people from other nations. However, the reason God gave was not that these people were from a different ethnicity but that they did not worship the one true God. Thus they were breaking the very first of the Ten Commandments.

As we previously mentioned, in the ancestry of Jesus Himself there are two women who are not Jewish. One was from Moab and the other was from Jericho. However, both of them abandoned the false gods of their own people and chose to worship the one true God.

JESUS, THE I AM

At the end of His debate with the Pharisees, Jesus made another profound yet peculiar statement. He said, "Before Abraham was, I AM" (John 8:58 CSB).

So what did He mean by this? We see that the Pharisees reacted to it quite strongly. In fact, they immediately wanted to even kill Jesus for saying that. So what was it about this particular sentence that drew such a violent response?

Jesus had claimed just prior to this statement that Abraham himself had rejoiced at the thought of seeing His day—the time of Jesus. Jesus also declared that Abraham did, in fact, see His day. Now, Abraham had lived two thousand years earlier, so it was impossible that he could have somehow seen Jesus. If Jesus were just an ordinary man, this would have been completely absurd. Yet Jesus was no ordinary Man.

There are two important implications of this last statement: "Before Abraham was, I AM." First, Jesus asserted that He not only saw Abraham but that His own origins go back even further than that—to *before* Abraham. Recall the prophecy we looked at from Micah that spoke of a ruler who would come, but "whose origins are from of old, from ancient times" (Micah 5:2 NIV). Jesus was making a very clear assertion that He Himself fulfilled that prophecy—that He Himself was eternal.

The second claim was even bolder than that. When God made Himself and His plan known to Moses, Moses had asked God what His name was. God replied by revealing that His name was "I AM." Thus there was no doubt what claim Jesus was making when He identified Himself as the "I AM." He was not only claiming to be the ruler who would come out of Bethlehem, whose origins were from ancient times. He was also unmistakably claiming to be God Himself—the God of

Abraham, Isaac, and Jacob—who had introduced Himself to Moses many years before.

In response to this claim to deity, the Pharisees, believing Jesus had just committed blasphemy, picked up stones to stone Him. Death was the penalty for blasphemy. However, it would only have been blasphemy if it were not true.

It was, in fact, *true*. Jesus was and is the Light of the World, the Lamb of God, the Son of Man, the King of Israel, the Bread of Life, the Son of God, and the I Am!

JESUS, THE GATE, THE GOOD SHEPHERD
JOHN 10

T he next passage contains two additional I Am statements of Jesus. Just before this, Jesus had healed a man who was blind from birth, and the same people who witnessed that were still with Jesus in this passage.

After He made these statements about Himself, the people once again struggle with the question of who He really was and who He was claiming to be.

In His response, Jesus again made it very clear.

Jesus, the Gate and the Good Shepherd

[1] *"Truly I tell you, anyone who doesn't enter the sheep pen by the gate but climbs in some other way is a thief and a robber. [2] The one who enters by the gate is the shepherd of the sheep. [3] The gatekeeper opens it for him, and the sheep hear his voice. He calls his own sheep by name and leads them out. [4] When he has brought all his own outside, he goes ahead of them. The sheep follow him because they know his voice. [5] They will never follow a stranger; instead they will run away from him, because they don't know the voice of strangers." [6] Jesus gave them this figure of speech, but they did not understand what he was telling them.*

⁷ Jesus said again, "Truly I tell you, I am the gate for the sheep. ⁸ All who came before me are thieves and robbers, but the sheep didn't listen to them. ⁹ I am the gate. If anyone enters by me, he will be saved and will come in and go out and find pasture. ¹⁰ A thief comes only to steal and kill and destroy. I have come so that they may have life and have it in abundance.

¹¹ "I am the good shepherd. The good shepherd lays down his life for the sheep. ¹² The hired hand, since he is not the shepherd and doesn't own the sheep, leaves them and runs away when he sees a wolf coming. The wolf then snatches and scatters them. ¹³ This happens because he is a hired hand and doesn't care about the sheep.

¹⁴ "I am the good shepherd. I know my own, and my own know me, ¹⁵ just as the Father knows me, and I know the Father. I lay down my life for the sheep. ¹⁶ But I have other sheep that are not from this sheep pen; I must bring them also, and they will listen to my voice. Then there will be one flock, one shepherd. ¹⁷ This is why the Father loves me, because I lay down my life so that I may take it up again. ¹⁸ No one takes it from me, but I lay it down on my own. I have the right to lay it down, and I have the right to take it up again. I have received this command from my Father."

¹⁹ Again the Jews were divided because of these words. ²⁰ Many of them were saying, "He has a demon and he's crazy. Why do you listen to him?" ²¹ Others were saying, "These aren't the words of someone who is demon-possessed. Can a demon open the eyes of the blind?"

²² Then the Festival of Dedication took place in Jerusalem, and it was winter. ²³ Jesus was walking in the temple in Solomon's Colonnade. ²⁴ The Jews surrounded him and asked, "How long are you going to keep us in suspense? If you are the Messiah, tell us plainly."

²⁵ "I did tell you and you don't believe," Jesus answered them. "The works that I do in my Father's name testify about me. ²⁶ But you don't believe because you are not of my sheep. ²⁷ My sheep hear my voice, I know them, and they follow me. ²⁸ I give them eternal life, and they will never perish. No one will snatch them out of my hand. ²⁹ My Father, who has given them to me, is greater than all. No one is able to snatch them out of the Father's hand. ³⁰ I and the Father are one."

³¹ Again the Jews picked up rocks to stone him.

³² *Jesus replied, "I have shown you many good works from the Father. For which of these works are you stoning me?"*

³³ *"We aren't stoning you for a good work," the Jews answered, "but for blasphemy, because you—being a man—make yourself God."*

³⁴ *Jesus answered them, "Isn't it written in your law, I said, you are gods? ³⁵ If he called those to whom the word of God came 'gods'—and the Scripture cannot be broken— ³⁶ do you say, 'You are blaspheming' to the one the Father set apart and sent into the world, because I said: I am the Son of God? ³⁷ If I am not doing my Father's works, don't believe me. ³⁸ But if I am doing them and you don't believe me, believe the works. This way you will know and understand that the Father is in me and I in the Father." ³⁹ Then they were trying again to seize him, but he escaped their grasp.*

Many Believe in Jesus

⁴⁰ *So he departed again across the Jordan to the place where John had been baptizing earlier, and he remained there. ⁴¹ Many came to him and said, "John never did a sign, but everything John said about this man was true." ⁴² And many believed in him there. (John 10 CSB)*

JESUS, THE GATE

In the Jewish culture of that day, sheep pens were often built with a circular or rectangular wall of moderate height with a single small opening. The shepherd would bring his sheep into the pen at night and then sleep at the doorway to the pen, thereby protecting his sheep from the wolves.

Jesus begins this passage by identifying Himself as the Gate for the sheep. In essence, there was one way for the sheep to escape the danger of the wolves, and that was to enter through that one gate.

You will recall that in the account of Noah, there was also a single door into the ark through which mankind could enter to escape the judgment of God. In the same way, there is only one way for us to escape the penalty of our own sins, and that is through faith in Jesus.

JESUS, THE GOOD SHEPHERD

Jesus also identified Himself as the Good Shepherd. The great King David had been a shepherd king. We even read a psalm of his where he referred to God as his own shepherd—the Shepherd's Shepherd.

Jesus, as a descendent of David and heir to the throne, was the true Shepherd King—the One to whom David was referring in his psalm. Jesus, however, did not merely identify Himself as the Good Shepherd, but He also described the qualities He possessed as the Good Shepherd. First and foremost, this included laying down His own life for the sheep. We will see this unfold very soon.

Being the Good Shepherd also included knowing His sheep and being known by them. There is a significant familiarity, comfort, and trust that develops between a shepherd and his sheep. They know his unique voice and respond to him alone. This is the kind of relationship God desires to have with us. God didn't create us and then abandon us. He is not aloof, disinterested, or far away. He is near us, speaking to us, leading us to green pastures, and protecting us from harm, if we will only listen to His voice and follow Him.

JESUS AND THE FATHER

Jesus did not, however, speak only about our relationship with God but also about His own relationship with the Father. This statement was once again met with a very violent response.

The people had asked Jesus specifically about whether or not He was the Christ—the Messiah, the Promised One, and the Savior of the World. In Jesus' response, He asserted that He had already answered that question but that they had not been listening. He had already claimed to be the Bread of Life, the Son of Man, the Light of the World, and the I AM. So, of course, He was the Christ. Who else could He be?

Nonetheless, Jesus reaffirmed His identity in a way that left no doubt as to exactly who He was claiming to be. He declared, "I and the Father are *one*" (John 10:31 CSB, emphasis added). In context, He had just affirmed that the miracles He was doing were performed in the Father's name. Additionally, those who were His sheep had been given to Him by the Father Himself. Finally, He Himself gives His sheep eternal life, and no one can remove them from His hand. The Father Himself joins Him in the protection of His sheep.

So He already had emphasized that He and the Father worked in partnership with each other. His final statement, though, takes it even further, emphatically declaring His absolute union with the Father—the union that we have seen described within the Trinity.

Such a relationship with God is impossible for man, as our sin separates us from God. Jesus affirms this by restating His claim to *not* be a mere man but the very Son of God. The people who heard Him that day understood perfectly well who He was claiming to be, but they didn't believe Him. If Jesus was not who He claimed to be, then He would have just committed blasphemy against God—a sin that was punishable by death according to God's law.

For this reason, they picked up stones to stone Him, although it was all to no avail. Jesus was speaking the truth, and though the Good Shepherd would, indeed, lay down His life for the sheep one day, today would not be that day.

JESUS, THE RESURRECTION AND THE LIFE

JOHN 11

We come now to the story of a man named Lazarus, the brother of two women named Mary and Martha. These were all very close friends of Jesus, and we are specifically told Jesus loved each of them.

As you read this account, be sure to observe the faith expressed first by Martha and then by Mary. They are similar but still different, with Martha exhibiting a bit more faith than Mary. Additionally, Martha also reveals her own understanding of who Jesus really is.

We will also see yet another I AM statement of Jesus, and, like all of the others, this is very significant.

¹ Now a man was sick, Lazarus from Bethany, the village of Mary and her sister Martha. ² Mary was the one who anointed the Lord with perfume and wiped his feet with her hair, and it was her brother Lazarus who was sick. ³ So the sisters sent a message to him: "Lord, the one you love is sick."

⁴ When Jesus heard it, he said, "This sickness will not end in death but is for the glory of God, so that the Son of God may be glorified through it." ⁵ Now Jesus loved Martha, her sister, and Lazarus. ⁶ So when he heard that he was sick, he stayed two more days in the place where he was. ⁷ Then after that, he said to the disciples, "Let's go to Judea again."

⁸ "Rabbi," the disciples told him, "just now the Jews tried to stone you, and you're going there again?"

⁹ "Aren't there twelve hours in a day?" Jesus answered. "If anyone walks during the day, he doesn't stumble, because he sees the light of this world. ¹⁰ But if anyone walks during the night, he does stumble, because the light is not in him."

¹¹ He said this, and then he told them, "Our friend Lazarus has fallen asleep, but I'm on my way to wake him up."

¹² Then the disciples said to him, "Lord, if he has fallen asleep, he will get well."

¹³ Jesus, however, was speaking about his death, but they thought he was speaking about natural sleep. ¹⁴ So Jesus then told them plainly, "Lazarus has died. ¹⁵ I'm glad for you that I wasn't there so that you may believe. But let's go to him."

¹⁶ Then Thomas (called "Twin") said to his fellow disciples, "Let's go too so that we may die with him."

The Faith of Martha

¹⁷ When Jesus arrived, he found that Lazarus had already been in the tomb four days. ¹⁸ Bethany was near Jerusalem (less than two miles away). ¹⁹ Many of the Jews had come to Martha and Mary to comfort them about their brother.

²⁰ As soon as Martha heard that Jesus was coming, she went to meet him, but Mary remained seated in the house. ²¹ Then Martha said to Jesus, "Lord, if you had been here, my brother wouldn't have died. ²² Yet even now I know that whatever you ask from God, God will give you."

²³ "Your brother will rise again," Jesus told her.

²⁴ Martha said to him, "I know that he will rise again in the resurrection at the last day."

²⁵ Jesus said to her, "I am the resurrection and the life. The one who believes in me, even if he dies, will live. ²⁶ Everyone who lives and believes in me will never die. Do you believe this?"

²⁷ "Yes, Lord," she told him, "I believe you are the Messiah, the Son of God, who comes into the world."

The Faith of Mary

²⁸ Having said this, she went back and called her sister Mary, saying in private, "The Teacher is here and is calling for you."

²⁹ As soon as Mary heard this, she got up quickly and went to him. ³⁰ Jesus had not yet come into the village but was still in the place where Martha had met him. ³¹ The Jews who were with her in the house consoling her saw that Mary got up quickly and went out. They followed her, supposing that she was going to the tomb to cry there.

³² As soon as Mary came to where Jesus was and saw him, she fell at his feet and told him, "Lord, if you had been here, my brother wouldn't have died!"

³³ When Jesus saw her crying, and the Jews who had come with her crying, he was deeply moved in his spirit and troubled. ³⁴ "Where have you put him?" he asked.

"Lord," they told him, "come and see."

³⁵ Jesus wept.

³⁶ So the Jews said, "See how he loved him!" ³⁷ But some of them said, "Couldn't he who opened the blind man's eyes also have kept this man from dying?"

The Resurrection of Lazarus

³⁸ Then Jesus, deeply moved again, came to the tomb. It was a cave, and a stone was lying against it. ³⁹ "Remove the stone," Jesus said.

Martha, the dead man's sister, told him, "Lord, there is already a stench because he has been dead four days."

⁴⁰ Jesus said to her, "Didn't I tell you that if you believed you would see the glory of God?"

⁴¹ So they removed the stone. Then Jesus raised his eyes and said, "Father, I thank you that you heard me. ⁴² I know that you always hear me, but because of the crowd standing here I said this, so that they may believe you sent me." ⁴³ After he said this, he shouted with a loud voice, "Lazarus, come out!" ⁴⁴ The dead man came out bound hand and foot with linen strips and with his face wrapped in a cloth. Jesus said to them, "Unwrap him and let him go."

The Plot to Kill Jesus

⁴⁵ Therefore, many of the Jews who came to Mary and saw what he did believed in him. ⁴⁶ But some of them went to the Pharisees and told them what Jesus had done.

⁴⁷ So the chief priests and the Pharisees convened the Sanhedrin and were saying, "What are we going to do since this man is doing many signs? ⁴⁸ If we let him go on like this, everyone will believe in him, and the Romans will come and take away both our place and our nation."

⁴⁹ One of them, Caiaphas, who was high priest that year, said to them, "You know nothing at all! ⁵⁰ You're not considering that it is to your advantage that one man should die for the people rather than the whole nation perish." ⁵¹ He did not say this on his own, but being high priest that year he prophesied that Jesus was going to die for the nation, ⁵² and not for the nation only, but also to unite the scattered children of God. ⁵³ So from that day on they plotted to kill him.

⁵⁴ Jesus therefore no longer walked openly among the Jews but departed from there to the countryside near the wilderness, to a town called Ephraim, and he stayed there with the disciples.

⁵⁵ Now the Jewish Passover was near, and many went up to Jerusalem from the country to purify themselves before the Passover. ⁵⁶ They were looking for Jesus and asking one another as they stood in the temple, "What do you think? He won't come to the festival, will he?" ⁵⁷ The chief priests and the Pharisees had given orders that if anyone knew where he was, he should report it so that they could arrest him. (John 11 CSB)

THE RESURRECTION AND THE LIFE

It is quite interesting, indeed, to see the faith of both Mary and Martha in this passage. Both of them came to Jesus and declared that if He had only been there, their brother would not have died. Perhaps they had discussed this possibility with each other before He came.

Both of them believed that Jesus had the power to heal those who were sick. However, Lazarus was no longer merely sick. He was dead. Still, Martha seems to suspect that even death might be something Jesus could overcome.

Jesus comforts her with the promise that her brother will rise again. Martha already understood that life really doesn't end in death. Our bodies die, but our souls and spirits live on. God had revealed that one day all of mankind will be raised to life again. So Martha responded by acknowledging this resurrection.

Jesus, however, identified that He Himself is the Resurrection and the Life. He is the one who first breathed into mankind the breath of life, and He is the Author of life. Death is, indeed, no match for Jesus.

Martha responds by acknowledging that Jesus is, in fact, the Christ, the Son of God.

THE RESURRECTION OF LAZARUS

Mary expressed a similar but somewhat lesser faith than Martha. Perhaps she was just more overcome with grief at the time. Even the crowd suspected that Jesus could have kept Lazarus from dying, though they stopped short of wondering if He could raise him from the dead.

Jesus, knowing full well what He is about to do, first entered into their grief with them. He observed the great pain and sorrow that comes with the loss of a loved one, and He wept with them in their grief.

Ever since Adam and Eve had sinned, death had reigned supreme as mankind's greatest enemy. Everyone fights against it, but every one of us will eventually lose.

One day the Offspring of the woman would crush the head of Satan. Death would win some battles, but God would ultimately win the war. On this particular day, Jesus, the Offspring of the woman, demonstrated that great truth. When He came to the tomb and told them to take away the stone, it seemed that all their faith had dwindled away. Jesus assured them that they were about to see the glory of God, and that's exactly what happened! Death was defeated, and Lazarus was raised to life again! Jesus demonstrated that He not only has the power to prevent death by healing those who are sick but that He even holds power over death. Death itself must bow at the feet of Jesus.

Lazarus had most likely been buried in a family tomb that contained the remains of several generations past. Jesus specifically called out to Lazarus. As the Mighty God and Creator of the world, had He not specified to whom He was speaking, every one of them could have come out.

Such is the power of God.

THE REACTIONS OF THE PEOPLE

It is interesting to ponder how the people responded to the resurrection of Lazarus. Many of them concluded, like Martha had, that Jesus was, indeed, the Christ, the Son of God, and they put their faith in Him.

Strangely enough, though, some of them still did not believe. It strains the imagination to think how anyone could see such an incredibly miraculous sign as this and still reject Jesus as the Son of God. Who else could hold such power over death? Yet this was exactly what happened when God was leading the Israelites to the Promised Land, so it really shouldn't be too big of a surprise.

As we have mentioned before, many people today claim that if they themselves could only see miracles like these, they would surely believe in Jesus. Yet that is simply not true, and we see the proof of that in this passage.

Remember that their refusal to accept Jesus as their Messiah was exactly what God had foretold long before in Isaiah 53—He was despised and rejected—not unknown or unproven. They saw unmistakable proof of who He was, yet they rejected Him.

THE PROPHECY OF CAIAPHAS

Lastly, we see the reaction of the religious leaders to the resurrection of Lazarus. In their response, their true motives are exposed. They were afraid that if they let Jesus go on doing miracles, everyone would believe in Him. But what would be wrong with that? If He was the Messiah, then everyone *should* believe in Him.

However, their fear was not just that everyone would believe in Jesus. John reveals that what they were really afraid of was that Rome would remove them from their positions of authority. So rather than acknowledge that Jesus was, in fact, the promised Messiah, they sought to protect their own power and prestige. However, just forty years later, the city of Jerusalem was destroyed by the Roman emperor Titus. As it turned out, their attempts to protect themselves didn't succeed for long.

As the discussion continued between the religious leaders, Caiaphas stepped forward and proposed a solution to the problem. The solution was to kill Jesus. His reasoning turned out to be quite prophetic. He specifically prophesied that Jesus should die in order to save the people of Israel.

You will recall that when Joseph found out that Mary was pregnant and began considering what to do about it, an angel came to him and told him to name the child Jesus, "because he will save his people from their sins" (Matthew 1:21 CSB).

The prophecy of Caiaphas matches that of the angel—Jesus would save His people from their sins, and He would save them by dying on the Cross.

THE PRODIGAL SON

LUKE 15:11-32

U p to this point, we have looked at who Jesus claimed to be, what other people said about Him, prophecies He fulfilled, historical events that foreshadowed His coming, and miracles He performed. Now we turn to one of the most beloved teachings in the entire Bible—a story that has come to be known as the parable of the prodigal son. The word *prodigal* means "wasteful."

Whenever Jesus spoke to large crowds, He often taught by using parables. A parable is essentially a story that does not represent actual events or people. It speaks about something physical, but its purpose is to illustrate a spiritual truth.

Despite its title, the parable of the prodigal son actually mentions two sons. Ultimately, though, it isn't really about either one of them. The central figure in the story is actually the father. As you read the passage, take note of the contrast between the two sons, but pay closest attention to the father.

¹¹ He also said, "A man had two sons. ¹² The younger of them said to his father, 'Father, give me the share of the estate I have coming to me.' So he distributed the assets to them.

¹³ "Not many days later, the younger son gathered together all he had and traveled to a distant country, where he squandered his estate in foolish living. ¹⁴ After he had spent everything, a severe famine struck that country, and he had nothing. ¹⁵ Then he went to work for one of the citizens of that country, who sent him into his fields to feed pigs. ¹⁶ He longed to eat his fill from the pods that the pigs were eating, but no one would give him anything.

[17] *"When he came to his senses, he said, 'How many of my father's hired workers have more than enough food, and here I am dying of hunger! [18] I'll get up, go to my father, and say to him, "Father, I have sinned against heaven and in your sight. [19] I'm no longer worthy to be called your son. Make me like one of your hired workers."'*

[20] *"So he got up and went to his father. But while the son was still a long way off, his father saw him and was filled with compassion. He ran, threw his arms around his neck, and kissed him. [21] The son said to him, 'Father, I have sinned against heaven and in your sight. I'm no longer worthy to be called your son.'*

[22] *"But the father told his servants, 'Quick! Bring out the best robe and put it on him; put a ring on his finger and sandals on his feet. [23] Then bring the fattened calf and slaughter it, and let's celebrate with a feast, [24] because this son of mine was dead and is alive again; he was lost and is found!' So they began to celebrate.*

[25] *"Now his older son was in the field; as he came near the house, he heard music and dancing. [26] So he summoned one of the servants, questioning what these things meant. [27] 'Your brother is here,' he told him, 'and your father has slaughtered the fattened calf because he has him back safe and sound.'*

[28] *"Then he became angry and didn't want to go in. So his father came out and pleaded with him. [29] But he replied to his father, 'Look, I have been slaving many years for you, and I have never disobeyed your orders, yet you never gave me a goat so that I could celebrate with my friends. [30] But when this son of yours came, who has devoured your assets with prostitutes, you slaughtered the fattened calf for him.'*

[31] *"'Son,' he said to him, 'you are always with me, and everything I have is yours. [32] But we had to celebrate and rejoice, because this brother of yours was dead and is alive again; he was lost and is found.'" (Luke 15:11-32 CSB)*

THE GREAT DISGRACE

The parable begins with a very shameful request made by the younger son. He was due an inheritance upon the death of his father. To ask for it while his father was still alive revealed that he didn't really care about his father at all. All he wanted was the money.

We might wonder why the father would even grant such a request. The reality was, though, that he had already lost his son at that point. Declining the request would not have changed his son's heart in the least. That was the father's only concern after all—that both of his sons would live in the joy of his presence.

It is interesting to note that the younger son, after having received his inheritance, journeys to a distant land. But why was this necessary? Why couldn't he have lived just a short distance from his father? The answer is that he knew the life he was going to be living would not be one of which the father would approve. The distance would help him avoid that shame.

It isn't long, however, until the foolishness of his choice becomes evident. He loses everything and has to get the worst possible job a Jewish man could ever have. In the Law of Moses, a pig was an unclean animal, so feeding pigs was unthinkable. Yet that was the level to which he had been reduced.

The story turns as it records that this younger son "came to his senses," and he begins to think of his father again for the first time in a long time. He acknowledges that what he has done has brought great disgrace to his family. He believes he could never truly be a son again. That wonderful life was now gone for good.

Perhaps, though, he could just be a servant there. To live as a servant to his father would be much better than dying of starvation as a servant to someone else. However, whether or not that would even be possible was not up to him. It depended on the heart of his father. Could his father possibly forgive him? Could he have at least enough compassion to let him be a hired hand? Or would he turn him away and throw him out forever? Was the shame he had brought his father just too great?

He didn't know the answers to those questions, but he decided it was worth the risk to find out. After all, he had already lost everything, so he had absolutely nothing more to lose. If he had stayed where he was, he would have surely died. If he returned, at least there was hope.

THE JOURNEY HOME

The journey home must have been a long one, filled with every range of emotion imaginable. His steps were likely slower on his return than they had been on his departure. His body was now diminished from lack of food, and his heart was broken from his own folly and shame. Yet still he walked on.

Meanwhile, the father was waiting. The father was watching. The father was hoping.

While he was on his way, the son had carefully prepared the speech that he would give to his father. It had three points: (1) I have sinned, (2) I am not worthy, and (3) may I be your servant?

I imagine how the son must have felt when the scenery started getting familiar again and then when he drew near his father's house—near *his* home. It wouldn't be long now before the heart of the father toward him would be revealed once and for all. The closer he got, the bigger the lump in his throat became.

Finally, the house came into view, and he began to see a few vague figures in the distance. Oh, if he could just be forgiven, if he could just be accepted, if he could just be welcomed home again!

A FATHER WHO RUNS

It was then that he noticed one of the figures in the distance running toward him. At first he couldn't make out just who it was. But then, could it possibly be? Was that his father? He had never seen him run before. A man of dignity did not do that. But it *was* his father.

Fear and trembling turned to joy and peace as his father's arms wrapped around him and as he felt the father's kiss on his cheek. He would not be turned away or driven off. Perhaps he really could live as his father's servant after all.

He then began his carefully prepared three-point speech—but he didn't get to finish it. His father interrupted him after he only made it through the first two.

The finest robe on his back, shoes on his bruised feet, and even the family's ring on his finger again—then the fattened calf and a celebration. All of this was too good to be true, but perhaps it was the father's words that meant the most to him. He had called him, "My son." He had hoped for forgiveness. He had longed for the chance to somehow work off some of his debt. He had dreamed of some degree of acceptance. What he received was extravagant grace and mercy and love. In essence, his father's answer to him was, "No, you can *never* be my servant—you are forever my *son!*"

THE OLDEST SON

Admittedly, if the parable ended there, it would still be my favorite by far. However, it continues with the account of the older son. This son had stayed faithful to his father the entire time, working diligently every day. Yet, when he learns of the arrival of his long-lost younger brother and the celebration that is being had, he becomes filled with jealousy and anger and refuses to join in.

When his father goes out to him, his character is revealed. All he is concerned about is his own merit and his own rights. He has no use for forgiveness. In fact, he really isn't interested in being with his father either.

Admittedly, the older son lived the kind of life that we typically admire. His life was one of duty and work and diligence. These are good things indeed. However, this is not a story about earning an honest day's work or responsibility. It is a story about relationship and forgiveness and love and restoration.

As I mentioned before, though, this story is a parable—a story that talks about something physical but is intended to illustrate something spiritual. Thus it really isn't about a man and his two sons. It's about a much greater truth.

THE MORAL OF THE STORY

So what is this parable really about? Why did Jesus tell this story? What was it that He was trying to teach us? Is it just a touching story, or was there more to it?

By now you may have probably guessed that the great father in this story represents God—full of love and compassion and mercy and grace and forgiveness. He deeply longs for a relationship with His people.

The two sons represent you and me. We may prefer to think of our lives as being more like the older son—responsible, diligent, hardworking, and dutiful. However, in the eyes of God, we are all like the younger son, like Adam and Eve, like the world in Noah's day and like the people of Israel. We have rejected God and dishonored Him. We have gone our own ways and have sought to fill the emptiness inside us with the things of this world, all to no avail. Eventually, our foolishness will be evident. Everything we have will be gone, and we will be left desperate and desolate, vainly trying to survive on food that does not satisfy and trying to quench our thirst with salt water.

The questions for us are, *Will we, like the younger son, come to our senses? Will we decide that it's time to come home? Will we take the risk? Will we trust the heart of the father to welcome us and forgive us and restore us?*

If we choose not to come home, spiritual death will be the outcome, and we will be separated from the Father forever. If, however, we do make the decision to return home, we are assured that we will be received with open arms, just like the younger son was. We will receive the Father's embrace, His kiss on our cheeks, the finest robes on our backs, shoes on our bruised feet, rings on our fingers, and a celebration to welcome us home. We will experience His eternal love and mercy and grace and forgiveness.

Will you return home to the Father today?

PART V
PARADISE RESTORED:
THE CULMINATION

THE RETURN OF THE KING

MATTHEW 21:1-17

We come now to the very last week of Jesus' life. His ministry had probably lasted about three years, beginning when He was about thirty years of age.

Matthew had previously summarized the ministry of Jesus by stating, "Jesus continued going around to all the towns and villages, teaching in their synagogues, preaching the good news of the kingdom, and healing every disease and every sickness" (Matthew 9:35 CSB). In these three years, though, His focus had not been on the masses but on the few. As Mark records, "He appointed twelve, whom he also named apostles, to be with him [and] to send them out to preach" (Mark 3:14 CSB). These twelve men were the ones who would be crucial to the next phase of God's plan of restoration. They were the ones who would take the message of Jesus throughout the world, and that is why Jesus focused His efforts on them. The closer the time came for Jesus' death, the more time He spent with these twelve men and the less time He spent with the multitudes.

This last week of Jesus' life takes place in and around the city of Jerusalem just before and during the Passover feast. As Jesus enters Jerusalem at the start of the week, the people welcome Him and are hoping that He will become their new King. But Jesus had already been their King from ages past, so this was merely *the return of the King*.

> ¹ *As they approached Jerusalem and came to Bethphage on the Mount of Olives, Jesus sent two disciples, ² saying to them, "Go to the village ahead of you, and at once you will find a donkey tied there, with her colt by her. Untie them and bring them to me. ³ If anyone says anything to you, say that the Lord needs them, and he will send them right away."*
>
> ⁴ *This took place to fulfill what was spoken through the prophet:*
> ⁵ *"Say to Daughter Zion,*
> *'See, your king comes to you,*
> *gentle and riding on a donkey,*
> *and on a colt, the foal of a donkey.'"*

⁶ The disciples went and did as Jesus had instructed them. ⁷ They brought the donkey and the colt and placed their cloaks on them for Jesus to sit on. ⁸ A very large crowd spread their cloaks on the road, while others cut branches from the trees and spread them on the road. ⁹ The crowds that went ahead of him and those that followed shouted,

"Hosanna to the Son of David!"

"Blessed is he who comes in the name of the Lord!"

"Hosanna in the highest heaven!"

¹⁰ When Jesus entered Jerusalem, the whole city was stirred and asked, "Who is this?"

¹¹ The crowds answered, "This is Jesus, the prophet from Nazareth in Galilee."

Jesus at the Temple

¹² Jesus entered the temple courts and drove out all who were buying and selling there. He overturned the tables of the money changers and the benches of those selling doves. ¹³ "It is written," he said to them, "'My house will be called a house of prayer,' but you are making it 'a den of robbers.'"

¹⁴ The blind and the lame came to him at the temple, and he healed them. ¹⁵ But when the chief priests and the teachers of the law saw the wonderful things he did and the children shouting in the temple courts, "Hosanna to the Son of David," they were indignant.

¹⁶ "Do you hear what these children are saying?" they asked him.

"Yes," replied Jesus, "have you never read,
"'From the lips of children and infants
you, Lord, have called forth your praise'?"

¹⁷ And he left them and went out of the city to Bethany, where he spent the night. (Matthew 21:1-17 NIV)

HOSANNA TO THE SON OF DAVID

Yet another prophecy is fulfilled in this passage. This one was given by Zechariah, one of the minor prophets who lived around 500

B.C. The text of that prophecy is abbreviated in this passage. The full prophecy reads, "Rejoice greatly, Daughter Zion! Shout in triumph, Daughter Jerusalem! Look, your King is coming to you; he is righteous and victorious, humble and riding on a donkey, on a colt, the foal of a donkey" (Zechariah 9:9 CSB).

The people welcomed Him with cries of "Hosanna to the Son of David." The word *hosanna* literally means "save us." The reference to Jesus as the Son of David identified Him both as the descendant of David who would reign forever and also as the Messiah. Thus the prophecy and the proclamation of the people are complementary. The prophecy identified the King as coming on a donkey, and the people identified Him as the Son of David, who was heir to the throne. The prophecy spoke of the King being righteous and victorious, and the people cried out to Him to give them salvation.

Jesus is also, once again, acknowledged as the Prophet, referring to the one of whom Moses had spoken—the Prophet like Moses. Thus Jesus is identified here as the King of Israel, the Son of David, and the Prophet like Moses.

THE CLEANSING OF THE TEMPLE

After Jesus entered Jerusalem, He went into the temple courts where He found, much to His displeasure, people buying and selling. This may seem a bit strange at first, as you may wonder what could possibly be wrong with this. However, it is likely *where* this was occurring that was the problem.

Jesus asserted, quoting from Isaiah, that the temple was to be "a house of prayer"—and not just for the people of Israel but "for *all nations*" (Isaiah 56:7 CSB, emphasis added). Yet they had disregarded this and made it into a place of *profit* instead of a place of prayer.

It is also likely that this was the place in the temple that was specifically designated for non-Jewish people to come and worship the one true God. God is the God of all people. He had chosen Abraham and his descendants for the purpose of proclaiming His name throughout the world and for being the nation through whom the Messiah would come. This place, then, was specifically set aside for Gentiles who came to worship God.

Thus Jesus drove these buyers and sellers out of the temple because it was intended to be a place of prayer and worship. God does not respond well when anyone prevents others from worshiping Him.

THE LAST SUPPER
MATTHEW 26:1-35

We come now to the final night of Jesus' life. Everything comes together in the next few chapters, from the fulfillment of many more prophecies to the full realization of what had been foreshadowed in so many ways in times past.

At this point, however, the disciples are seemingly unaware of all that is about to happen. They were slow to comprehend God's purpose and plan, even though He had spoken often to them about it.

In this account, the disciples again do not seem to present themselves in the best light. They were not the heroes of the story. Rather, they are depicted as just a bunch of ordinary men who were nothing special. They would seem to be the last people on earth anyone would have ever chosen for any great task, let alone the greatest mission the world has ever known.

This is beautifully refreshing because if God would choose to do great things through men such as these, He just might choose to do something special through you and me!

In this passage, we will see an extravagant act of worship, a traitor revealed, and the New Covenant established.

¹ When Jesus had finished saying all these things, he said to his disciples, ² "As you know, the Passover is two days away—and the Son of Man will be handed over to be crucified."

³ Then the chief priests and the elders of the people assembled in the palace of the high priest, whose name was Caiaphas, ⁴ and they schemed to arrest Jesus secretly and kill him. ⁵ "But not during the festival," they said, "or there may be a riot among the people."

Jesus Anointed at Bethany

⁶ While Jesus was in Bethany in the home of Simon the Leper, ⁷ a woman came to him with an alabaster jar of very expensive perfume, which she poured on his head as he was reclining at the table.

⁸ When the disciples saw this, they were indignant. "Why this waste?" they asked. ⁹ "This perfume could have been sold at a high price and the money given to the poor."

[10] *Aware of this, Jesus said to them, "Why are you bothering this woman? She has done a beautiful thing to me.* [11] *The poor you will always have with you, but you will not always have me.* [12] *When she poured this perfume on my body, she did it to prepare me for burial.* [13] *Truly I tell you, wherever this gospel is preached throughout the world, what she has done will also be told, in memory of her."*

Judas Agrees to Betray Jesus

[14] *Then one of the Twelve—the one called Judas Iscariot—went to the chief priests* [15] *and asked, "What are you willing to give me if I deliver him over to you?" So they counted out for him thirty pieces of silver.* [16] *From then on Judas watched for an opportunity to hand him over.*

The Last Supper

[17] *On the first day of the Festival of Unleavened Bread, the disciples came to Jesus and asked, "Where do you want us to make preparations for you to eat the Passover?"*

[18] *He replied, "Go into the city to a certain man and tell him, 'The Teacher says: My appointed time is near. I am going to celebrate the Passover with my disciples at your house.'"* [19] *So the disciples did as Jesus had directed them and prepared the Passover.*

[20] *When evening came, Jesus was reclining at the table with the Twelve.* [21] *And while they were eating, he said, "Truly I tell you, one of you will betray me."*

[22] *They were very sad and began to say to him one after the other, "Surely you don't mean me, Lord?"*

[23] *Jesus replied, "The one who has dipped his hand into the bowl with me will betray me.* [24] *The Son of Man will go just as it is written about him. But woe to that man who betrays the Son of Man! It would be better for him if he had not been born."*

[25] *Then Judas, the one who would betray him, said, "Surely you don't mean me, Rabbi?"*

Jesus answered, "You have said so."

26 While they were eating, Jesus took bread, and when he had given thanks, he broke it and gave it to his disciples, saying, "Take and eat; this is my body."

27 Then he took a cup, and when he had given thanks, he gave it to them, saying, "Drink from it, all of you. 28 This is my blood of the covenant, which is poured out for many for the forgiveness of sins. 29 I tell you, I will not drink from this fruit of the vine from now on until that day when I drink it new with you in my Father's kingdom."

30 When they had sung a hymn, they went out to the Mount of Olives.

Jesus Predicts Peter's Denial

31 Then Jesus told them, "This very night you will all fall away on account of me, for it is written:

"'I will strike the shepherd,
and the sheep of the flock will be scattered.'
32 But after I have risen, I will go ahead of you into Galilee."

33 Peter replied, "Even if all fall away on account of you, I never will."

34 "Truly I tell you," Jesus answered, "this very night, before the rooster crows, you will disown me three times."

35 But Peter declared, "Even if I have to die with you, I will never disown you." And all the other disciples said the same. (Matthew 26:1-35 NIV)

AN ACT OF WORSHIP

We don't know much about the woman named Mary in this passage. There was another woman of the same name whom Jesus had freed from demonic influence earlier in His ministry, and she could certainly be the same one mentioned here. We just don't know for sure. Whoever she was, her act was, indeed, an extravagant act of worship. The perfume she used was very expensive, so it had to cost her a great deal. But she gave it freely and without reservation.

Jesus' own disciples, however, were upset at this. They argued that the perfume could have been sold for a great price, and the money could have been given to the poor. Nevertheless, Jesus is honored by her gift, and He praises her for what she did.

True worship for God is always extravagant. Yet the greatest thing that we can give God today is certainly not financial in nature. To be sure, giving financially is an act of worship, and we who are believers should certainly be generous in that. Yet the greatest act of worship today is the offering of our own lives to glorify God.

A TRAITOR REVEALED

Judas had been one of Jesus' twelve disciples—a very exclusive group of men. He had been an eyewitness of countless miracles, including healings, the feeding of the five thousand, the walking on the water, the giving of sight to the blind, and even the raising of Lazarus from the dead. He had heard Jesus teach the multitudes and confound the most educated scholars of the day. If anyone had reason to put their faith in Jesus, Judas certainly did. Nonetheless, all the miracles in the world had not been enough to make him believe.

Perhaps he realized what the Pharisees were about to do to Jesus at this time, and he just wanted to save his own life. We don't know for sure. Still, the fact that Jesus was betrayed by one of His own companions was a fulfillment of yet another prophecy, proving once again that God makes known the end from the beginning.

THE NEW COVENANT

In this account, Jesus and His disciples observed the Passover feast together. You will recall that the first Passover occurred when the Israelites were enslaved in Egypt. God had pronounced judgment but provided a way of escape. The Jewish people had celebrated this in remembrance ever since then, for over fifteen hundred years. This feast was the last meal Jesus ate before He was crucified. As such, it has come to be known as the Last Supper.

The Passover feast encompasses many different stages and can last a few hours. Bread is broken at one point in the evening, and there are also four different cups of wine that are shared, each with its own particular name and meaning. One of the cups is known as the *cup of redemption*. To redeem something is to buy something back that was lost. God had promised to redeem Israel from slavery in Egypt, and He had fulfilled that promise. This *cup of redemption* is likely the one to which Jesus is referring in this passage.

Now that His betrayer had departed, and as Jesus has eaten the Passover meal with His disciples for the last time, He reveals the true meaning that the bread and wine had been foreshadowing for centuries.

The broken bread symbolized His own body, as He Himself was the Bread of Life that had come down from heaven to give life to the world. Like the bread in the Passover ceremony that is broken, His *body* would soon be broken. The wine symbolized the blood of Jesus, which He would soon shed on the Cross. In Egypt, the Jewish people had to put the blood of the Passover lamb on the doorframes of their houses. Jesus, the true Passover Lamb, was about to be offered as a sacrifice.

Jesus also identified this cup of wine with a particular covenant—a *new* one! In the Old Testament, God had made covenants with Adam, Noah, Abraham, Moses, and the people of Israel. Yet we saw that the prophet Jeremiah had spoken of another final covenant that would one day be established—the *New Covenant*—that would be superior to all the others. Jesus declared that this New Covenant was being established at that moment, and it would be connected with His death.

Today, Christians all over the world celebrate the portion of the Passover celebration that is recorded here—the breaking of bread and the drinking of the cup. It is referred to as communion, the Lord's Supper, or the Eucharist.

JESUS ON TRIAL
MATTHEW 26:36-75

A fter supper, Jesus and His disciples left the house where they had eaten and went to a garden. Judas had left them earlier and would soon return to betray Him.

Jesus was then arrested and put on trial. At this time in history, you will recall that the Jewish nation was under the control of Rome. They were able to enforce their own laws to a certain extent. However, Rome reserved the right to punish crimes that were punishable by death.

Since the Jewish leaders wanted to have Jesus put to death, they would have to convince the Roman governor that He had done something deserving of that. So, after they arrested Jesus, they first hold their own trial. Then they take Him to the Roman governor, whose name was Pilate. Understanding this will make more sense of what is going on in the passage. Jesus stands trial here before the Jewish court and then again before the Roman court in the next chapter.

³⁶ Then Jesus went with his disciples to a place called Gethsemane, and he said to them, "Sit here while I go over there and pray." ³⁷ He took Peter and the two sons of Zebedee along with him, and he began to be sorrowful and troubled. ³⁸ Then he said to them, "My soul is overwhelmed with sorrow to the point of death. Stay here and keep watch with me."

³⁹ Going a little farther, he fell with his face to the ground and prayed, "My Father, if it is possible, may this cup be taken from me. Yet not as I will, but as you will."

⁴⁰ Then he returned to his disciples and found them sleeping. "Couldn't you men keep watch with me for one hour?" he asked Peter. ⁴¹ "Watch and pray so that you will not fall into temptation. The spirit is willing, but the flesh is weak."

⁴² He went away a second time and prayed, "My Father, if it is not possible for this cup to be taken away unless I drink it, may your will be done."

⁴³ When he came back, he again found them sleeping, because their eyes were heavy. ⁴⁴ So he left them and went away once more and prayed the third time, saying the same thing.

⁴⁵ Then he returned to the disciples and said to them, "Are you still sleeping and resting? Look, the hour has come, and the Son of Man is delivered into the hands of sinners. ⁴⁶ Rise! Let us go! Here comes my betrayer!"

Jesus Arrested

⁴⁷ While he was still speaking, Judas, one of the Twelve, arrived. With him was a large crowd armed with swords and clubs, sent from the chief priests and the elders of the people. ⁴⁸ Now the betrayer had arranged a signal with them: "The one I kiss is the man; arrest him." ⁴⁹ Going at once to Jesus, Judas said, "Greetings, Rabbi!" and kissed him.

⁵⁰ Jesus replied, "Do what you came for, friend."

Then the men stepped forward, seized Jesus and arrested him. ⁵¹ With that, one of Jesus' companions reached for his sword, drew it out and struck the servant of the high priest, cutting off his ear.

52 "Put your sword back in its place," Jesus said to him, "for all who draw the sword will die by the sword. 53 Do you think I cannot call on my Father, and he will at once put at my disposal more than twelve legions of angels? 54 But how then would the Scriptures be fulfilled that say it must happen in this way?"

55 In that hour Jesus said to the crowd, "Am I leading a rebellion, that you have come out with swords and clubs to capture me? Every day I sat in the temple courts teaching, and you did not arrest me. 56 But this has all taken place that the writings of the prophets might be fulfilled." Then all the disciples deserted him and fled.

Jesus on Trial

57 Those who had arrested Jesus took him to Caiaphas the high priest, where the teachers of the law and the elders had assembled. 58 But Peter followed him at a distance, right up to the courtyard of the high priest. He entered and sat down with the guards to see the outcome.

59 The chief priests and the whole Sanhedrin were looking for false evidence against Jesus so that they could put him to death. 60 But they did not find any, though many false witnesses came forward.

Finally two came forward 61 and declared, "This fellow said, 'I am able to destroy the temple of God and rebuild it in three days.'"

62 Then the high priest stood up and said to Jesus, "Are you not going to answer? What is this testimony that these men are bringing against you?" 63 But Jesus remained silent.

The high priest said to him, "I charge you under oath by the living God: Tell us if you are the Messiah, the Son of God."

64 "You have said so," Jesus replied. "But I say to all of you: From now on you will see the Son of Man sitting at the right hand of the Mighty One and coming on the clouds of heaven."

65 Then the high priest tore his clothes and said, "He has spoken blasphemy! Why do we need any more witnesses? Look, now you have heard the blasphemy. 66 What do you think?"

"He is worthy of death," they answered.

67 Then they spit in his face and struck him with their fists. Others slapped him 68 and said, "Prophesy to us, Messiah. Who hit you?"

Peter Disowns Jesus

69 Now Peter was sitting out in the courtyard, and a servant girl came to him. "You also were with Jesus of Galilee," she said.

70 But he denied it before them all. "I don't know what you're talking about," he said.

71 Then he went out to the gateway, where another servant girl saw him and said to the people there, "This fellow was with Jesus of Nazareth."

72 He denied it again, with an oath: "I don't know the man!"

73 After a little while, those standing there went up to Peter and said, "Surely you are one of them; your accent gives you away."

74 Then he began to call down curses, and he swore to them, "I don't know the man!"

Immediately a rooster crowed. 75 Then Peter remembered the word Jesus had spoken: "Before the rooster crows, you will disown me three times." And he went outside and wept bitterly. (Matthew 26:36-75 NIV)

THE TEMPLE DESTROYED

The irony of Jesus' trial is quite intriguing. The holy Son of God was put on trial by sinful men. How could any fault be found in Him? Simply put, there was no way. They would have to fabricate something.

In His trial, Jesus was specifically accused of claiming that He would destroy the temple and rebuild it in three days. The account of this is recorded in the second chapter of the book of John, quite early on in Jesus' ministry. This was *not* one of the passages that we read together, so I'll give you a brief summary here.

Jesus had entered the temple and saw the same thing He saw three years later and what we just read about—people turning the place of worship into a place of profit. His response then was the same as it was in the passage we read.

After He had cleared the temple area, the people demanded He show them proof of His authority to do that. He responded by saying,

"Destroy this temple, and I will raise it up in three days" (John 2:19 CSB). Note that He did not say that He Himself was going to destroy the temple but that if they dared to destroy the temple, then He would raise it again in three days. (Thus those who accused Him in this passage had misrepresented what He had said.)

John then explains that Jesus was not talking about destroying the *building* that was called the temple. Rather, Jesus was referring to His own body as a temple. If a temple is the place where God's presence dwells, then Jesus' body was most certainly a temple! So in essence, Jesus declared that the proof of His authority would be that three days after they had killed *Him*, He would rise again from the dead.

Indeed, the resurrection of Jesus is proof of His identity as the Christ, the Son of God, the Ruler from Bethlehem, and the King of Israel—and the Judge of all the earth. One day, those who had put Jesus on trial and had falsely accused Him will have to stand before Him once again. This time, however, Jesus will be the Judge.

THE SON OF MAN

This trial of Jesus was actually a complete disgrace—an embarrassment to justice. They had begun with the punishment in mind and then searched for a crime that would merit that penalty. However, even with all their evil intent, nothing worked out as they had planned.

Finally, as a last resort, the high priest attempted to get Jesus to incriminate Himself. Jesus, knowing full well what it would mean, gave them exactly what they wanted.

You will recall that in Daniel's vision, there was *one like a son of man* who approached the throne of God, was given divine authority, was worshiped by all nations, and reigned as king forever. This Son of Man had specifically approached God by coming on the clouds of heaven. Jesus' response to the high priest's question was shocking. He said, "From now on you will see *the Son of Man* sitting at the right hand of the Mighty One and *coming on the clouds of heaven*" (Matthew 26:64b NIV emphasis added).

There was no doubt about it. Jesus had claimed to be the very Son of Man whom Daniel had seen in his vision—the same Son of Man who would receive divine authority, be worshiped by the nations as God, and reign as King forever. Jesus had just claimed to God!

The religious leaders were astonished that He dared to give such a response. They could now accuse Him of blasphemy, which was punishable by death. So they led Him away to Pilate, the Roman governor. Yet it really wasn't blasphemy at all because Jesus really was that Son of Man.

PETER'S DENIAL

Peter is well known today for failing miserably, but that's certainly not the whole story. Earlier in the evening, he had voiced great confidence in his own commitment to Jesus, claiming that he would be willing to give his life for Him—even if everyone else fell away.

A few hours later, when Jesus was being arrested, it was Peter who put his commitment into action, drew a sword, and, with all the refined combat skills of a fisherman, attacked the soldiers. His attempt was a huge failure, as he only managed to cut off the ear of one servant. (Though Matthew does not record who did this, John identifies him as Peter in his account.)

Jesus immediately stopped his attack, though, and this probably confused Peter. How could Jesus being arrested be part of God's plan? He just didn't understand. Peter then followed the soldiers from a distance and found himself waiting outside as the trial began.

Then he who had been so bold and willing to die just a short time before quickly lost all confidence when asked a simple question by an unarmed bystander. When he later realized his horrible failure, he was overwhelmed with grief.

JESUS CONDEMNED
MATTHEW 27:1-26

We now come to the final part of the trial of Jesus as He is taken before Pilate, the Roman governor. Surprisingly enough, Judas again enters the story as he faces the grim reality of what he had done.

Another person of interest also appears, whose name is Barabbas. Be sure to pay close attention to who he is and what part he plays in the story, as that will turn out to be of great significance.

> *¹ Early in the morning, all the chief priests and the elders of the people made their plans how to have Jesus executed. ² So they bound him, led him away and handed him over to Pilate the governor.*

³ When Judas, who had betrayed him, saw that Jesus was condemned, he was seized with remorse and returned the thirty pieces of silver to the chief priests and the elders. ⁴ "I have sinned," he said, "for I have betrayed innocent blood."

"What is that to us?" they replied. "That's your responsibility."

⁵ So Judas threw the money into the temple and left. Then he went away and hanged himself.

⁶ The chief priests picked up the coins and said, "It is against the law to put this into the treasury, since it is blood money." ⁷ So they decided to use the money to buy the potter's field as a burial place for foreigners. ⁸ That is why it has been called the Field of Blood to this day. ⁹ Then what was spoken by Jeremiah the prophet was fulfilled: "They took the thirty pieces of silver, the price set on him by the people of Israel, ¹⁰ and they used them to buy the potter's field, as the Lord commanded me."

Jesus Before Pilate

¹¹ Meanwhile Jesus stood before the governor, and the governor asked him, "Are you the king of the Jews?"

"You have said so," Jesus replied.

¹² When he was accused by the chief priests and the elders, he gave no answer. ¹³ Then Pilate asked him, "Don't you hear the testimony they are bringing against you?" ¹⁴ But Jesus made no reply, not even to a single charge—to the great amazement of the governor.

¹⁵ Now it was the governor's custom at the festival to release a prisoner chosen by the crowd. ¹⁶ At that time they had a well-known prisoner whose name was Jesus Barabbas. ¹⁷ So when the crowd had gathered, Pilate asked them, "Which one do you want me to release to you: Jesus Barabbas, or Jesus who is called the Messiah?" ¹⁸ For he knew it was out of self-interest that they had handed Jesus over to him.

¹⁹ While Pilate was sitting on the judge's seat, his wife sent him this message: "Don't have anything to do with that innocent man, for I have suffered a great deal today in a dream because of him."

²⁰ But the chief priests and the elders persuaded the crowd to ask for Barabbas and to have Jesus executed.

²¹ "Which of the two do you want me to release to you?" asked the governor.

"Barabbas," they answered.

²² "What shall I do, then, with Jesus who is called the Messiah?" Pilate asked.

They all answered, "Crucify him!"

²³ "Why? What crime has he committed?" asked Pilate.

But they shouted all the louder, "Crucify him!"

²⁴ When Pilate saw that he was getting nowhere, but that instead an uproar was starting, he took water and washed his hands in front of the crowd. "I am innocent of this man's blood," he said. "It is your responsibility!"

²⁵ All the people answered, "His blood is on us and on our children!"

²⁶ Then he released Barabbas to them. But he had Jesus flogged, and handed him over to be crucified. (Matthew 27:1-26 NIV)

SILENT BEFORE HIS ACCUSERS

When the religious leaders accused Jesus, He remained silent. This was a fulfillment of the prophecy of the Suffering Servant in Isaiah 53, where "as a sheep before its shearers is silent, so he did not open his mouth" (Isaiah 53:7 NIV). This silence is quite intriguing. The usual response in the face of an accusation is to object and defend oneself. Even the guilty will attempt to put the blame on others, deny reality, and make excuses. Those who are falsely accused will protest just as much, if not more. The accusation is deeply insulting to their integrity and character. Still, the fear of punishment is enough to cause the loudest of protestations. After all, who would ever willingly suffer a punishment he could avoid, especially if the person were truly innocent?

So what kind of man is this who doesn't say anything at all? What kind of innocent man remains silent in the face of false accusations? The only kind of man that does this is one who is willingly taking on someone else's penalty—a substitute. That is precisely what Jesus was doing.

WHY DIDN'T THE JEWISH PEOPLE ACCEPT JESUS AS THEIR MESSIAH?

Christianity strongly affirms that Jesus is the Savior whom God promised and foreshadowed all throughout the Old Testament. However, the vast majority of Jewish people, both then and now, have rejected Jesus as their Messiah.

So if the Jewish people, who were chosen by God and who received all these promises and prophecies, have rejected Jesus, then how could He really be their Messiah? That is a very important question. Yet the answer is quite simple.

God had specifically prophesied that the Messiah would be "despised and rejected by men" and that the Jewish people themselves would not esteem Him (Isaiah 53:3 NIV). They would *reject* Him as their Messiah.

As we have seen, this rejection of God is completely consistent with the history of the Jewish people. As we read in Psalm 78, they continually rebelled against God and the prophets He sent to them. They complained often, seldom trusted, frequently doubted, consistently disobeyed, and only sporadically followed Him. So the fact that the Jewish people rejected Jesus is *not* evidence against the claim that Jesus is their promised Messiah. It is actually evidence that supports that claim. In fact, if Jesus had been fully embraced by the Jewish people of His day, then He would certainly not have been their Messiah since the prophecy of their rejection would not have been fulfilled.

Nevertheless, God has not forgotten His chosen people Israel, nor has He ever stopped loving them. He has longed for them to return to Him like the prodigal sons and daughters that they are, yet for centuries most of the Jewish people have refused to do so.

However, in the last half century or so, something has begun to change. The Jewish people are beginning to return to God and embrace Jesus as their Messiah, and the numbers are growing more and more rapidly!

THE GOSPEL ACCORDING TO BARABBAS

The entire message of the Bible is actually captured in the brief account of the man named Barabbas. Barabbas was a guilty criminal, before both Rome and God. He well deserved the penalty of death for the crimes he had committed. No one would argue that his sentence was unjustified. A cross had already been prepared for him to carry to his own death that very day.

However, through a somewhat bizarre turn of events, Barabbas did not carry his cross up the hill that day. *Jesus* did. And Barabbas was not nailed to his cross that day. *Jesus* was. And Barabbas did not die that day. *Jesus* did. Barabbas was set free because *Jesus* took his place. Jesus was his *Substitute*. In fact, if someone had seen Barabbas later that day and knew that he had been sentenced to death, he might have asked him what had happened and how he was still alive. Barabbas could have answered simply, "Jesus died in my place."

That is the message of the Bible. It is the message of Christianity. It is God's message to all mankind. It is God's message to you and me. You and I are both guilty of sin before God, just like Barabbas. We, too, deserve God's punishment for our own sin, and that punishment is death—both physical and spiritual. However, Jesus Himself took *our* place. He died on *our* behalf and paid the penalty for *our* sins. The penalty could not simply be ignored. It had to be paid, and Jesus paid it in full. There is no penalty left for us to pay.

We are set free when we put our complete trust in Jesus and in His death on the Cross. We become God's children, not through anything that we have ever done or ever could do but only through what Jesus Himself did on that day. Thus salvation is not based on our works or heritage or any religious ceremony but only on our faith alone in His work on the Cross.

In a sense, we are all Barabbas. The only question that remains is whether or not we will accept what Jesus did for us. Like Barabbas, we must say, "Jesus died in my place too."

Salvation is available to all people, but no one is compelled to receive it. Will you accept it today?

JESUS CRUCIFIED
MATTHEW 27:27-50

After having been sentenced first by the Jewish leaders and now by Pilate, Jesus is led out of the city to be crucified. This is where He will endure His greatest suffering, both physically and emotionally.

Yet this is the culmination of God's plan of restoration that had begun in the Garden of Eden. It is important, then, to take note of every detail that we are given, as everything is packed with meaning.

[27] *Then the governor's soldiers took Jesus into the Praetorium and gathered the whole company of soldiers around him. [28] They stripped him and put a scarlet robe on him, [29] and then twisted together a crown of thorns and set it on his head. They put a staff in his right hand. Then they knelt in front of him and mocked him. "Hail, king of the Jews!" they said. [30] They spit on him, and took the staff and struck him on the head again and again. [31] After they had mocked him, they took off the robe and put his own clothes on him. Then they led him away to crucify him.*

[32] As they were going out, they met a man from Cyrene, named Simon, and they forced him to carry the cross. [33] They came to a place called Golgotha (which means "the place of the skull"). [34] There they offered Jesus wine to drink, mixed with gall; but after tasting it, he refused to drink it. [35] When they had crucified him, they divided up his clothes by casting lots. [36] And sitting down, they kept watch over him there. [37] Above his head they placed the written charge against him: this is Jesus, the King of the Jews.

[38] Two rebels were crucified with him, one on his right and one on his left. [39] Those who passed by hurled insults at him, shaking their heads [40] and saying, "You who are going to destroy the temple and build it in three days, save yourself! Come down from the cross, if you are the Son of God!" [41] In the same way the chief priests, the teachers of the law and the elders mocked him. [42] "He saved others," they said, "but he can't save himself! He's the king of Israel! Let him come down now from the cross, and we will believe in him. [43] He trusts in God. Let God rescue him now if he wants him, for he said, 'I am the Son of God.'" [44] In the same way the rebels who were crucified with him also heaped insults on him.

[45] From noon until three in the afternoon darkness came over all the land. [46] About three in the afternoon Jesus cried out in a loud voice, "Eli, Eli, lema sabachthani?" (which means "My God, my God, why have you forsaken me?").

[47] When some of those standing there heard this, they said, "He's calling Elijah."

[48] Immediately one of them ran and got a sponge. He filled it with wine vinegar, put it on a staff, and offered it to Jesus to drink. [49] The rest said, "Now leave him alone. Let's see if Elijah comes to save him."

⁵⁰ *And when Jesus had cried out again in a loud voice, he gave up his spirit. (Matthew 27:27-50 NIV)*

THE CROWN OF THORNS

Pilate had ordered the Roman soldiers to flog Jesus prior to sentencing Him to death. This was something that they had done many times before. I imagine that the first time each of them had to participate in this horror would have probably been quite difficult, as they had to observe the deep anguish in their victim's eyes and the mutilation of his body. After hundreds of floggings, though, they had likely grown callous to the dreadful task.

When they flogged Jesus that day, they knew that He was accused of being the King of Israel. One of the soldiers decided to mock this King, and perhaps he just happened to notice the thorn tree nearby. It was then that the idea occurred to him to twist the thorns into a crown and make that a cruel tool of mockery. Thus this crown would not be a crown of honor but a crown of pain and suffering and shame. Yet even in this depraved act, this soldier unknowingly but symbolically acted out the deeper reality of what was taking place.

You will recall that thorns came about as the result of sin in the Garden of Eden, when God cursed the ground. Thus thorns are symbolic of sin. Centuries later, as we saw, Isaiah prophesied that God would place upon the Suffering Servant the sin of us all (Isaiah 53:6).

The crown of thorns represented the reality that God was, at that moment in time, placing upon Jesus the sins of the whole world—including your sins and mine.

THE TREE OF LIFE AND THE TREE OF DEATH

There were two named trees in the Garden of Eden that God had made for Adam and Eve. One was the Tree of Life. The other was the Tree of Death—the Tree of the Knowledge of Good and Evil. Though the Tree of Death was alive, the fruit that hung on it brought death to any who partook of it.

On the day that Jesus died, though, there was another kind of tree. Unlike the trees in the Garden, this tree was dead. It had been cut up and formed into the shape of a Cross. This Cross would be the Tree of Death for Jesus, the Son of God. Although it had been mankind who had chosen the Tree of Death originally, it was Jesus who chose it for Himself on this day. In doing so, what was the Tree of Death for Jesus became the Tree of Life for the world.

In the Garden of Eden, whoever would eat from the Tree of Life would live forever. Today, whoever goes to the ultimate Tree of Life—the Cross of Jesus—receives eternal life.

THE PLACE OF THE SKULL

The place of the crucifixion was known as Golgotha, which means "The Place of the Skull." The Jewish people had apparently used this site originally to quarry rocks for the building of the temple but had abandoned it when they began to hit air pockets and could no longer get good stones. The result of the quarrying had inadvertently left the appearance of a skull—and, thus, the name.

Recall, though, that this was not the first time a beloved son had been bound to wood that he himself had carried up the hill. As we have already mentioned, it was, at the very least, in the same region where Abraham and Isaac had walked some two thousand years before. Abraham had proclaimed then that God Himself would one day provide a Lamb. On this day, God fulfilled that prophecy as Jesus, the Lamb of God, was offered for the sins of the world.

HIS CRIME

Whenever anyone was crucified, a sign was nailed to the top of his cross. This sign identified the crime of which that person was guilty. This served as a warning to all who passed by that this gruesome fate awaited all who did the same thing.

However, when it came time to make the sign for the Cross of Jesus, there must have been a bit of confusion. After all, He hadn't been convicted of any crime at all. In John's account of the trial, Pilate actually proclaimed, "I find no basis for a charge against Him" (John 19:6 NIV). When Pilate had demanded of the Jews what crime He had committed, their only response was to continue shouting for His death. So what were they supposed to write for His crime?

In another place, the Bible indicates that Pilate himself was the one who determined what would be written (John 19:19-22). The sign simply read, "This is Jesus, the King of the Jews" (Matthew 27:37 NIV). Thus Jesus was not put to death because of anything He had done. He was put to death because of who He was.

THE DARKNESS

Just before Jesus died, there was a period of darkness that lasted for a total of three hours. Some have suggested that this may have been a solar eclipse with a greatly exaggerated duration. However, the Jews were celebrating the Passover feast at this time. This feast is always held during a new moon—not a full moon. Thus an eclipse was scientifically impossible. The moon was as far away as it could possibly be from being able to cause an eclipse at that time.

Yet this wasn't the first time that darkness had come upon the land. Long before, when God was showing His supremacy over the false gods of Egypt in the time of Moses, He had brought darkness on that land for three days. Jesus, of course, was the Prophet like Moses that God had raised up. Thus there seems to be a direct correlation between these two periods of darkness.

We also remember that Jesus had identified Himself as the Light of the World who had spoken light into existence. Thus, as the true Light of the World was being extinguished, the physical light of the world refused to shine.

More than that, the darkness suggests complete isolation. The penalty for sin was not merely physical death but spiritual death as well—separation from God. In order for Jesus to pay the penalty for our sins, He had to make a full payment—a payment that would include both physical death and spiritual separation from the Father. As Jesus died on the Cross, He did make that full and complete payment for all sin.

WHAT AM I WORTH?

You and I both struggle from time to time with the question of self-worth. *Do I matter? Am I valued? What worth do I really have?* The true value of something is determined by the price that is paid for it. In an auction, there can be many bids that are offered. The first bid can be as low as one dollar, but that is not what determines the value of the item. It is the last bid that does that.

In the same way, the world sometimes ascribes very low value to individuals. Yet that is not what determines our worth. Our value is determined by the highest bidder—not the lowest. The price that Jesus, the Son of God, paid for us was the giving of His own life. There is nothing more valuable than that. It follows, then, that there is absolutely nothing in all creation that is worth more than you and me.

THE AGONY OF ABANDONMENT

The agony of Jesus' separation from the Father is expressed in one of the last statements He made on the Cross: "My God, my God, why have You forsaken Me?" (Matthew 27:46b NIV). You may recall that this is the first verse of Psalm 22, which we read earlier. It was a psalm of David, of whom Jesus was a descendant. The psalm described a truly horrific event and depicted with remarkable accuracy the scene at the Cross. It spoke of abandonment by God, of scorn and mockery. In fact, it actually quoted the mockers as saying, "He relies on the LORD; let him save him. Let the LORD rescue him, since he takes pleasure in him" (Psalm 22:8 CSB). These were essentially the same words the religious leaders used to mock Jesus moments before He quoted from this psalm. It was as if Jesus was proving to them yet again that He really was the Messiah.

The psalm goes on to speak of physical thirst, being surrounded by enemies and Gentiles, of having His hands and feet pierced and His clothes divided among them, and of much more. Still, the last words of the psalm are truly wonderful. They speak of future generations being told about the Lord and of His righteousness being proclaimed to the nations.

That is all possible because the psalm also declared that God will, in fact, hear the cry of this Suffering One. Even though Jesus did die on the Cross that day, the story was far from over!

THE DEATH AND BURIAL OF JESUS

MATTHEW 27:50-66

We come now to the truly unimaginable—the death of Jesus Christ. How is it even possible for the Author of Life Himself to die? Even for those who have studied the Bible their whole lives, this question is still a profound mystery in many ways, even though we understand it was God's plan all along. Jesus is described in one place as "The Lamb slain from the creation of the world" (Revelation 13:8 NIV). Thus God knew the end from the beginning—that the Son of God would enter the world to die in our place. However, it is still difficult to comprehend how this is really possible.

As you read this passage, take special note of all that happens at the very moment Jesus dies.

⁵⁰ And when Jesus had cried out again in a loud voice, he gave up his spirit.

⁵¹ At that moment the curtain of the temple was torn in two from top to bottom. The earth shook, the rocks split ⁵² and the tombs broke open. The bodies of many holy people who had died were raised to life. ⁵³ They came out of the tombs after Jesus' resurrection and went into the holy city and appeared to many people.

⁵⁴ When the centurion and those with him who were guarding Jesus saw the earthquake and all that had happened, they were terrified, and exclaimed, "Surely he was the Son of God!"

⁵⁵ Many women were there, watching from a distance. They had followed Jesus from Galilee to care for his needs. ⁵⁶ Among them were Mary Magdalene, Mary the mother of James and Joseph, and the mother of Zebedee's sons.

The Burial of Jesus

⁵⁷ As evening approached, there came a rich man from Arimathea, named Joseph, who had himself become a disciple of Jesus. ⁵⁸ Going to Pilate, he asked for Jesus' body, and Pilate ordered that it be given to him. ⁵⁹ Joseph took the body, wrapped it in a clean linen cloth, ⁶⁰ and placed it in his own new tomb that he had cut out of the rock. He rolled a big stone in front of the entrance to the tomb and went away. ⁶¹ Mary Magdalene and the other Mary were sitting there opposite the tomb.

The Guarding of the Tomb

⁶² The next day, the one after Preparation Day, the chief priests and the Pharisees went to Pilate. ⁶³ "Sir," they said, "we remember that while he was still alive that deceiver said, 'After three days I will rise again.' ⁶⁴ So give the order for the tomb to be made secure until the third day. Otherwise, his disciples may come and steal the body and tell the people that he has been raised from the dead. This last deception will be worse than the first."

⁶⁵ "Take a guard," Pilate answered. "Go, make the tomb as secure as you know how." ⁶⁶ So they went and made the tomb secure by putting a seal on the stone and posting the guard. (Matthew 27:50-66 NIV)

THE TORN CURTAIN

At the very moment that Jesus died, the curtain of the temple was torn in two. The temple was the one place where the Jewish people worshiped God. It had just two rooms in it. The first room was called the Holy Place, and the second was called the Holy of Holies. Dividing the two rooms was an enormous and ornate curtain.

Only a select group of people who were descendants of Levi, one of the sons of Jacob, could serve as priests of God. Moses and Aaron were both from this tribe. These priests were the only ones who were permitted to enter the first room of the temple to perform their duties. The other people would come *to* the temple to worship but could never go inside.

The very presence of God Himself dwelt in the second room, the Holy of Holies. Therefore no one was permitted to go into the second room. In fact, the purpose of the curtain was to make sure no one would ever accidentally look into the very presence of God. Sinful men do not last long in the presence of holiness.

However, once a year, the high priest was commanded to go *behind* this curtain and into God's presence. When he did so, he had to carry the blood of a lamb, offered as a sacrifice for the sins for himself and all the people of Israel. It was the most sacred and holiest ceremony of all.

This very curtain was the one that was torn from top to bottom at the moment Jesus died.

So why did this happen? And who tore it? Well, when Jesus, the true Lamb of God, died, everything changed! The full penalty of all the sins of mankind in all of human history, past, present, and future, had been paid for once and for all. Consequently, there was then nothing more that needed to be done—no more lambs to be offered, no more ceremonies to be observed, and no more rituals to be performed.

Access to the very presence of God Himself was now possible— not just for the high priest once a year, not even just for priests, not even just the Jewish people, but for all people of every nation! The Lamb of God had been sacrificed once for all! Thus it was God Himself who tore the curtain to proclaim that everything had changed!

THE CENTURION'S FAITH

The Roman centurion had perhaps been a mostly disinterested party in all that had occurred that day. After all, he was merely doing his job. As a Roman soldier, he likely didn't have any particular interest in this Jewish teacher from Nazareth. However, as the day unfolded, his interest likely started to grow. The silence of Jesus before His accusers, the strange three hours of darkness, the crime of which He was accused, and the very manner in which Jesus had died—all of this had been anything but ordinary.

He had also heard the mockery and insults that had been hurled at Jesus. Why did they hate this man so much?

The religious leaders of the day had seen the miracles Jesus had performed and had heard His teaching for the past three years, but they had refused to believe. This Roman Centurion hadn't seen any of that. He had only observed Him for a few hours while He was dying a painful death. Nevertheless, this non-Jewish solider, in a very short time, concluded that Jesus had to be the very Son of God.

Thus, on that day, those who had seen the most miracles rejected Jesus as the Son of God entirely, but one who had seen hardly any miracles at all embraced Him completely.

THE TWO OTHER CROSSES AND THE RICH MAN'S TOMB

When Jesus was crucified, two other criminals hung on crosses next to Him. Thus the prophecy in Isaiah was fulfilled that said He would be "numbered with the transgressors" (Isaiah 53:12 NIV).

After He had died and was taken down from the Cross, He was placed in the tomb of a rich man named Joseph of Arimathea, fulfilling another prophecy of Isaiah that He would be "assigned a grave with the wicked, and with the rich in His death" (Isaiah 53:9 NIV). God had again made known the end from the beginning.

IT IS FINISHED

In John's parallel account of the death of Jesus, he records that the last statement He made on the Cross before His death was, "It is finished" (John 19:30 CSB). At first glance this might appear to be referring to the end of Jesus' suffering, but that is not the meaning of the verb that is used here. It could well be translated as, "It is accomplished!" Thus it is not a statement of resignation but of achievement—of victory even.

So what exactly was accomplished when Jesus died? That was the moment in history when Jesus made the full payment for the sin of the whole world once for all. That was what was now accomplished.

ARMED GUARDS

After the burial of Jesus, armed soldiers were assigned to guard His tomb. Now that is certainly something you don't see every day. Armed guards are usually assigned to prisons—not cemeteries! Prisoners can escape, but no one expects that from those who are dead.

What would anyone want with the body of a crucified man anyway? He hadn't been buried with anything of any value—even His clothes had been divided up among the soldiers. And even if someone did steal the body, what could they possibly do with it? Yet the religious leaders, even after Jesus was dead and buried, were still afraid of His influence. What kind of man is this who was so feared even after His death?

Still, since Jesus really *was* the Son of God, all the soldiers in the world would not be enough to keep Him in the grave! In fact, the guards were all facing the wrong direction!

JESUS IS RISEN!
MATTHEW 28

Upon the death and burial of Jesus, the disciples were devastated and confused. They still did not understand that this was the fulfillment of God's purpose and plan. All their hopes and dreams seemed to be lost now, and they hid in fear for their own lives.

Three days later, they were still hiding, unaware of the wonder that was about to occur. Death would not win!

¹ After the Sabbath, at dawn on the first day of the week, Mary Magdalene and the other Mary went to look at the tomb.

² There was a violent earthquake, for an angel of the Lord came down from heaven and, going to the tomb, rolled back the stone and sat on it. ³ His appearance was like lightning, and his clothes were white as snow. ⁴ The guards were so afraid of him that they shook and became like dead men.

⁵ The angel said to the women, "Do not be afraid, for I know that you are looking for Jesus, who was crucified. ⁶ He is not here; he has risen, just as he said. Come and see the place where he lay. ⁷ Then go quickly and tell his disciples: 'He has risen from the dead and is going ahead of you into Galilee. There you will see him.' Now I have told you."

⁸ So the women hurried away from the tomb, afraid yet filled with joy, and ran to tell his disciples. ⁹ Suddenly Jesus met them. "Greetings," he said. They came to him, clasped his feet and worshiped him. ¹⁰ Then Jesus said to them, "Do not be afraid. Go and tell my brothers to go to Galilee; there they will see me."

The Telling of a Lie

¹¹ While the women were on their way, some of the guards went into the city and reported to the chief priests everything that had happened. ¹² When the chief priests had met with the elders and devised a plan, they gave the soldiers a large sum of money, ¹³ telling them, "You are to say, 'His disciples came during the night and stole him away while we were asleep.' ¹⁴ If this report gets to the governor, we will satisfy him and keep you out of trouble." ¹⁵ So the soldiers took the money and did as they were instructed. And this story has been widely circulated among the Jews to this very day.

The Great Commission

¹⁶ Then the eleven disciples went to Galilee, to the mountain where Jesus had told them to go. ¹⁷ When they saw him, they worshiped him; but some doubted. ¹⁸ Then Jesus came to them and said, "All authority in heaven and on earth has been given to me. ¹⁹ Therefore go and make disciples of all nations, baptizing them in the name of the Father and of the Son and of the Holy Spirit, ²⁰ and teaching them to obey everything I have commanded you. And surely I am with you always, to the very end of the age." (Matthew 28 NIV)

NOT-SO-GREAT EXPECTATIONS

Early on a Sunday morning, two thousand years ago, a few women went to a grave to honor the remains of a beloved teacher and friend. They expected to find His body still in the tomb, sealed behind a large stone, wrapped in strips of linen, and guarded by a detachment of soldiers.

Jesus' closest disciples, however, were hiding in fear for their own lives, believing that He was now dead and gone. They feared that soldiers would come for them next and put them to death as well.

The religious leaders also believed that Jesus was still in the grave. They expected to go on about their business and never have to worry about the Prophet from Nazareth again.

The Romans believed that they had appeased the Jewish people and could look forward to a period of stability in the region, now that the troublemaker was gone for good.

The last thing that anyone expected at that time was that the tomb would be empty. But that is precisely what the women found!

THE FIRST EYEWITNESSES

The very first witnesses to the resurrection of Jesus were a few women, and this is rather intriguing. In the culture of the day, women were not considered to be reliable witnesses and could not even testify in legal proceedings. So it is quite surprising to find that women are listed as the very first witnesses to the resurrection.

If the disciples had made up the story of Jesus' resurrection, they certainly would not have included something like this. That would have made their story *less* believable—not *more*. Instead, they would have listed the most reliable witnesses possible to strengthen their case. Thus the fact that the first witnesses to the resurrection would have been considered unreliable actually bolsters the reliability of the account. If it didn't really happen this way, no one would have made such a story up.

THE UNBELIEF OF THE RELIGIOUS LEADERS

The response of the religious leaders to the news of the empty tomb is interesting as well. The soldiers had told them everything that had happened. Thus they were the first to be told of the resurrection of Jesus, and the evidence was overwhelming.

So how did they respond? Did they rush to the tomb to verify the truth for themselves? Did they acknowledge that they had been wrong about Jesus? Did they confess their sin and unbelief? Did they accept that Jesus *was* the promised Messiah? Did they cry out to God for forgiveness? No. They did none of that. In fact, they did the exact opposite. Instead of believing the reality that was right in front of their eyes, they continued to stubbornly reject the truth and even believed a lie of their own making. They then passed this lie on to others to prevent anyone else from believing the truth.

Again, many people will say that if only they could see miracles themselves, then they would believe in Jesus. The religious leaders of that day were witnesses to many miracles and even Jesus' resurrection, yet they still refused to believe.

THE MEANING OF THE EMPTY TOMB

It is certainly true that all of Christianity rests on the reality of the empty tomb and the resurrection of Jesus. If Jesus did not rise from the dead, then Christianity is based on a lie, wishful thinking, and mere fabrications. It is of absolutely no importance and is utterly meaningless. The world remains completely separated from God. There is no means by which our sins can be forgiven, and there is no hope.

However, Jesus *did* rise from the dead. This fact makes Christianity of supreme importance. Jesus is, indeed, the Christ, the Son of God. The penalty for the sins of the world has been paid. Death has been conquered. The New Covenant has been established. Hope abounds, and you and I can become the sons and daughters of God.

THE GREAT COMMISSION

In three short days, the disciples had gone from a state of complete despair to one of complete joy. In fact, the transformation of the disciples from fearful followers to fearless leaders who turned the world upside down is compelling evidence for the truth of the resurrection. At first they couldn't comprehend that Jesus had actually died. Now they had difficulty grasping the reality that He had risen from the dead. As the days passed, they continued struggling to understand what it all meant for their own lives.

The Great Commission is the answer to that question, not only for them but for all believers everywhere in all of history. This Great Commission Jesus gave them was to take the message of His death, burial, and resurrection to all the nations of the world.

God's commandment to Adam in the Garden had been to fill the earth with people who walked with God and reflected His image. He had given the same command to Noah as well to fill the earth. Then, after dividing the people into languages at the Tower of Babel, He had chosen Abraham and promised that through him all the peoples of the earth would be blessed. In Daniel's vision, He revealed that all nations would one day worship the Son of Man.

The Great Commission was God's reaffirmation of that very same vision and promise. Jesus was the Savior of the whole world, not just the Jewish people. Their mission now was to proclaim the New Covenant to all the world.

THAT YOU MAY HAVE LIFE

JOHN 20:30-31

The majority of the passages we have read in the New Testament have come from the book of John, whose author was one of the closest disciples of Jesus. He knew Jesus better, saw more of His miraculous signs, and heard more of what He said than almost anyone else in the world. Toward the end of his book, there is a short passage that is quite profound, and it has become one of my very favorites.

At this point in his book, John has carefully and thoughtfully recorded the life of Jesus from its beginning, including several miracles, the I AM statements, and finally the death and resurrection of Jesus. Then he pauses. In fact, it's almost as if he puts down his pen, looks across the table into the eyes of his readers, and then speaks directly to them—to you and me. And this is what he says:

> *30 Jesus performed many other signs in the presence of his disciples, which are not recorded in this book. 31 But these are written that you may believe that Jesus is the Messiah, the Son of God, and that by believing you may have life in his name. (John 20:30-31 NIV)*

JOHN'S PURPOSE

John's purpose in writing his account of the life of Jesus is not left to speculation. He told us exactly what it was. He wanted you and I to believe something—something about Jesus, something that specifically has to do with who He is. He didn't merely want us to believe that Jesus was a great teacher. If that were the case, then he could merely have written about His great teaching. All the world could read it, and there would be near unanimous consent that He was, in fact, a great teacher. John didn't want us to believe that Jesus was merely a great example either. If that were all he wanted, he could have just recorded the account of Jesus caring for people and doing good things. Again, there would be near unanimous agreement that He was, in fact, a great example.

John wanted us to believe something much more significant than that. He wanted us to believe that Jesus is, in fact, the promised Messiah, the Christ, and the very Son of God, who came from heaven, entered the world, died for our sins, rose from the dead, and reigns forever as King of heaven and earth.

To be sure, this is no small thing to believe. We would need very strong evidence to believe something as significant as that. This evidence would have to prove not that He was merely a great man but was divine. This is the reason John gives for why he recorded the miracles we have read about. He himself had seen many other miraculous signs, and these had served to convince him of who Jesus was. They showed Jesus' power over nature, His power over disease, His power over sin, and His power even over death itself. Only God has that kind of power. Thus the best conclusion from the evidence is that Jesus is, in fact, the Christ, the Son of God.

John then gives the reason why he wants us to believe this about Jesus. He asserts that there is a life to be gained through this faith—and a life that can be missed out on as well. This life is not a physical one but a spiritual one. It is a life of knowing Jesus Christ—of knowing God! John himself experienced this life, and his desire is that you and I experience it too.

That is my own personal desire for you as well. I do hope and pray that you also will believe that Jesus is the Christ, the Son of God, because, by believing, you also can have life in His name.

JESUS ASCENDED
ACTS 1:1-11

We have already stated that the resurrection of Jesus from the dead is the most significant event in all of Christianity. All of Christianity rests on the truth of that historical event. But what happened after that? Jesus is no longer physically in the world today, so what happened to Him? Where did He go?

This next passage answers that question for us and also details the reality of the New Covenant that Jesus established. This comes from the book of Acts, from which we have already read. This book gives the history of how Christianity began to spread rapidly throughout the world immediately after the resurrection of Jesus, beginning with His ascension. A man named Luke is the author of this particular book, and he also wrote one of the four accounts of the life of Jesus. His book is the only one that contains the parable of the prodigal son, which we previously read together. He also appears to be the only non-Jewish person to write any book of the Bible.

Luke addresses both of his books to an individual named Theophilus. This name itself actually means "Lover of God." Thus it is at least possible that there was no particular person to whom he was writing. Instead, he may have been writing to each and every person who is a lover of God.

> [1] In my former book, Theophilus, I wrote about all that Jesus began to do and to teach [2] until the day he was taken up to heaven, after giving instructions through the Holy Spirit to the apostles he had chosen. [3] After his suffering, he presented himself to them and gave many convincing proofs that he was alive. He appeared to them over a period of forty days and spoke about the kingdom of God. [4] On one occasion, while he was eating with them, he gave them this command: "Do not leave Jerusalem, but wait for the gift my Father promised, which you have heard me speak about. [5] For John baptized with water, but in a few days you will be baptized with the Holy Spirit."
>
> [6] Then they gathered around him and asked him, "Lord, are you at this time going to restore the kingdom to Israel?"
>
> [7] He said to them: "It is not for you to know the times or dates the Father has set by his own authority. [8] But you will receive power when the Holy Spirit comes on you; and you will be my witnesses in Jerusalem, and in all Judea and Samaria, and to the ends of the earth."
>
> [9] After he said this, he was taken up before their very eyes, and a cloud hid him from their sight.
>
> [10] They were looking intently up into the sky as he was going, when suddenly two men dressed in white stood beside them. [11] "Men of Galilee," they said, "why do you stand here looking into the sky? This same Jesus, who has been taken from you into heaven, will come back in the same way you have seen him go into heaven." (Acts 1:1-11 NIV)

MANY CONVINCING PROOFS

Luke declared that Jesus gave "many convincing proofs" that He was, indeed, alive after His death and resurrection. This is very important, too, as Jesus knew full well that people throughout history would make every attempt imaginable to deny the truth of His real, physical resurrection.

You will recall that when Jesus was walking on the water, the disciples had first thought that they were seeing a ghost. Throughout the forty days after He rose from the dead, Jesus made sure they knew with absolute certainty that He was truly risen from the dead in a *physical* body and not merely a *spiritual* one. He was not a ghost or a spirit. Luke included one of these proofs here, in particular, when he records that Jesus was eating with His disciples. Only physical beings can consume physical food.

One of the attempts other people have made to discount the resurrection of Jesus is the idea of mistaken identity. They assert that someone else who merely looked like Jesus was crucified. Then Jesus just waited around for a few days before pretending that He had risen from the dead. Again, we see that this attempt to change the story quickly becomes absurd. First of all, Judas betrayed Jesus with a kiss, as was the common greeting in the Jewish culture of the day. Having walked with Jesus for three years, it would strain the imagination to think that he could get that close to someone and not realize it wasn't Jesus.

Furthermore, Peter almost died trying to prevent the soldiers from apparently seizing the wrong person. Did Peter not realize who was there? Was he risking his life to save a stranger from being arrested? And what about the religious leaders? Did they not recognize their mistake either? And what about the man himself? Did he never protest and tell them his name wasn't *Jesus*? Did he draw back from the greeting of a kiss from someone he didn't know? Did he just go along with it and let himself be crucified?

Finally, John recorded that after the resurrection, Jesus appeared to Thomas with the other disciples (John 20). Jesus had appeared to the disciples before, but Thomas was not with them then. Thus Thomas had not yet seen Jesus and was himself doubting the reality of the resurrection. When Jesus appeared to him, He specifically showed him His hands and His side. He even told Thomas to put his own finger into the nail prints in His hands and to put his own hand into His pierced side.

Of course, Jesus would not have had these wounds if He Himself had not been crucified. Thus in order for the mistaken identity idea to be real, Jesus would have had to have someone nail Him to a Cross and pierce His side just so He would have the right wounds. This mistaken identity idea, along with all the other attempts to explain away the resurrection of Jesus, quickly becomes absurd at the highest level.

Jesus gave many convincing proofs, and these were more than sufficient to convince all of the disciples, including Thomas. These men had been scared to death of losing their lives at first, yet, after having been convinced beyond a reasonable doubt of the resurrection, all of them were willing to give up their lives in order to proclaim Jesus to the world.

THE GIFT OF THE HOLY SPIRIT

As we have said before, the Bible is really the story of God redeeming us from our sins and restoring our relationship with Him, and this occurred in three distinct phases. First, the Father came to be *near* us. Then, the Son came to be *with* us. Here, Jesus Himself speaks of the third and final phase that will soon begin, when the Spirit will come to be *within* us.

He specifically states that the disciples would be baptized with the Holy Spirit. The word *baptize* literally means "to immerse." When the Bible was first translated into English, they came to this word and chose not to really translate it at all. Instead, they just made it into a new English word.

The prophet John, who first introduced Jesus as the Messiah, was actually referred to as "John the *Baptist*" because he *baptized* people in the Jordan River. Baptism was, then, a religious ceremony where people were immersed in the water of the river. That, however, was a ceremony that was physical in nature and merely a shadow of the spiritual reality that was to come. John actually baptized Jesus Himself and then introduced Jesus as the Lamb of God.

The baptism with the Holy Spirit occurs when a person puts his or her faith in Jesus. At that moment, He is immersed in the Spirit of God who comes to live in him from that day on and forever. We sometimes refer to this as the *indwelling*. When Jesus came to earth, He was called Immanuel, because then God was *with* us. To everyone who believes in Jesus, however, God makes His dwelling place *within* us. The Holy Spirit works in the lives of believers to reveal God to them, convict them of sin, guide them into truth, and work through them to glorify God.

This is a truly wonderful reality! Never before in history has mankind had the benefit of God working to transform him into His likeness from the inside out. Before Jesus had paid the penalty for sins, God could not indwell us. Only after the penalty for our sins had been paid could this occur.

Forty years after the resurrection, the great temple in Jerusalem was destroyed and has never been rebuilt. The place where God was supposed to be worshipped no longer exists. Instead, God refers to each of *us* as "a temple of the Holy Spirit" (1 Corinthians 6:19 CSB). Thus the primary place where God is to be worshipped *now* is in the life of every believer.

ALL NATIONS

Once again, we see that Jesus spoke about taking the message of His death and resurrection to the ends of the earth. At that moment in time, this had to sound quite impossible to the disciples. The total number of believers in the entire world at that point in history was only in the hundreds. These were mostly ordinary people from a conquered nation, possessing little education and limited resources. On top of that, the leaders of their own society fiercely opposed them. Also, the might of Rome was always poised to crush anything that could be viewed as a threat to its authority.

So again, the thought of the message of Jesus going from Jerusalem to the ends of the earth at that time was, by human standards, absolutely impossible. However, that is certainly not true today! In fact, today we are seeing the message of Jesus growing ever closer to reaching every nation, tribe, and language. The finish line is in sight!

THE ASCENSION

Now we know where Jesus is today. He had come from the Father and entered the world. Then He had left the world and had returned to the Father in heaven, being taken up and hidden by a cloud.

We read before of Daniel's dream of one like a Son of Man coming on the clouds of heaven, who would be worshiped by all nations and reign forever. Jesus had identified Himself as that very Son of Man.

We already read about His birth, and there was no mention of Him coming on the clouds of heaven then. He was merely born in Bethlehem and laid in a manger. So how does He fulfill the prophecy of Him coming on the clouds of heaven? The answer is that there will actually be a second time when Jesus comes into the world. The first time, He came as a Suffering Servant and was born in Bethlehem. The second time, He will come on the clouds of heaven and will reign as King forever.

When will that take place? That's a good question! The disciples were asking that very thing, and Jesus told them plainly that it was not for them to know. They were simply called to take the message of Jesus to the entire world. However, before they began doing this, Jesus instructed them to wait until the Holy Spirit would come. They would not have to wait long!

THE HOLY SPIRIT COMES

ACTS 2

The coming of the Holy Spirit took place on the Jewish feast of Pentecost. This was fifty days after the celebration of the Passover. We just saw that Jesus had appeared to the disciples over a period of forty days after the resurrection. If you add in the three days that Jesus was in the grave, then that means Pentecost occurred perhaps a week after they had last seen Jesus at His ascension.

As you read this account, remember that God's heart had been and will always be for all the nations of the world. With this in mind, it is fascinating to see what exactly happens when the Holy Spirit comes to be *within* us!

¹ When the day of Pentecost came, they were all together in one place. ² Suddenly a sound like the blowing of a violent wind came from heaven and filled the whole house where they were sitting. ³ They saw what seemed to be tongues of fire that separated and came to rest on each of them. ⁴ All of them were filled with the Holy Spirit and began to speak in other tongues as the Spirit enabled them.

⁵ Now there were staying in Jerusalem God-fearing Jews from every nation under heaven. ⁶ When they heard this sound, a crowd came together in bewilderment, because each one heard their own language being spoken. ⁷ Utterly amazed, they asked: "Aren't all these who are speaking Galileans? ⁸ Then how is it that each of us hears them in our native language? ⁹ Parthians, Medes and Elamites; residents of Mesopotamia, Judea and Cappadocia, Pontus and Asia, ¹⁰ Phrygia and Pamphylia, Egypt and the parts of Libya near Cyrene; visitors from Rome ¹¹ (both Jews and converts to Judaism); Cretans and Arabs—we hear them declaring the wonders of God in our own tongues!" ¹² Amazed and perplexed, they asked one another, "What does this mean?"

13 Some, however, made fun of them and said, "They have had too much wine."

Peter Addresses the Crowd

14 Then Peter stood up with the Eleven, raised his voice and addressed the crowd: "Fellow Jews and all of you who live in Jerusalem, let me explain this to you; listen carefully to what I say. 15 These people are not drunk, as you suppose. It's only nine in the morning! 16 No, this is what was spoken by the prophet Joel:

17 "In the last days, God says,
I will pour out my Spirit on all people.
Your sons and daughters will prophesy,
your young men will see visions,
your old men will dream dreams.
18 Even on my servants, both men and women,
I will pour out my Spirit in those days,
and they will prophesy.
19 I will show wonders in the heavens above
and signs on the earth below,
blood and fire and billows of smoke.
20 The sun will be turned to darkness
and the moon to blood
before the coming of the great and glorious day of the Lord.
21 And everyone who calls
on the name of the Lord will be saved.'

22 "Fellow Israelites, listen to this: Jesus of Nazareth was a man accredited by God to you by miracles, wonders and signs, which God did among you through him, as you yourselves know. 23 This man was handed over to you by God's deliberate plan and foreknowledge; and you, with the help of wicked men, put him to death by nailing him to the cross. 24 But God raised him from the dead, freeing him from the agony of death, because it was impossible for death to keep its hold on him. 25 David said about him:

"'I saw the Lord always before me.
Because he is at my right hand,
I will not be shaken.
26 Therefore my heart is glad and my tongue rejoices;
my body also will rest in hope,

*²⁷ because you will not abandon me to the realm of the dead,
    you will not let your holy one see decay.
²⁸ You have made known to me the paths of life;
    you will fill me with joy in your presence.'*

²⁹ *"Fellow Israelites, I can tell you confidently that the patriarch David died and was buried, and his tomb is here to this day. ³⁰ But he was a prophet and knew that God had promised him on oath that he would place one of his descendants on his throne. ³¹ Seeing what was to come, he spoke of the resurrection of the Messiah, that he was not abandoned to the realm of the dead, nor did his body see decay. ³² God has raised this Jesus to life, and we are all witnesses of it. ³³ Exalted to the right hand of God, he has received from the Father the promised Holy Spirit and has poured out what you now see and hear. ³⁴ For David did not ascend to heaven, and yet he said,*

*"'The Lord said to my Lord:
    "Sit at my right hand
³⁵ until I make your enemies
    a footstool for your feet."'*

³⁶ *"Therefore let all Israel be assured of this: God has made this Jesus, whom you crucified, both Lord and Messiah."*

³⁷ *When the people heard this, they were cut to the heart and said to Peter and the other apostles, "Brothers, what shall we do?"*

³⁸ *Peter replied, "Repent and be baptized, every one of you, in the name of Jesus Christ for the forgiveness of your sins. And you will receive the gift of the Holy Spirit. ³⁹ The promise is for you and your children and for all who are far off—for all whom the Lord our God will call."*

⁴⁰ *With many other words he warned them; and he pleaded with them, "Save yourselves from this corrupt generation." ⁴¹ Those who accepted his message were baptized, and about three thousand were added to their number that day.*

The Fellowship of the Believers

⁴² *They devoted themselves to the apostles' teaching and to fellowship, to the breaking of bread and to prayer. ⁴³ Everyone was filled with awe at the many wonders and signs performed by the apostles. ⁴⁴ All*

*the believers were together and had everything in common. *[45] *They sold property and possessions to give to anyone who had need. *[46] *Every day they continued to meet together in the temple courts. They broke bread in their homes and ate together with glad and sincere hearts, *[47] *praising God and enjoying the favor of all the people. And the Lord added to their number daily those who were being saved. (Acts 2 NIV)*

ALL LANGUAGES

The coming of the Holy Spirit marked the true beginning of the New Covenant, and that beginning is truly marvelous! God's heart for the nations is wonderfully revealed in the miraculous ability given to the disciples to speak in many languages that they did not know—languages spoken in many other places in the world. The account seems to suggest that there were as many as fourteen different languages spoken that day. Pentecost was an important feast of the Jews, so many of them had come from very far away. All of them heard about the wonders of God *in their own language.*

This is God's plan. This is God's passion. This is God's purpose.

God first created the language families of the world more than two thousand years earlier at the Tower of Babel. His purpose in choosing Abraham shortly thereafter was to be a blessing to all the dispersed nations and languages. *Jesus* was that blessing.

Thus it is fitting that Christianity began like this, with the proclamation to the nations of the death and resurrection of Jesus—the descendant of Abraham through whom all nations would be blessed!

After hearing this, many of the people responded by putting their faith in Jesus. Soon afterward, they would all return to their home countries, taking with them this message, which they then proclaimed to even more people. This helped foster the rapid spread of Christianity throughout the world.

BIBLE TRANSLATION STATISTICS

God's heart for the world continues to this very day, and Christianity enthusiastically embraces His call to take the gospel to all people. One of the ways this is being done is through Bible translation—translating the Bible into all the languages of the world. After all, the Bible presents itself as God's message to all mankind. It follows, then, that every man, woman, and child in the world should be able to read or hear God's message in his or her native tongue.

Wycliffe Global Alliance is an association of various Bible translation organizations throughout the world.[3] According to their website, there are about 7,350 unique languages in the world. You will recall that there were probably around seventy different languages created at the Tower of Babel. Over time, however, these root languages split into multiple other languages. For instance, the Slavic family of languages today includes Ukrainian, Russian, Slovakian, Czech, and others. Still, these grew out of one root language but are distinct enough today to be considered unique.

So just how many languages has the Bible been translated into so far? How does this compare to other books? One of the most read books in the world for centuries is *The Imitation of Christ*, written by Thomas A. Kempis in 1418. This book has been translated into about one hundred languages.

Pilgrim's Progress, an allegory of the Christian life written by the American John Bunyan in 1678, boasts around two hundred languages. Estimates for *The Little Prince*, written by Antoine de Saint Exupery in 1943, approach three hundred languages.

However, the Bible reigns supreme over every book. According to Wycliffe, the entire Bible has now been translated into over seven hundred languages! Many other translation efforts are currently underway but not yet complete. However, these efforts have produced the entire New Testament in over fifteen hundred additional languages. Smaller portions of the Bible have been translated into more than one thousand other languages. In all, there are currently over thirty-four hundred languages in which at least portions of the Bible have been translated!

Admittedly, this is still less than half of the total number of languages in the world, yet these typically represent the languages with the largest numbers of native speakers. In fact, the total number of people who speak languages in which at least part of the Bible has been translated, meaning the number of people in the world who can read or hear at least some of God's message in their native tongue, totals nearly *seven billion*!

There remain less than two hundred million people in the world today who speak a language in which there is currently no portion of the Bible translated and no active translation project. Those people are certainly valued, and Wycliffe and other organizations are pressing hard toward the goal of completing this work and reaching these last groups

---

3. All Bible translation statistics are taken from Wycliffe Global Alliance's website: Wycliffe.net.

of people—people who are made in the image of God and who God deeply desires to know Him and walk with Him.

It is truly exciting to see how quickly Bible translation is nearing the ultimate goal of reaching every nation, tribe, and language. Estimates of the completion date are now typically given in years—not centuries! What a wonderful time to be alive!

PETER'S MESSAGE

Responding to the confusion that had begun with the sound of the mighty wind and the speaking of so many languages, Peter stepped forward, first to explain to them what they were observing, then to proclaim God's message to them.

The people there that day were all Jewish and had likely attended the Passover feast just fifty days before. They would probably have known, then, that Jesus had been crucified. Perhaps some of them had even been among those who had called for His death. Some might have even been witnesses to it. After the feast, however, many of them had likely returned to their own countries. Thus they may have not yet even heard about the resurrection or even about the lie that the religious leaders had begun to spread.

Peter proclaimed Jesus not as some new religious faith but as the promised Messiah who fulfilled all the prophecies God had given their forefathers throughout the centuries. God had not, in fact, forgotten His people. He had now established the New Covenant just as He had promised.

As we have seen for ourselves, the evidence was quite compelling, and many people that day responded in faith.

THE COUNSEL OF GAMALIEL
ACTS 5:12-42

Christianity continued to spread very rapidly. There had been just a few hundred believers at the beginning, but that number had grown to over five thousand in just a short time. God was proving to the world that this was, indeed, from Him, as He continued to perform many miraculous signs through the believers.

The religious leaders had put Jesus to death because they saw Him as a threat to their power. Now, they began to see that the same threat still existed in those who now proclaimed His resurrection. Thus the religious leaders began to attack the disciples.

¹² The apostles performed many signs and wonders among the people. And all the believers used to meet together in Solomon's Colonnade. ¹³ No one else dared join them, even though they were highly regarded by the people. ¹⁴ Nevertheless, more and more men and women believed in the Lord and were added to their number. ¹⁵ As a result, people brought the sick into the streets and laid them on beds and mats so that at least Peter's shadow might fall on some of them as he passed by. ¹⁶ Crowds gathered also from the towns around Jerusalem, bringing their sick and those tormented by impure spirits, and all of them were healed.

¹⁷ Then the high priest and all his associates, who were members of the party of the Sadducees, were filled with jealousy. ¹⁸ They arrested the apostles and put them in the public jail. ¹⁹ But during the night an angel of the Lord opened the doors of the jail and brought them out. ²⁰ "Go, stand in the temple courts," he said, "and tell the people all about this new life."

²¹ At daybreak they entered the temple courts, as they had been told, and began to teach the people.

When the high priest and his associates arrived, they called together the Sanhedrin—the full assembly of the elders of Israel—and sent to the jail for the apostles. ²² But on arriving at the jail, the officers did not find them there. So they went back and reported, ²³ "We found the jail securely locked, with the guards standing at the doors; but when we opened them, we found no one inside." ²⁴ On hearing this report, the captain of the temple guard and the chief priests were at a loss, wondering what this might lead to.

²⁵ Then someone came and said, "Look! The men you put in jail are standing in the temple courts teaching the people." ²⁶ At that, the captain went with his officers and brought the apostles. They did not use force, because they feared that the people would stone them.

[27] *The apostles were brought in and made to appear before the Sanhedrin to be questioned by the high priest.* [28] *"We gave you strict orders not to teach in this name," he said. "Yet you have filled Jerusalem with your teaching and are determined to make us guilty of this man's blood."*

[29] *Peter and the other apostles replied: "We must obey God rather than human beings!* [30] *The God of our ancestors raised Jesus from the dead—whom you killed by hanging him on a cross.* [31] *God exalted him to his own right hand as Prince and Savior that he might bring Israel to repentance and forgive their sins.* [32] *We are witnesses of these things, and so is the Holy Spirit, whom God has given to those who obey him."*

[33] *When they heard this, they were furious and wanted to put them to death.* [34] *But a Pharisee named Gamaliel, a teacher of the law, who was honored by all the people, stood up in the Sanhedrin and ordered that the men be put outside for a little while.*

[35] *Then he addressed the Sanhedrin: "Men of Israel, consider carefully what you intend to do to these men.* [36] *Some time ago Theudas appeared, claiming to be somebody, and about four hundred men rallied to him. He was killed, all his followers were dispersed, and it all came to nothing.* [37] *After him, Judas the Galilean appeared in the days of the census and led a band of people in revolt. He too was killed, and all his followers were scattered.*

[38] *"Therefore, in the present case I advise you: Leave these men alone! Let them go! For if their purpose or activity is of human origin, it will fail.* [39] *But if it is from God, you will not be able to stop these men; you will only find yourselves fighting against God."*

[40] *His speech persuaded them. They called the apostles in and had them flogged. Then they ordered them not to speak in the name of Jesus, and let them go.*

[41] *The apostles left the Sanhedrin, rejoicing because they had been counted worthy of suffering disgrace for the Name.* [42] *Day after day, in the temple courts and from house to house, they never stopped teaching and proclaiming the good news that Jesus is the Messiah. (Acts 5:12-42 NIV)*

THEUDAS AND JUDAS THE GALILEAN

So who are Theudas and Judas the Galilean? You have never heard of them, have you? Don't worry, though. Almost no one else knows who they are either. The word *Theudas* is still underlined in red as I am typing this, indicating that it must be spelled incorrectly. It isn't recognized by the program I'm using. Judas, of course, was also the name of the disciple who betrayed Jesus, so that name is at least recognized, but not because of this person. The reality is that history has forgotten about these two men long ago, but that is certainly not true of Jesus!

While these two men were alive, they were apparently viewed as having some significant influence. Theudas had claimed four hundred followers. The people of Israel were looking for the Messiah at that time. They desperately wanted Him to come and free them from being subject to Rome. Yet the reality was that everything Theudas and Judas sought to achieve had failed. This served to prove that neither of them were truly from God.

THE WISDOM OF GAMALIEL

The counsel of Gamaliel was simple, yet profound. He asserted that if Jesus were not from God, then they didn't need to do anything about Him at all. The movement would collapse on its own, just like it had with the other two who had made similar claims. However, if this was, indeed, from God, then nothing they could do would stop it anyway. After all, who can hold back the hand of God? What can feeble men do against the force of one who spoke the universe into existence? *Is there anything too hard for the LORD?*

Keep in mind that this was the reasoning of Gamaliel who was *not* a believer in Jesus. He merely understood the reality of the circumstances and spoke accordingly. In essence, Gamaliel was saying that if Christianity was false and Jesus was just a mere man, then in two thousand years the world wouldn't even recognize His name—just like we don't recognize the names of Theudas or Judas the Galilean. In fact, if Jesus hadn't risen from the dead, then His name would also be underlined in red in all of our word processors today.

So which was it? Does the world today know the name of Jesus? Has history completely forgotten about Him? The answer is obvious. The name of Jesus is known all over the world. At the beginning, there were only a few hundred people who believed in Jesus, and they were all in the capitol of a conquered nation. Today, there are well over two billion people who identify as followers of Jesus from every nation of the world, and that number is still growing rapidly today!

UNSTOPPABLE!

Despite the counsel of Gamaliel, the religious leaders did everything they could to destroy Christianity from the very beginning. They flogged Peter and John in this very chapter (Acts 5) in an attempt to silence them. But because it was, indeed, from God, Peter and John proclaimed Jesus all the more, and Christianity continued to spread.

A short time later, the religious leaders murdered a believer named Stephen. You will recall that we previously read his defense against the false accusations when he recounted the history of Israel and its rebellion against God. After he was killed, there was great fear among the believers. In response, many of them left Jerusalem and went back to their homes in Judea and Samaria. Then they continued to proclaim Jesus in those places. And because it was from God, Christianity spread all the more.

Later on, the Roman Empire unleashed its tremendous might in the persecution of Christians, killing them by the thousands. Yet, because it was of God, it continued to spread all the more. In fact, the city of Rome itself had a growing number of believers within only a few decades of the resurrection. Still, the persecution continued.

A few hundred years later, one Roman emperor proclaimed that he had successfully destroyed all of the writings of the Christians. The next emperor, however, was Constantine, who declared Rome as a Christian nation and even sponsored the Bible to be copied and sent throughout his kingdom. Because it was from God, it could not be stopped.

In more modern times, the Soviet Union persecuted Christianity intensely, but it has collapsed now. And because it is from God, Christianity continues on.

In many countries still today, Christians suffer under varying degrees of persecution. Some of these are extremely harsh. Believers are murdered, imprisoned, and abused, while church buildings are destroyed. The Bible itself is either illegal or restricted in one out of every four countries in the world today. Yet, because it is from God, it continues to expand further and further—and it does so not *with* the sword, but *against* it.

Even in countries where Christianity is legal, there are many who devote their lives to destroying it. Some of these have set out to prove once and for all that Christianity is false. However, as they faced the evidence honestly, many of them became convinced that it was true after all. Among these are Josh McDowell and Lee Strobel, both of whom have become powerful defenders of the Christian faith. (See the appendix for some of their works.)

Still others, like Richard Dawkins, continue seeking desperately to destroy Christianity through philosophy and reason, all to no avail. In fact, all those throughout history who have given their lives to destroying Christianity or God's Word have ended up living lives of complete futility. Their efforts have all miserably failed. This will be the outcome of all such efforts.

Because it is of God, Christianity continues on, growing ever stronger, reaching ever further. Christianity will never be stopped. The strongest armies, the most brilliant philosophers, and the most vicious rulers are all completely powerless to stand against the God who spoke the world into existence by the power of His word.

Despite what many atheists claim, God is *not* dead. He did die, but He's not dead anymore! He is alive all over the world today, drawing men and women to Himself and thwarting all attempts to crush the gospel. Even in the greatest tragedies and horrors, God is working. His purpose and plan will surely prevail. It is the same purpose He had from the very beginning—that people from all over the world would know and love Him, walk with Him, and reflect His image.

My prayer is that you will be one of them.

WHO DO YOU SAY I AM?

MATTHEW 16:13-16

Two thousand years have passed since the resurrection of Jesus. Still today, He stands alone as the central figure in all of human history. In fact, we actually measure time based on when He Himself was born into the world. Right now, it is the year 2020 A.D.—2,020 years after the birth of Jesus. *A.D.* is Latin for *anno domino*, which means "in the year of our Lord," or how long it has been since our Lord Jesus came into the world. When we speak of time before Jesus, we use *B.C.*, which stands for *before Christ*.

In recent times, seemingly in an attempt to obscure the obvious impact of Jesus on the world, these terms have been changed to *C.E.* and *B.C.E.*, meaning *current (or common) era* and *before current era*. Still, the dates are the same, and the division still takes place at the time of His birth. No matter what abbreviations we use, Jesus remains the central figure in all of human history.

So the question remains for you and for everyone in the world, *Who do you say Jesus is?* A short time before Jesus was crucified, He discussed this very question with His disciples. Thus we will use this passage as the conclusion of our time together.

> *¹³ When Jesus came to the region of Caesarea Philippi, he asked his disciples, "Who do people say the Son of Man is?"*
>
> *¹⁴ They replied, "Some say John the Baptist; others say Elijah; and still others, Jeremiah or one of the prophets."*
>
> *¹⁵ "But what about you?" he asked. "Who do you say I am?"*
>
> *¹⁶ Simon Peter answered, "You are the Messiah, the Son of the living God." (Matthew 16:13-16 NIV)*

THE CHRIST, THE SON OF THE LIVING GOD

The disciples responded to Jesus' question with a few different answers they had heard from the crowds. Some claimed He was John the Baptist, who had been killed not long before. Yet John was the one who introduced Jesus as the Lamb of God, so that really wasn't a valid option.

Others claimed He was Elijah, an Old Testament prophet. He and Enoch share the distinction of being the only two people in the Bible who never died but were taken up to heaven. A prophecy in the Old Testament says that Elijah will come back to the earth before God returns to establish His kingdom. However, this prophecy is talking about the second coming of the Messiah—not the first. So the timing was off for this idea. Still others suggested another prophet had returned, but again, none of these were accurate.

Then Jesus turned the question back on His disciples. Who did *they* say He was? Then Simon Peter expressed the timeless truth—Jesus is the Christ, the Son of the Living God.

WHO IS JESUS?

At the outset of our journey, I told you that this was going to be all about Jesus. I'm sure you can now see just how true that statement was. Jesus is foreshadowed in Adam even before the Fall, as His side is pierced for the sake of His bride. He is the Offspring of the woman who would crush the head of Satan. He is the One who was sacrificed to cover over the shame of Adam and Eve's sin.

In the time of Noah, He is the one door through which mankind could escape His judgment. For Abraham, He is the promised Descendant through whom all the world would be blessed. His death is then foreshadowed as Abraham offers up his one and only son to God. He is the Lamb that Abraham said God would one day provide, and He is the ram that was the substitute given for Isaac.

He is portrayed in the entire life of Joseph, the beloved son of his father, who was betrayed by his brothers, cast down into a pit as a type of death, and then raised back up—then later he left for a distant land, became ruler over all, and brought salvation to his own family and many others. He is the Prophet like Moses whom God raised up to lead the whole world out of slavery to sin. He is the pure, spotless Passover Lamb, whose blood was applied to the doors of their homes in order to escape the judgment of God.

He is the true Bread from heaven and the Water from the rock. He is the One lifted up, that all who look on Him in faith may be healed of the poison of sin. He is the Shepherd's Shepherd, the Shepherd King, the virgin's Son, and God with us. He is the Suffering Servant who would be pierced, mocked, and rejected by men, but who would rise from the dead as the Victor. He is the Ruler whose origins are from ancient times, who would one day be born in Bethlehem.

He is the One who would establish the New Covenant between God and man—a new covenant in His blood. He is *Jesus*, meaning "God saves," because He is God, and He came to this world to save us from our sins. He is the Word made flesh, Son of God and Son of Man, the One about whom Moses wrote, the King of Israel, the Messiah, the Light of the World, and the Great I AM.

He is the Good Shepherd, the Gate for the sheep and the Resurrection and the Life. He is the Risen Lord, our Savior, who defeated death and triumphed over sin. He is the One who will soon return on the clouds of heaven as the Conquering King.

WHO ELSE COULD HE BE?

So again, who is Jesus? If He is not the Christ, the Son of God, then who else could He possibly be? Just a good man? A great moral teacher? A misunderstood rabbi? Both C. S. Lewis and Josh McDowell address this question far more eloquently than I ever could. However, here is my humble attempt to do the same.

Jesus clearly claimed to be God. If He was not God, then the question is whether or not He *knew* He was not God. If Jesus was not God and He knew He was not God, then He was the biggest fraud the world has ever seen. Indeed, that would make Him a fake, a liar, and a deceiver at the very core of who He was.

If, however, Jesus was not God but He truly believed that He was, then He would have had to have been mentally ill—a lunatic. There are some people today who believe themselves to be God, but this is diagnosed as a mental disorder. If Jesus was not God but truly believed that He was, then He would have to be classified along with them.

Both of these alternatives are absurd at the highest level. In reading the full accounts of His life on earth, we see a man of the humblest nature and the highest integrity. He touched those who were deemed untouchable. He loved those who were considered unlovable. He forgave those who had done the unforgivable. He was full of compassion yet upheld the highest standards of morality. He was uninterested in fame and fortune, as he often avoided the crowds and had no earthly possessions.

Christians throughout history have followed His example and brought immeasurable good to the world. Wherever there is a humanitarian need in the world, you will find Christians meeting it, including orphanages, free medical clinics and hospitals, women's shelters, homeless shelters, pregnancy centers, drug recovery programs, food banks—the list goes on and on.

Samaritan's Purse, World Vision, Mercy Ships, Compassion International, and countless other Christian organizations do incredible work all over the world. Just reading through some of their programs often brings tears to my eyes as I realize all the wonderful things they are doing. All of this happens because of people whose lives have been transformed by following Jesus, who volunteer and give financially to make all of this possible.

The followers of other religions do some charitable work as well, but no other religion even comes close to Christianity. It stands alone at the top in this area.

Again, if Jesus is not God, then the only other options are that He was a complete fraud or insane. If that is true, then all that Jesus did and taught along with the overwhelming good that His followers carry out all over the world—all of this would have to be the product of either a fraud or a lunatic. Neither of those options is even plausible. Jesus is not a lunatic, and He's not a liar. The only reasonable conclusion, considering all the evidence, is that Jesus is, in fact, the Christ, the Son of God—just as Peter declared.

Still, the question for you is not what C. S. Lewis said about Jesus. It's not about what Peter concluded. The question for you is, *Who do you say Jesus is?* My longing and prayer for you is that you will agree with Peter that Jesus truly is the Christ, the Son of the Living God, and that you will come to Him in faith.

IN CHRIST ALONE

The Bible emphatically declares there is one and only one way for mankind to receive forgiveness of sins. There is one and only one means by which he may be reconciled to God. There is one and only one path that leads to heaven. All of this comes through faith in Jesus Christ alone. There is no other way, no other means, and no other path. Before He was crucified, Jesus declared that He Himself is "the way, the truth and the life" and that no one can come to God the Father in heaven except through Him (John 14:6 CSB).

No other religion, no other faith, no other lifestyle, no other ceremony—nothing else is sufficient. Only faith in Christ can do this. This is certainly a very exclusive statement, and many people strongly object to it for that reason. However, Christianity is hardly alone in such a claim. All religions make truth statements that are by nature exclusive.

But why does Christianity make this particular truth statement? What is the basis for it? Only the death of Jesus pays the penalty for our sin. It's that simple. We all have sinned against God. The penalty for that sin is physical and spiritual death. Either we pay that penalty ourselves, or we receive the payment of Jesus as our Substitute. No other religion offers any suitable payment for sin. They all leave sin unpunished. They all leave mankind in his sins. They all leave us condemned.

You may object and claim that you have lived a good life. Perhaps you have even lived a truly noble life. But what about your sin? You may have given to the poor and served the needy. You may have voted for equality and spoke out against injustice. This is to be admired. But what about your sin? You may have been a good son or daughter, brother or sister, father or mother. You may have been a caring and faithful friend. That is honorable. But what about your sin? You may have been greatly devoted to a particular place of worship and followed all the rituals and requirements with great zeal. That is commendable. But what about your sin?

Has the penalty for your sin been paid? Has Someone paid it on your behalf? Have you trusted in the death of Jesus on your behalf? If not, the penalty for your sin remains unpaid. One day that payment will come due.

ARE YOU READY?

Are you ready now to put your faith in Jesus? Are you ready now to have the penalty for your sin paid in full? Are you ready now to become a child of God?

Be assured that today God is calling out to you just as He called out to Adam in the Garden. He is searching for you and asking, *Where are you?* Do you sense His calling now?

Though the evidence is overwhelming, it is doubtful that any Christian has ever gotten *every one* of his intellectual questions answered. To be sure, there are answers for most questions people ask, and there are plenty of places that can help you find them. Still, just how convinced do you have to be?

Just how convinced would you have had to have been to go and look at the snake on the pole—ninety percent? seventy-five percent? fifty-one percent? thirty-three percent? ten percent? There was nothing else that could have saved you, so even if you thought there was only a small chance, would you not have at least given it a try? Why not go and put your faith in Him who was raised up on the Cross so that you may be spiritually healed? You do not need great faith—only enough faith to take the step and make the decision to come.

No matter how little or how much you are convinced of the truth of Christianity, God's primary call to you is not merely intellectual in nature. He calls out to you and speaks to the deepest places in your heart. He offers love and hope and meaning and purpose and forgiveness and joy and belonging. Do you sense His calling now?

You will recall that we discussed the Ultimate Story of Beauty Established, Beauty Threatened, and Beauty Restored. Jesus is calling you into the Restored Beauty of a relationship with Him. Paradise was lost, but now it has been restored. That paradise is available to you if you will only come.

Even if your mind is not completely convinced, perhaps your heart will lead you. After all, it is often the stronger of the two in its demands. I pray that you will choose to come home to God like so many prodigals before you. Be assured that He is calling to you, waiting for you, hoping for you, longing for you, ready to run to you and welcome you home, and preparing a celebration the moment you arrive. However, the door will not be opened forever, so I urge you to come home now.

THE SINNER'S PRAYER

If you are, indeed, ready to take this step, you might be wondering how exactly you do that. To be sure, there are no magic words you have to say, there is no special ceremony you need to go through, and there is no church or organization you have to join. It won't cost you anything. Be assured that the God who made the heavens and the earth doesn't need any money from you. He's doing quite well. So, though it doesn't cost you anything, it did cost Him everything—but He gave it freely!

The Bible is clear that it only requires faith. You must believe that Jesus is who He claimed to be and that He died on the Cross in your place to pay the penalty for your sins. You must trust that His penalty will be credited to your account and that He will then make you His own.

Typically, when a person is ready to respond to Christ in faith, he or she is encouraged to voice that faith in what has come to be known as the Sinner's Prayer. This doesn't come from any place in the Bible but is the essence of what the Bible teaches about coming to Him. Again, there are no magic words, but these are the ones you might use:

Jesus, I do admit that I am a sinner. I have broken Your laws, I have rejected You as my God, and I have gone my own way. I have committed sins in my heart, in my mind, and in my actions.

I understand that the penalty for my sins is spiritual death, which is separation from You for all eternity.

Jesus, I believe that You are the Christ, the Son of God. I believe that You came into this world to pay the penalty for my sins by dying on the Cross, just as the prophets foretold.

I believe that You also rose from the dead, defeating death once and for all.

I ask You to forgive my sins and to give me eternal life.

I put my faith completely in You, Jesus, and in Your death on the Cross. I put no faith in my own works.

Make me Your child. Be my Shepherd. Be my Lord. Be my Guide.

Again, the words are not magic. Simply saying them without meaning them will surely not fool God. Yet, if these words really do express your heart, and if you have just made the decision to put your faith completely in Jesus as the Christ, the Son of God, then He has just now welcomed you into His family as His very own child. He has forgiven your sins and given you eternal life, and He is ready to be your Father, your Shepherd, your Lord, and your Guide.

If you have not yet put your faith in Jesus, the door is still open today, but it won't always be so. There was a time when the door to the Ark was closed. There was a time when it was too late to sacrifice the Passover lamb and apply the blood to the doorframes of the house. It was possible for one who was bitten in the desert to wait too long to go look at the snake on the pole. And there will also be a day when it will be too late to come to Jesus.

Won't you come today?

EPILOGUE

FOR THE SEEKER

If you are new to the Bible or Christianity, then I hope our journey through the Scriptures together has been helpful for you. We have certainly discussed a great many topics and read a lot of passages. I personally find the foreshadowing and the prophecies to be incredibly beautiful, and I hope you appreciated them as well.

Most of all, I hope you have considered putting your trust in Jesus as your Savior. If you haven't *come home* yet, let me encourage you to continue your search. Recall that God's desire for you is that you would seek Him and reach out for Him and find Him.

One way to continue seeking God is to read the Bible for yourself. I would suggest starting with the Gospel of John. We have already read several portions from it, so it should be somewhat familiar to you. However, there are several passages we didn't cover that you can enjoy for the first time.

The three other Gospels are very similar to each other, so picking one of those to read would be good as well. However, if you read them all one after the other, you will find quite a bit of material that is repeated.

The book of Acts shows how the gospel spread after the ascension of Jesus, so I would recommend that also. Most of the other books in the New Testament are written primarily for believers and deal more with correcting doctrine and living the Christian life. They are certainly worth reading but may not be as relative to you for your search in particular. Nonetheless, you might enjoy Romans and 1 John. As far as Old Testament books, check out the rest of Genesis and Exodus, and then Ruth, Esther, Ecclesiastes, Psalms, and Proverbs.

Another way to continue your search is to find a good church. I need to warn you, though, that there are many so-called churches that don't view the Bible as truly God's Word. They are much like Israel was in the desert. Although they still referred to themselves as God's people, they reject Him when they reject His Word. Such churches won't be of much help to you. A good way to distinguish between the two is to see how much time they spend reading and discussing the Bible. If it really isn't discussed much and isn't believed, then try somewhere else.

There are a few churches that read the Bible a lot but misuse it. So if you ever feel uncomfortable or pressured, you might need to leave and find another one. Many of these churches focus on works and earning their way to heaven rather than on the grace of God. This didn't work for Adam and Eve, and it doesn't work for us today either. Such people have the appearance of happiness but are usually exhausted from their futile attempts to earn God's favor.

A few other warning signs common in such churches are exclusivity and church publications. Some so-called churches believe they are the only ones who are truly Christians and going to heaven. In conjunction with this, they sometimes produce their own literature that interprets the Scriptures for you. They assert that you can't understand the Bible for yourself and should rely on them to tell you what it means. Be assured that God did not reveal His Message to the world in such a way that only a select few can understand it. God is much bigger than that.

I also need to warn you that some churches have highly entertaining services but lack real substance and aren't focused on the Word of God at all. Attending such services can be really fun and even emotionally uplifting. However, if you walk away without hearing or reading much from the Bible, you're probably in the wrong place.

Definitely try do some research on churches before you go. This could save you a lot of time going to the wrong churches. Try to find their statements of faith and study them carefully. If they affirm that salvation is by faith alone in Christ alone, that's a great start. If, however, they assert that salvation is by faith *and works,* then you should look elsewhere. Salvation is received *by faith*—not by faith *and anything else.* When I myself began looking for a publisher for this book, I was very pleased to come across Innovo Publishing, in large part due to their own statement of faith. If you find a church with a statement of faith like theirs, you have a great chance of being in the right place.

It might just be good to try a few different churches, but also ask God to guide you. After trying one, ask yourself if you learned more about God *through His Word.* If the answer is yes, that's a good sign. Even if you are not a believer, God very well may intervene to help you find Him and find a good church! After all, He is more interested in your journey home than you are. He will be the one running, even if you aren't.

FOR THE NEW BELIEVER

If you have recently decided to take the next step and put your faith in Jesus, then let me be the first to congratulate you and welcome you to the family of God! You are now my brother or sister. You should know, too, that we are all equals in the family of God. No shame, no guilt, no blue collars or white collars, no rich or poor, no proper or improper—we are all just prodigals who have returned home to the welcome embrace of the Father! We boast not about how great we are but about how wonderful He is! He forgave *even me!*

There are a few things that will really help you as you begin this new life as a Christian. First and foremost is reading and studying God's Word. Most new believers find the New Testament the easiest to read and understand, but I would certainly encourage you to consider Genesis, Exodus, Deuteronomy, Psalms, Proverbs, Daniel, Esther, Ruth, Ecclesiastes, the Psalms, and Proverbs as well.

Secondly, fellowship with other believers is crucial. It will be most helpful, though, for you to associate with the most committed believers possible. There are a lot of people who go to church but aren't really serious about their faith. You will want much more than that, so try to find someone who truly loves the Word of God and whose life is as much like Jesus as possible. True Christians should be humble, love God's Word deeply, be enthusiastic about Jesus and His death on the Cross, and be forgiving, loving, generous, kind, and at peace.

Another thing to watch for is how someone who claims to be a believer responds to God's Word when they find something in it that is contrary to their beliefs or lifestyle. One person will conclude that God is wrong. Another person will conclude that he himself is wrong. Be assured that whenever my life or beliefs disagree with God's Word, *I'm* the one who is wrong. Look for someone who has that same perspective.

As a word of caution, you will probably start your journey as a Christian with a great deal of excitement. There will probably come a point in the near future, though, when this fades a bit. You will most certainly go through some trials and doubts. Be assured that this is quite normal. A spiritual battle is still being waged, and Satan will certainly try to make you question the Word of God and the goodness of God. That's what he always does.

Whenever you face such doubts, the best way to handle them is with the truth of God's Word. Believe what God says and reject the lies of the world. If you do come across a question that bothers you, definitely check out the appendix of this book for some helpful resources. Remember, though, that questions, doubts, and trials are normal. Your faith will be tested many times in this life, but that will just make it stronger. The storms of life come to both the believer and the unbeliever. The Christian life is one of peace and joy, not in the absence of any storms but in the very midst of the very worst of them.

FOR THE BELIEVER

If you are already a believer, then I hope this book was an encouragement to you. Perhaps you have seen a beauty in the Scriptures that you hadn't seen before, or maybe this was just a good refresher course for you. At any rate, I pray that, with this encouragement, you will have a renewed fervor in seeking God's presence in your life and loving His Word. I also pray that you and I both learn to trust, and not doubt, that God is good and will be our Provider and Protector.

If you have enjoyed this book, I would encourage you to give it away to someone else, perhaps someone who is not a believer. Better yet, ask them if they would like to read through it together and discuss it with you!

FOR EVERYONE

There is an old adage that says, "A burden shared is halved; a joy shared is doubled." In the appendix, I have included a list of several books and other resources that have been a great help for me. Some of them have captivated my heart, and others have instructed my mind. Either way, they have been a source of great delight and encouragement for me, and I hope they can be that for you as well. If so, my joy will be doubled.

May this book be for the glory of Jesus Christ alone and for the furtherance of His kingdom!

APPENDIX

APOLOGETICS (REASONS TO BELIEVE)

BOOKS

The Case for Grace: A Journalist Explores the Evidence of Transformed Lives, by Lee Strobel. Strobel is the author of many books that defend the Christian faith, which we call *apologetics*. This is my favorite one by far. I call it *apologetics for the heart*, as it looks at the evidence of transformed lives. His other books are great, and I will recommend a few of them as well. However, this one just grabbed my heart like no other. Chapter two is well worth the price of the entire book.

The Case for Christ: A Journalist's Personal Investigation of the Evidence for Jesus, by Lee Strobel. This book traces Strobel's own spiritual journey from atheism to faith in Jesus. His approach is that of a journalist, so he interviews and challenges various experts with questions. The book is very readable and keeps the interest of the reader. There is also a DVD version and a great movie by the same title that recounts the author's journey to faith in Jesus. All of them are excellent.

The Case for Faith: A Journalist Investigates the Toughest Objections to Christianity, by Lee Strobel. This is another very readable book on reasons to believe in Jesus.

The Case for a Creator: A Journalist Investigates Scientific Evidence that Points Toward God, by Lee Strobel. You may have heard about intelligent design, but if you're like I was, you might not know much about it. This book uncovers that and details how the universe has overwhelming evidence for design and, by implication, a Designer.

Cold-Case Christianity: A Homicide Detective Investigates the Claims of the Gospels, by J. Warner Wallace. The author is a former L. A. County homicide detective and atheist, who used his detective skills to consider the claims of Christianity, specifically the death, burial, and resurrection of Jesus. Through his investigation, he became a believer. In this book, he shares that evidence with us. There's also a DVD.

I Don't Have Enough Faith to be an Atheist, by Norman Giesler and Frank Turek. This book starts with the question of God's existence, then logically works through successive questions until it comes to Christianity. For those who appreciate a complete argument from start to finish, this is an excellent resource.

Letters from a Skeptic: A Son Wrestles with His Father's Questions about Christianity, by Greg Boyd. This format is really captivating the way the son and his father go back and forth. Another very readable and interesting book.

Mere Christianity, by C. S. Lewis. Lewis is one of the most celebrated Christian thinkers of the twentieth century. He is a former skeptic turned Christian. This classic of his is still relevant today.

More than a Carpenter, by Josh McDowell. Written by a former skeptic turned believer, this classic presents logical evidence for the claims of Christianity. Very readable.

The New Evidence that Demands a Verdict, by Josh McDowell. An exhaustive work on many challenges to Christianity. Not for the faint of heart, but a fantastic resource.

OTHER RESOURCES

Jews for Jesus: This is an organization of Jewish believers in Jesus. They have a multitude of resources that show clearly that Jesus is, in fact, the promised Jewish Messiah (jewsforjesus.org).

EVIDENCE FOR THE TRUTH OF THE BIBLE

God's Promise to the Chinese, by Nelson, Broadberry, and Chock. God has not left Himself without witness, and this is true in China as well. This book reveals evidence that the original Chinese believed in one God. A truly fascinating read.

The Discovery of Genesis: How the Truths of Genesis Were Found Hidden in the Chinese Language, by C. H. Kang and Ethel R. Nelson. An illustrated presentation of how the truths of Genesis are found hidden in the Chinese characters. We covered some of these already, but this book covers many more and goes into much greater detail.

Ancient Post-Flood History: Historical Documents that Point to Biblical Creation, by Ken Johnson. This book provides historical evidence that supports the genealogies and stories in the first part of Genesis.

Tower of Babel, by Bodie Hodge. Another work that examines the evidence for the Genesis account, particularly the Tower of Babel.

Patterns of Evidence. A series of DVDs, each providing compelling evidence of Moses and the Exodus.

Flood Legends, by Charles Martin. A record of some of the many worldwide flood stories.

CREATION VS. EVOLUTION

Evolution's Achilles' Heels, by Robert Carter. There is both a book and a DVD for this title. The DVD is amazing. Several PhDs in various scientific specialties discuss the insurmountable obstacles that the theory of evolution faces. In my opinion, the evidence is quite overwhelming.

Tornado in a Junkyard: The Relentless Myth of Darwinism, by James Perloff. This book deals with the growing scientific evidence against the theory of Evolution.

Answers in Genesis: This is an organization that is all about the scientific evidence in support of Genesis. I once got to shake hands with Ken Ham, the founder of this organization, and that was a great honor for me. Check out their website (answersingenesis.org) for their books and DVDs. I also encourage you, if it's at all possible, to visit the Creation Museum and Ark Encounter in Kentucky.

THE SPREAD OF THE GOSPEL

Eternity in their Hearts, by Don Richardson. "God has not left Himself without witness." That would be how I would describe this book. A former missionary, Richardson shares beautiful accounts of remote tribes that were strangely and powerfully prepared for the gospel of Jesus Christ. It's a book that is really hard to put down. God's heart is for the nations.

Peace Child, by Don Richardson. In Richardson's own missionary work, a strange custom is revealed that provides the perfect way to present the gospel to a remote tribe.

I Dared to Call Him Father: The Miraculous Story of a Muslim Woman's Encounter with God, by Bilquis Sheikh. A Muslim woman in Pakistan wasn't seeking God, but God was seeking her. As she begins to investigate who God really is, she is told by Christians that He is a loving Father. Could she possibly call God by such a personal name? When she does, everything changes!

Miracle of Miracles: A Muslim Woman's Conversion to Christ and Flight from the Perils of Islam, by Mina Nevisa. A young Muslim girl in the Middle East finds a Bible among her things. She begins to read it and becomes a Christian. When a husband is chosen for her, she is terrified. How will she survive as a Christian married to a Muslim man in the Middle East?

Betrayed, by Stan Telchin. What would you do if your daughter called you from college and told you she believed in Jesus? As a Jewish businessman, Telchin felt *betrayed.* So he decided to read the New Testament for himself to prove to his daughter it wasn't true. It did not turn out as he expected.

The Costly Call: Modern-Day Stories of Muslims Who Found Jesus, by Emir Fethi Caner and H. Edward Pruitt. Modern-day stories of Muslims who found Jesus. It is so wonderful to see how God is touching so many lives and bringing them to faith in Jesus, even in the most difficult places.

THE GOSPEL

All of Grace, by Charles Spurgeon. Known as the prince of preachers, Spurgeon eloquently presents that salvation is not of any works but is *all of grace.* This book was, in part, the inspiration for my own. I love the way he speaks directly to the reader. I have tried to follow his example.

GOD

The Knowledge of the Holy, by A. W. Tozer. In this work, Tozer explores and meditates on the attributes of God. It reveals a God who is far beyond what we could ever imagine. Indeed, finite beings can never fully comprehend an infinite God, but we can grow in our knowledge of Him.

CPSIA information can be obtained
at www.ICGtesting.com
Printed in the USA
LVHW050803300623
751144LV00005B/333